WAYS
to the
WEST

WAYS
to the
WEST

How Getting Out of Our Cars Is
Reclaiming America's Frontier

TIM SULLIVAN

UTAH STATE UNIVERSITY PRESS
Logan

© 2015 by the University Press of Colorado

Published by Utah State University Press
An imprint of University Press of Colorado
5589 Arapahoe Avenue, Suite 206C
Boulder, Colorado 80303

 The University Press of Colorado is a proud member of
Association of American University Presses.

The University Press of Colorado is a cooperative publishing enterprise supported, in part, by
Adams State College, Colorado State University, Fort Lewis College, Metropolitan State College
of Denver, Regis University, University of Colorado, University of Northern Colorado, Utah State
University, and Western State College of Colorado.

∞ This paper meets the requirements of the ANSI/NISO Z39.48–1992 (Permanence of Paper).

Cover design by Daniel Pratt
ISBN: 978-0-87421-992-0 (paper)
ISBN: 978-0-87421-993-7 (ebook)

Library of Congress Cataloging-in-Publication Data
Sullivan, Tim, 1978–
  Ways to the West : how getting out of our cars is reclaiming America's frontier / Tim Sullivan.
     pages cm
    ISBN 978-0-87421-992-0 (pbk.) — ISBN 978-0-87421-993-7 (ebook)
  1. Transportation, Automotive—Social aspects—West (U.S.) 2. Transportation, Automotive—
Environmental aspects—West (U.S.) 3. Cities and towns—West (U.S.) 4. Sustainable develop-
ment—West (U.S.) 5. West (U.S.)—Description and travel. I. Title.
  HE5629.S85 2015
  388.3'210978—dc23

                    2014038130

24   23   22   21   20   19   18   17   16   15   10   9   8   7   6   5   4   3   2   1

Cover photograph collage and all text illustrations by Jonah Chiarenza

To Erin, my traveling companion.

Contents

Acknowledgments

The long and winding journey of this project passed many mileposts and by them stood people who offered help, wisdom, and sorcery to turn an idea into a book. I give them the deepest thanks. My friend and colleague Jonah Chiarenza was *Ways to the West*'s earliest adopter. Yes, he drew the illustrations for the book and designed the cover, but he also gave perspective on the venture as a planner, reader, and friend and subjected himself to helping me work through the minutiae of trip preparations. Jon Wilde joined me on one of the loneliest roads in the West. Phil Erickson and everyone at CD+A gave me an understanding of the connection between transportation and communities, and this understanding shaped me as a planner and urbanist and drove this book. I wrote 90 percent of this book in early mornings at World Ground Café in Oakland, the greatest neighborhood café ever. Michael Spooner read potential in the manuscript and took the leap and, along with my wonderful peer reviewers, gave affirmation and suggestions. Everyone at Utah State University Press and University Press of Colorado ably transformed my vision and words into a finished book. My colleagues at InterPlan supported me during later stages of the book's publication. I owe the most to the dozens of people who talked (and walked) with me for the book; their perspectives and insights bring *Ways to the West* to life. My dad carefully read the manuscript and offered great advice, as did my mom, who, in a surprise twist, also saw me through Wyoming. Finally, my wife and family let me take a three-week road trip that might or might not find its way to a book. E, J, and T—next time you can come along.

Prologue: Selling the Truck

I used to take road trips. On my sixteenth birthday, when I received my driver's license, I inherited my parents' 1988 red and white Isuzu Trooper, a garish, dangerously top-heavy vehicle that was quick to overheat. The Trooper always had a rugged demeanor. We had broken it in—and I emphasize *broken*—on a drive over Elephant Hill in Canyonlands National Park a week after buying it new. Elephant Hill was a mound of sandstone in the desert that a road pretended to go over, a foreboding barrier for four-wheelers, with steep grades and drop-offs. We banged the undercarriage and dented the tailpipe of our brand-new sport utility vehicle. It was just as well.

I could rally the Trooper a long way at a few hours' notice. I packed a sleeping bag and pad, a Coleman stove, a Gore-Tex coat, and some CDs and I was gone. Within five hours of my Salt Lake City house was enough public land to explore for five lifetimes. I drove the Trooper south to the desert and north to the mountains. My parents always worried that the Trooper wouldn't make it out of the city.

A few years later, after the Trooper died, I bought a silver Toyota pickup truck. I installed a lighted camper shell over its bed so I could sleep in it.

A few days after I bought the pickup I drove it alone to Oregon—to the Cascades, the coast, then on to Portland. The next year I took my brother to the Olympic Peninsula. I drove the truck to British Columbia and Alberta, Baja and Chihuahua.

Spending time on the road led me to work as a reporter for various newspapers. A job that allowed me to travel the West's byways in search of good stories seemed too good to be true, and I loved chewing up miles in my truck between obscure western places. I camped in the truck a lot. One night my girlfriend and I slept in it to wait out a blizzard in Carbondale, Colorado. We froze in our sleeping bags as the blinking plows scraped up and down Main Street all night. I lived in western Colorado, southern Colorado, northern Arizona, and eastern Utah, but they were more like stops on one long road trip. I kept my stuff in the truck.

As these trips accumulated, I sensed something about the West that I was able to pinpoint only later. The mountains and deserts I explored were plenty scenic, but they possessed something else, and it was this: So many of the aspects of America that defined our country, for better and for worse, had always lay westward. They were the persona Jackson carved out of Appalachia, the designs Jefferson had on Louisiana, the dams Floyd Dominy built on the Colorado, the sublimity John Muir saw in the Sierra. The West was the frontier of a young frontier nation, its biggest mystery box of what might come next. The West owned opportunity, freedom, adventure, and America's most spectacular landscapes. A mobility-addicted nation went fastest in the West. The West had always been a well for what we valued about our country.[1] Making all of this possible, of course—this big multi-century westward reach—was transportation, and on the road I was part of the story. That's what I felt as I drove all those miles.

When my truck turned ten, we had a party for it. I had driven it in the neighborhood of 150,000 miles, to all ends of North America. By then the road trips had tailed off. I had moved to the Bay Area and my life had been in stasis, on a happy circular track of work, neighborhood, and family. Every day my wife and I woke up our two-year-old daughter. I took her to school. I went to work. I got lunch at the same places at the same time of day. I visited the same sports websites, took a break at the same time, and came home along the same route. We bought a house and rebuilt our yard and sank ourselves into our neighborhood like the young trees we planted. My pickup, once the vehicle of choice among my friends and I, seemed out of place among the Priuses and MINIS that populated the area. The truck sat in the driveway.

I sold my truck when it couldn't safely transport our daughter's new car seat. We didn't get much for it. We traded it for a new family car. The man at the dealership who negotiated with me explained that my truck would be bundled with a bunch of other old beaters and put on a barge to Asia, or something like that. An ignoble end for a traveling companion.

As spring came around last year, I got the urge for the road again. I felt cabin fever in the house and in the neighborhood. I had a surfeit of vacation time at work. My list of western places to visit still contained a lot of unchecked items. In my head, I began to plan a solo three-week road trip: California, Nevada, Utah, Oregon—I could cover a lot of ground in three weeks.

But I was also now painfully aware of something about the West that I loved. I had spent the last ten years studying cities in one way or another as a journalist or student or city planner. And having lived in large coastal cities, I had become used to getting around much of the time by modes other than cars. I biked or bused to work and took Bay Area Rapid Transit from my East Bay house to explore San Francisco. I lived in a neighborhood where a three-minute walk led to three grocery stores, a hardware store, a café, a few restaurants, a few bars, a bookstore, a music store, a dry cleaner, and my barber. I drove, sure. I mean, I lived in California. Our house's convenience to Oakland's gazillion freeways was one of its major selling points. But I did not choose to drive with the automation that I did growing up. As with many people my age, cars did not hold the appeal they once did. We realized there were other ways of getting around. We rediscovered the pleasures of walking, of riding a bike, and of public transportation. I reveled living in a place where the other options were close at hand. I started to spend fewer weekends driving to bike rides outside the city and did more biking inside the city. My daughter and I took the train to our adventures.

I knew that having a variety of options for getting around is a rarity in America. We have been the grounds for what Bill McKibben calls the "sunk costs" of oil-dependent auto infrastructure.[2] What has been best for America is what is best for cars. So eventually people suffered. Where, half a century ago, almost half of American school children walked or biked to school, now almost 90 percent do not.³ Most of the country cannot walk to their daily needs within ten or twenty minutes, let alone three.

The Interior West is the greatest offender: the square states are a web of freeways tying together knots of mega malls and subdivisions. The places where most of us westerners live are quasi cities that are too spread out to walk in or for mass transit but too close together to be a home on the range. They are perfect for one thing: driving cars.⁴

I had watched it happen. That I drove all those miles in my truck was no accident: the automobile built the West. And at first, automobility had heightened the things that made the West great. We arrived at more spectacular places faster. We lived in farther flung, prettier places where we could remove ourselves from the idea of million-person conurbations but still get to our metropolitan jobs in less than half an hour. The individual freedom that cars seemed to offer was in step with the open vistas of the West. And so we gave ourselves to cars and, outside of historic downtowns and central city neighborhoods, they dictated the shape of the places we lived. This is true throughout America, but it is especially true in the West, where cities emerged as factories began to produce internal combustion engines and grew as the auto became ubiquitous and all-powerful. In the twentieth century, the car paced everything we valued about America's frontier.

But even for a road-loving person like myself, it had become clear that love had become dependence, and dependence had become addiction. And the West's overdependence on autos had put in jeopardy all of these things we loved about it in the first place. Cars, seemingly providing a kaleidoscope of choice, actually narrowed the possibilities for living in such wide-open country. The course of this western experience, while appearing limitless, presented limited options. The enormous returns of mobility and opportunity seen decades before had begun to diminish rapidly.

Perhaps most important, the auto had jeopardized the West's mystic hold on the American future. In the wake of the Great Recession, the West's boom cities appear to be relics of a twentieth-century ethos that rode the auto until it broke down and then bought a new one. Western cities, once paragons of mobility, are constantly threatening to become congested messes. Once fashioned as clear mountain-aired sanitariums to heal the sick, they create some of the worst air quality in the nation. Once unique places that bore a connection to their landscapes, western metropolises began to look like everywhere else.[5] Take, for example, a drive down State Street in Salt Lake City. You start at the hilltop perch of the Utah State Capitol, looking down into the bowl of the Salt Lake Valley, clear across to the sharp peaks of the Wasatch—if the view is not mucked up by smog—and begin heading south, moving through the grandeur of Eagle Gate and the Beehive House, which optimistically marked a new kind of community in the open valleys of the West. As this community grew, State Street, as its name implies, became the string that connected the communities of Utah—eventually, as U.S. Highway 89, reaching to the Arizona border. A ribbon of asphalt and a car provided a day's ride from the Capitol through fruit orchards, Lombardy poplars, and big sagebrush to the far-flung communities of the state. But on the State Street of today it's only a few blocks until you see the toll the auto has taken on this profound road of the West. State Street has become a treeless seven-lane traffic canal that, despite its continuing throughput, produces a hostile public realm for people. Drive on it fifty miles to the southern tip of the Wasatch Front metro area and find few respites from car malls, strip malls, boat malls, empty malls, drive-throughs, drive-ins, drive-ups, double left turns, and Double Whoppers. Dozens of State Streets cross the West, and without the scene of the mountains rising behind them it would be very hard to distinguish one from another. Autos are their means, but they have no ends.

I dare say that cars have *betrayed* the American West by promising the best things about the West and then breaking those promises.

A big part of the problem is that we hold onto the old meanings of the words that have long defined the West as America's frontier. The ways we define opportunity, freedom, and mobility are too dependent on fossil fuels, freeways, low-density subdivisions, space between people, and free parking lots. Meanings from a mythic past, an insolvent present, and an unpleasant future. I've come to realize that the meanings of these words should evolve. We need to not only reclaim but also redefine these words in the West.

I grew up, I realize now, during the absolute height of automobility. For much of my childhood gas cost less than $1. Streets in Salt Lake City were wide and uncomplicated. The peak of the industrial dream similarly defined other aspects of life in the 1970s and 1980s. One of my earliest memories is of sitting in the back of my parents' car in a giant parking lot of a chain drugstore, eating a hamburger from the McDonald's drive-through.

And that's the thing. Mounting evidence tells us that we have seen the peak of cars. Yes, the private auto still constitutes the way 86 percent of America commutes to work, including 75 percent of us who drive alone.[6] These figures are even higher in the West, with autos having a 90 percent share of the commutes in most western metro areas. But throughout the 2000s, joining several other upward curves that defined twentieth-century American life—income growth, the expanding house, insane real estate appreciation, smoking—driving started to decline. Auto travel appeared to be slowing down for the first time since the invention of the car. The number of miles a person travels in a given time period, called Vehicle Miles Traveled, or VMT, leveled off in 2004 and then began to decline for the next decade.[7] One researcher estimated that the US VMT in 2010 was 10 percent below what it would have been had twentieth-century trends continued.[8] Although the Great Recession hastened the decline of VMT, the reduction began well before the downturn and has continued through the recovery (Yes, VMT started to increase again in mid-2014, likely due to plunging fuel prices, but has not returned to the historical trend). By late 2012 the total decline since 2004 amounted to 7.5 percent. This change has affected nearly all of the country's metropolitan areas,[9] where Americans began to commute less by private vehicle and own fewer cars.[10]

Meanwhile, Americans are once again discovering other ways to get around. The proportion of people who commute by transit in the United States remains small—averaging about 5 percent in the nation's metro areas—but since the 1990s, transit's share of American transportation has grown, especially in recent years.[11] From 2010 to 2011, as vehicle use declined, transit use jumped by 2.3 percent, reaching its second highest ridership since 1957 (after 2008) and increasing by another 5 percent from 2011 to 2012.[12] According to the Federal Transit Administration's National Transit Database, the total annual miles traveled on public transit increased by 20 percent from 2000 to 2011.[13] As more comfortable and classy urban rail systems become available and mobile device applications allow would-be passengers to use GPS to track buses, many people who can afford a car are choosing to ride transit.

The 2000s also saw a bicycle revolution. The largest changes in America's transportation behavior from 2000 to 2009 stemmed from an increase in city bicycling.[14] Bicycling's share of commutes in the nation's thirty largest metro areas' central cities increased by almost 60 percent from 2000 to 2009.[15]

America is slowly responding to the demand for alternative transportation.[16] Since 1981 a dozen formerly bus-only cities have built light rail systems.[17] Cities are building bike lanes by the tens of miles. They are becoming serious about walking, rewriting street standards and zoning codes to encourage getting around on foot.

On America's onetime frontier, the same trends are apparent, and in some cases westerners are leading the way. A report by the Maryland Public Interest Research Group found that interior western metro areas for which data was available all experienced declines in VMT for 2006–2011, including Salt Lake City, Tucson, Albuquerque, Spokane, and Denver, whose VMT decreased by over 10 percent.[18] The West offers many of the nation's best new rail systems and has experimented with train-like buses called bus rapid transit.[19] Western cities with new rail systems are seeing their populations ride transit significantly more, including 33 percent increases in per capita transit miles traveled in metropolitan Salt Lake City and Phoenix and almost a 300 percent increase in Albuquerque.[20] A recent Brookings Institution report ranked the best and worst cities in the United States for transit service to and from work, and all of the top ten cities were in the West. Considering that, unlike the older cities in the East and the Midwest, the largely post-auto metros of the West are building both their transit and transit-supportive communities from scratch, that's remarkable.

In addition, western cities have pioneered bike-sharing programs, doubled and tripled their bike lane miles, and brought mountain trails into urban transportation networks. The West has become home to America's most physically active populations.[21]

Clearly, in the West we have an opportunity to decide which way we want to point our arrow and to reconcile the contradictions between the soul of the West and our servitude to the auto. To redirect all the State Streets. It is clear the car is not going away, nor should it. But what we have are possibilities, options, choices in a world where only one choice existed for the last fifty years.

But back to my road trip. A solo journey by the station wagon that we bought to transport our daughter safely was less appealing than by my departed silver pickup. So I thought of another idea. When I had traveled to other countries, in Europe as well as in South America and Asia, I got around by train and bus without even thinking about it. Who would rent a car in those places? Who would want to? I had covered hundreds of miles by train and bus in China and Peru. I had traveled their cities by cabs, trains, bike, and foot without ever looking for parking. Why couldn't I do the same thing at home? And so I became intrigued by the prospect of a carless road trip through the West—what the West would feel like without the speed and convenience of a car or whether it was even possible.

Planning this trip also became an investigation of sorts, and I set out a few parameters for it. First, I would need to understand the West's cities, simply because most westerners lived there. Our lifestyles drove almost everything that shaped the West, from our footprint on the land to our economic opportunities. Changing the West had to happen in the cities. If the places we lived couldn't embody opportunity, freedom, and adventure, how could the rest of the West? I wanted to talk to people in the cities who were changing how we got around them, fundamentally shifting the foundation of the region.

I researched the changes taking place in the ways the urban West got around, and I picked six cities to visit on my trip. These cities embodied the important qualities I saw in the West, in the frontier of America, and were now beginning to rediscover the region's character and identity—and the common thread was ditching the car.

But I would also need to understand the vastness around the cities, the space of the American West. So in between my urban stops I would travel historic routes of the region in order to appreciate the origins of these qualities of the West and America and how we might recapture and reinterpret them. My hypothesis was that these historic routes—Spanish explorations, emigrant trails, railroads, early highways—created and shaped the modern West and the things we liked about it. I wanted to gain a history of the western road trip, if you will. As John Wesley Powell found out 150 years ago, explaining the West requires a mix of adventure and public policy. And I believed that the people I'd encounter in the twenty-first century would be caught in the same themes of this young American province as those in Powell's time.[22]

I drew my route from Las Vegas across the three deserts of the Mojave, the Colorado Plateau, and the Great Basin north to Salt Lake City, across the Rockies to Denver, down the Front Range into the Great Plains, back over the Continental Divide, through the Navajo Reservation and down to Phoenix, then due north a thousand miles to Boise, and finally out nearly

The trip.

to the West Coast to Portland. In a few places, I could not avoid the car, but mostly I found ways to travel without one—by bus, train, and on foot. My bicycle, packed with panniers and decked out with a GPS, would be my principal vehicle.

Each chapter in this book is focused on a segment of this trip. More importantly, though, it is focused on a quality, a characteristic, an ingredient of America that has traditionally been owned by the West: the future, the land, opportunity, freedom, adventure, and mobility. Each of these was born in the torturous historic transportation routes I would be exploring. Each was heightened by the automobile, just as each was threatened by overdependence on the automobile. And now, each is experiencing a revival in the cities of the West by people choosing to get out of their cars and explore other ways of getting around. Each of the six chapters follows this story arc: the West created, lost, and reclaimed.

With the auto's hold on the American West seemingly loosening, I set out to see how we are reclaiming America's frontier and the things we love about it. If not the car, what does define the West? I took to the road to find out.

Notes

1. By "our country," I mean the United States of America, separate from the Native American nations that lay in its path of westward expansion. The land that, through conquest, became the American West, likely meant different things to these communities and nations.

2. Bill McKibben, *Eaarth: Making a Life on a Tough New Planet* (New York: Times Books, 2010), 55.

3. According to the National Center for Safe Routes to School, 48 percent of children five to fourteen years of age usually walked or bicycled to school in 1969. In 2009, 13 percent of children five to fourteen years of age usually walked or bicycled to school. "How Children Get to School: School Travel Patterns from 1969 to 2009," The National Center for Safe Routes to School, accessed July 16, 2014, http://saferoutesinfo.org/sites/default/files/resources/NHTS_school_travel_report_2011_0.pdf.

4. And, as we will find out, they aren't even very good for that anymore.

5. This is to say nothing of the use of the auto as a tool to marginalize poor populations and communities. Freeways allowed middle- and upper-class residents to live in distant suburbs while working in the city while fragmenting and cleaving off the urban fabric of working-class communities. This was especially true in the industrial cities of the East, Midwest, and West Coast, but it happened in the Interior West as well.

6. "2009 American Community Survey," US Census Bureau, accessed July 16, 2014, http://www.census.gov/acs/www/data_documentation/2009_release/.

7. Eric Sundquist, "Per Capita VMT Ticks Down for Eighth Straight Year," State Smart Transportation Initiative, accessed February 25, 2013, http://www.ssti.us/2013/02/per-capita-vmt-ticks-down-for-eighth-straight-year/.

8. Todd Litman, "Changing Travel Demands: Implications for Planning," Planetizen, accessed August 22, 2010, http://www.planetizen.com/node/45665.

9. The proportion of workers commuting by private vehicle—either alone or in a carpool—declined in ninety-nine out of one hundred of America's largest urbanized areas between 2006–2011; the proportion of households without cars increased in eighty-four out of the one hundred largest urbanized areas from 2006 to 2011; and the proportion of households with two cars or more decreased in eighty-six out of the one hundred largest urbanized areas from 2006 to 2011. See "Transportation in Transition: A Look at Changing Travel Patterns in America's Biggest Cities," Maryland PIRG, last modified December 4, 2013, http://www.marylandpirg.org/reports/mdp/transportation-transition.

10. The 2000s were the first decade since the automobile era began in 1900 in which the number of vehicles per person was smaller at the end of the decade than at the beginning. See Norman Garrick, "The End of the Automobile Era?" Planetizen, last modified April 12, 2010, http://www.planetizen.com/node/43731.

11. A study by Steven E. Polzin and Xuehao Chu concluded that in the last few decades transit trips had risen overall. Polzin and Chu found that transit trips declined in the early 1990s, followed by ridership growth through 2001, at which point ridership began declining again before rising in 2004. "A Closer Look at Public Transportation Mode Share Trends," US Department of Transportation, Bureau of Transportation Statistics, *Journal of Transportation Statistics* 8, no. 3, accessed July 16, 2014, http://www.rita.dot.gov/bts/sites/rita.dot.gov.bts/files/publications/journal_of_transportation_and_statistics/volume_08_number_03/html/paper_03/index.html.

12. "10.4 Billion Trips Taken On U.S. Public Transportation In 2011: Second Highest Annual Ridership Since 1957," press release, American Public Transportation Association, last modified March 12, 2012, http://www.apta.com/mediacenter/pressreleases/2012/Pages/120312_2011Ridership.aspx.

13. "Transportation in Transition," Maryland PIRG.

14. A key force underlying these changes appeared to be a major generational shift in how Americans viewed urban life, which is to say, life for 80 percent of us. American cities had found new vitality as the focus of the latest generation to come into adulthood. This millennial generation was less likely to want to own a car and more likely to want to live in an urban place. In 2008, 82 percent of twenty- to twenty-four-year-olds had their driver's license, down from more than 87 percent in 1994, according to the Federal Highway Administration. The percentage of new cars sold to twenty-one- to thirty-four-year-olds hit a high of nearly 38 percent in 1985 but stands at around 27 percent today. Allison Linn, "Carmakers' Next Problem: Generation Y: People in Their Teens and Twenties Are More Interested in Gadgets than Cars," NBC News, last modified November 4, 2010, http://www.nbcnews.com/id/39970363/ns/business-autos/t/carmakers-next-problem-generation-y/.

15. Yonah Freemark, "Transit Mode Share Trends Looking Steady; Rail Appears to Encourage Non-Automobile Commutes," The Transport Politic, last modified October 13, 2010, http://www.thetransportpolitic.com/2010/10/13/transit-mode-share-trends-looking-steady-rail-appears-to-encourage-non-automobile-commutes/.

16. In March 2010, the US Department of Transportation (DOT) announced a new bike and pedestrian planning policy "to incorporate safe and convenient walking and bicycling facilities into transportation projects. Every transportation agency, including DOT, has the responsibility to improve conditions and opportunities for

walking and bicycling and to integrate walking and bicycling into their transportation systems. Because of the numerous individual and community benefits that walking and bicycling provide—including health, safety, environmental, transportation, and quality of life—transportation agencies are encouraged to go beyond minimum standards to provide safe and convenient facilities for these modes." http://www.fhwa.dot.gov/environment/bicycle_pedestrian/overview/policy_accom.cfm, accessed March 15, 2010.

17. Eric Jaffe, "Can Light Rail Carry a City's Transit System? It Can If It's Built Right, As in Portland Or San Diego, and New Research Explains Why," Citylab, last modified August 1, 2012, http://www.citylab.com/commute/2012/08/can-light-rail-carry-citys-transit-system/2786/.

18. "Transportation in Transition," Maryland PIRG.

19. Adie Tomer, Elizabeth Kneebone, Robert Puentes, and Alan Berube, "Missed Opportunity: Transit and Jobs in Metropolitan America," Brookings, last modified May 12, 2011, http://www.brookings.edu/research/reports/2011/05/12 jobs and -transit.

20. "Transportation in Transition," Maryland PIRG. The Salt Lake City metro area's per capita transit passenger miles traveled (PMT) increased from 138 to 174 (with the new TRAX light rail system); Phoenix's increased from 82 to 110 (with the new Valley Metro light rail system; and Albuquerque's increased 21 to 129 (with the new Rail Runner commuter rail system). These were all top-twenty-in-the-nation increases.

21. Seven of the top ten states with the highest percentages of highly physically active adults were in the West. "State Indicator Report on Physical Activity, 2010," Department of Health and Human Services, Centers for Disease Control and Prevention, accessed July 16, 2014, http://www.cdc.gov/physicalactivity/downloads/PA_State_Indicator_Report_2010.pdf.

22. And while it may seem odd to place the muddy theories that drive the shaping of cities alongside the clear(er) narratives of history—after all, city planning and western history each have their own canons, jargon, stories, and professions—each works at one end of the short timeline of the same remarkable American region; they can't help but to inform one another.

WAYS
to the
WEST

PART I

The Future

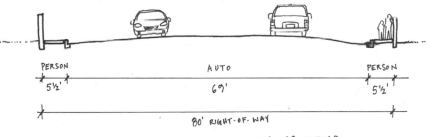

PERSON   AUTO   PERSON
5½'   69'   5½'

80' RIGHT-OF-WAY

TROPICAL PARKWAY, NORTH LAS VEGAS

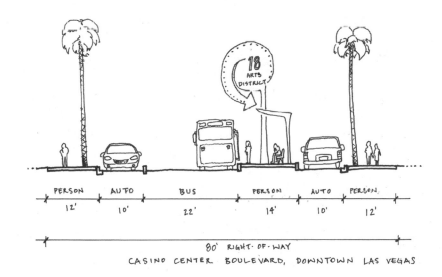

PERSON   AUTO   BUS   PERSON   AUTO   PERSON
12'   10'   22'   14'   10'   12'

80' RIGHT-OF-WAY

CASINO CENTER BOULEVARD, DOWNTOWN LAS VEGAS

DOI: 10.7330/9780874219937.c001

The First Ride

I began in Las Vegas, flying into McCarran International Airport with a plastic bag of bike touring panniers, a tent, a pad, and a bike in a cardboard box. In planning, I had quickly realized that from the moment of getting off the plane, I had to think through every detail of my trip differently than past road trips. With a car, you wander into the driveway, throw your stuff in, and go. With a bike as your central vehicle, supplemented by bus and train, you face obstacles at every turn. How do you carry your bags? How do you transport your bike? How do you get around safely? How do you protect your stuff from thieves? I spent weeks figuring out how to pack.

The first day's logistics were especially challenging: transporting, reassembling, and loading up my touring bike in what could be the most car-dependent city in America. My plan was to take my boxed bike and bags and board an express bus at the airport that would take me through Las Vegas to within a few hundred feet of where Google pinpointed the location of an REI. There, I could assemble and tune my bike and pack my panniers. My rig would then be operational, and I would ride to my hotel, the Stratosphere, on the Las Vegas Strip.

Most people who come to Las Vegas don't bring much luggage. My plane mates cruised by me wheeling small carry-ons, traveling light for the forty-eight-hour debauchery of the Las Vegas experience. I was practically alone in the baggage claim area. As I waited I admired all the signs around the baggage conveyors—Garth Brooks at the Wynn and some kind of show called "Toptional."

An airport employee saw my awkward load come off the conveyer and offered me a flatbed cart for wheeling my baggage. She led me to where I could catch my bus, which was down an elevator and out a back door into a parking area apparently used exclusively for limousines. Even early on a Sunday morning, several people waited for the bus. Three people talked about how Las Vegas was scary and spread out. A couple spoke to each other in a Native American language, smoking cigarettes.

My bus arrived on time. It was sparsely occupied, mostly by European tourists headed to Strip hotels: a few older women and a slew of backpackers, all satisfied to pay a quarter of the cost of the Strip shuttles that left from the airport's front door. They all disembarked where our route crossed the Strip, at the MGM Grand, and I rode alone up Interstate 15 to the US 95 freeway and out to the west end of the valley. We arrived at a newer shopping center, and the bus stopped at the curb. I got off with my plastic bag and bike box.

I plopped them down on the sidewalk and heard that sad sound of a bus driving away from a desolate place. It was a cool, silent desert morning—the calm before the daily Sunbelt city storm of heat and traffic. Surrounding me were hard surfaces ready to bake in the sun: asphalt, concrete, desert clay. New fan palm trees were planted on the street and two condo towers rose from parking lots in the distance. Beyond them, the morning sun lit the Spring Mountains in cool blue and tan. No person was in sight. I was alone in this sprawl of 2 million people.

I dragged my box and bag along the barren sidewalk toward the shopping center, hoping that the REI would make itself apparent. It did not. This was one massive center. The store didn't answer its phone, so I began walking though an empty parking lot, hoping I had chosen the right direction. If not, I could be correcting course for up to an hour. I still could see no other humans.

Providently, a golf cart emerged. It whirred across the empty parking lot in a careless diagonal direction, ignoring the drive aisles, which cast a sort of post-apocalyptic feeling over the scene. The cart came over to me and the driver, a heavy Latino in a white golf shirt, looked at my baggage and asked if I was looking for the REI. He was a member of the shopping center's security staff. I admitted that I was lost.

"I'll give you a lift," he said.

The store wasn't open yet, but the bike mechanic saw me on the way from his car to clock in and let me in the back door. The mechanic, a tall, tanned, rugged white guy who looked out of place in suburban Las Vegas, opened the box and went to work on reassembling and tuning my bike. I roamed the empty store and picked up a few other items: more bike tubes, sunscreen, a roll of Tenacious Tape to repair a hole in one of my panniers that had occurred during the plane trip.

At noon, I was ready to ride. My main vehicle for the next three weeks would be a black LeMond Poprad cyclocross bike, with two waterproof panniers hanging off the rack, a front pannier on my handlebars, a tent and sleeping pad bungeed onto my rack, and a bike computer to log my miles. I asked a couple I passed to take a picture of me and my rig in front of a marble fountain next to the Mixt Urban Beauty Bar.

My first ride was ten miles back toward the Strip to my hotel. I steered out of the parking lot and turned left onto a huge arterial street, the needle of the Stratosphere as my guiding beacon.

It took roughly fifteen seconds for a Cadillac Escalade to bear down on me, honk, and shriek by. My bike and I, we did not belong here.

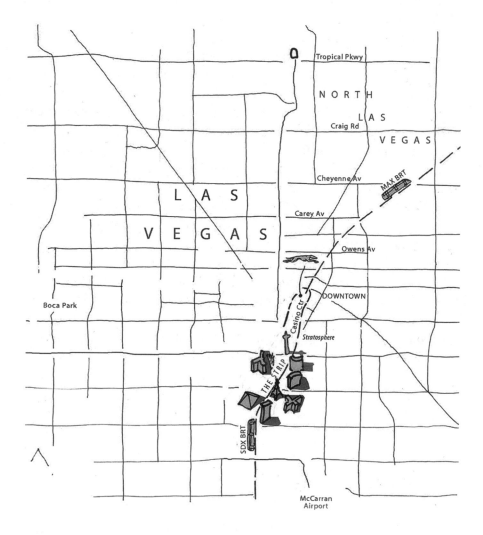

Las Vegas.

Insanity

Forty-five minutes later, I pulled into the Stratosphere driveway alongside the taxis and tour buses. Walking my bicycle though the casino on the way to the front desk, I was confident that it had been some time since they'd seen a two-wheel tourer pull up. I felt so out of place that I began to be nervous that they might not let me stay here with my bike, so I propped it in a corner out of view of the desk staff. I checked in and navigated without a problem to my $30 room, which had a huge bed and one small window in the corner. After a rest, I went down to stand in line for the double-decker elevator, billed as the world's sixth fastest. It shot you up 900 feet in thirty seconds, after which you discovered that you could tie into a bungee cord and free fall for almost the same distance in even less time.

The top of the Stratosphere housed a grotesque amusement park built to heighten the Las Vegas experience even more for its visitors. Out on the observation deck, a hot wind blew and the popular song "Dynamite" created a pool party atmosphere. The sun shone at the golden angle of evening. I stood against the railing and watched a series of people climb onto a ride called the X-Scream, in which a small car rolled down a short track mounted on a mechanical arm extending from the observation deck. After riders were told to buckle in, the arm wound up and dropped the car down the track, aiming toward the ground far below, leading to gravity and terror for two seconds, the shrieks drowning out Taio Cruz. The car slammed to a stop at the end of the track, then paused for the effect of suspension over the thin air before the arm retracted and the car emptied out for the next ride.

On the other side of the circular deck was a carousel that dangled passengers over the desert abyss at various angles so that eventually their torsos were spinning almost parallel to the sidewalk, visible distantly below. The passengers sat in pairs on the seats positioned at the ends of green levers that extended out over the tower. Once the machine was up to speed, the passengers stuck out their arms, like they were flying over the desert. This ride was called Insanity.

I looked over the sun-bleached splendor of the Mojave Desert in early April from almost a quarter mile up and wondered whether I was looking at the past or the future. In the daylight, from this high above, Las Vegas's old downtown didn't look different from the downtowns of unassuming small cities of the American West, like Cheyenne or Great Falls. The streets were dutifully named after western mountain men or military explorers: Lewis, Clark, Carson, Fremont, Ogden, Bonneville. The stumpy hotel casinos could have been office buildings for branch companies, and around them the land spread out into train tracks, a freeway, leafy neighborhoods, open desert, and gaunt mountains.

But the other side presented a totally different view. As Insanity continued to spin, I walked back around the deck. Below was the twenty-four-hour thrum of urban activity: world class, intimidating. It spread down Las Vegas Boulevard like the leavings of a lumbering giant or an archipelago of cooled eruptions. Pink Circus Circus, gold Trump, copper Wynn, blue-green MGM Grand. A tectonic place in constant motion.

This was why I had started here. Las Vegas was hardly representative of the greater West, but it was emblematic of it. Looking over this scene, I decided that what had happened to Las Vegas over the last fifty years is what all western boosters secretly had in mind when they put their stakes in the ground. This was the city they built as boys with erector sets and dreamed about in Pullman cars. Perhaps in one of the dreams an amusement park had topped a 1,000-foot tower. The sleepy small city had definitely been Plan B.

Las Vegas began as a train stop and exploded with the easy auto access from Los Angeles. The city's transportation network was still the thing that tenuously held together its clamoring growth. To the west and to the east, silvery arterial streets spread, and the grid of streets seemed to be a thin net. The freeways below arched over each other in ways that reminded me of carnival rides. I could see a few vehicles from the Las Vegas Monorail circulating. I could almost hear the streets breathing hard to keep up.

After the sun set on the Spring Mountains, the Insanity and X-Scream still running, I took the elevator down to street level and walked out into the night. I caught a bus traveling south on Las Vegas Boulevard. It was a bronze two-story double-decker, almost full with tourists bound for the Strip. I found a seat on the top level near the front and sat with a large family.

I alighted across the street from the Wynn and then walked past Treasure Island, the Mirage, and the Bellagio fountains beginning their show. Near Caesar's I got excited when I thought I saw another bike tourer, but his panniers were just full of stacks of cards with pictures of naked women to flick out toward tourists on the street.

At the Flamingo, I rode the escalator to the bridge over Las Vegas Boulevard and walked out into the middle of it. The bridge bounced with all the pedestrians moving across. Like the double-decker bus, the Strip's pedestrian bridges provided a good vantage point in all directions. Around was the thick mix of the old Vegas of the Flamingo, the 1990s themes of the Bellagio and Paris, and the new global urban sophistication of The Cosmopolitan and CityCenter. I counted a dozen video screens, probably a million lights. Below was Las Vegas Boulevard itself. It had to be the most congested street in the United States, if not the world: a dozen lanes, bumper to bumper, twenty-four hours a day, 365 days a year. A hundred modes of transport: cars, trucks, convertibles, limos, stretch limos, Hummer limos, trucks with ads in their beds, taxis, people walking, escalators, stairs, buses, double-decker buses, topless double-decker tour buses, monorail, kids on BMXs, Coors beer trucks (72 ounces for $18!), elevators, double-decker elevators, shuttle buses, motorcycles, jacked-up Suburbans, crotch rockets, trucks carrying crotch rockets, police on bikes, helicopters, bus coaches, semi trucks, Jazzys, Harleys. It went on.

I considered the modes of transportation not created yet, the visions of the future that Las Vegas conjured in the minds of Americans. Get off a plane at McCarran and have your bags already checked into your hotel; get on the monorail and in six minutes be at your hotel, keys in your pockets and bags in your room. Begin the Las Vegas experience in Victorville, California, by boarding the 150-mile-per-hour Desert X-Press bullet train and enjoy valet service, hotel check-in, and through-checking of baggage straight to the resorts. Or ride the Maglev train from Anaheim at 300 miles per hour without even touching the ground.

And so this place would seem to embody the promise of multiplicity in the new century, as the capital of a New West again ready, through rapidly developing technology and globalizing capitalism, to simulate the desires of the nation. The West has always projected America's future to the rest of our growing country. The West invented amusement parks, retirement communities, and women's suffrage. Historian Kevin Starr called the West a "testing ground for the national experience."[1] The strangeness and openness of its landscapes have always offered possibilities. Its population centers have not been cities as much as open-ended questions or upward arrows.

The late historian and Las Vegas chronicler Hal Rothman considered Las Vegas the first city of the twenty-first century. Like the transportation options along Las Vegas Boulevard, one had access to a plethora of new identities and corresponding experiences. The Strip, like the West, had always engaged the fantasies of its visitors. It promised a sense of mobility, of movement.

But the Strip was a false front. It was the ultimate fake western street. Behind the promenades of the Strip loomed oversized infrastructures of parking and highways and utilities sucking energy from the planet to create comfortable excitement along Las Vegas Boulevard frontages. Las Vegas's sense of the future was escape from an increasingly troubling present situation, nowhere more apparent than in Las Vegas itself. Despite the many transportation modes and choices streaming under me on the Strip, the city, and the West it embodied, was in the death grip of one mode.

These days, in the throes of the recession, the questions were darker and the arrows pointed down. Las Vegas, like the West itself, was caught between the future and the past. Behind the display pieces of the Strip, like I had seen from the top of the Stratosphere, Las Vegas was just a little city of the West taken to the extremes of the last century.

It took venturing off the Strip and into the rest of the Las Vegas Valley to see that insanity.

Polly Carolin: veteran planner, geologist, project manager. You put it on her desk and she figures out how to get it done. She came to Las Vegas in 1993 to help the Southern Nevada Water Authority put the second straw in Lake Mead, the dammed section of the Colorado River immediately below the Grand Canyon. Carolin was charged with buying land leases for the pipe. That was a heady time for Vegas, the beginning of what Hal Rothman called the "Mirage Phase," when a new set of casino hotels took their place along Las Vegas Boulevard, providing jobs for the thousands of newcomers moving into well-watered suburban houses. She had come to Las Vegas from Tucson, and she brought a suitcase full of water conservation ideas. At the onset of the Mirage Phase, Las Vegans didn't want to hear them. They lived in the Mojave oasis, the namesake Springs.[2]

Even stronger than the thirst for water was the zeal for automobility. In the 2000s, as the boom continued, the metropolis grew new subdivisions by the week. The Regional Transportation Commission of Southern Nevada (RTC), the agency in charge of a motley mix of transportation matters in the Las Vegas Valley—transit, funding, traffic signals—was looking for a planner to push the sacrificial cause of alternative transportation, and Carolin applied. Having grown up in California and worked in Chicago, she always liked getting around by transit and walking. She had moved into a Vegas neighborhood where she could actually walk to a grocery store, so she appreciated such things. And so she spent the last years of her career jousting with agencies, engineers, schools, real estate developers, and pretty much everyone in the valley over the token inclusion of sidewalks and crosswalks and trying to limit what became the bane of her workday, the 6-foot-high stucco-covered masonry wall.

The next morning Carolin gave me a different Las Vegas experience. We met at a Starbucks in a strip mall along Camino al Norte in North Las Vegas, an incorporated suburb that sat in the lap of its namesake like an overweight kid. North Las Vegas was the third-largest city in Nevada and occupied an area almost twice the size of San Francisco. The city had grown quickly. The streets around us had random names that seemed to have been flung on them like a child's art project—Ann Road, Journey Way, Wizard Wand Street, Carlos Julio Avenue. A few miles to the north was the Bruce Woodbury Beltway, which circulated eerily out through the desert past unfinished subdivisions.

This wasn't an arbitrary location. We were in the heart of zip code 89031, which in early 2012 became known as the foreclosure capital of the United States. While North Las Vegas had the highest rate of home foreclosures, 89031 had the highest rate within North Las Vegas. Within this zip code, 2,500 houses had recorded foreclosure filings in the last year, nearly one in ten homes.[3] Earlier in the year, the city had declared a financial state of emergency.[4] On its website, a special page offered "Key Things to Do If You Are Facing Foreclosure."

Places like North Las Vegas had signaled a stunning turn of events for the West. Just a few years earlier, many of the West's newest communities—once the nation's fastest-growing places and declared to be its future—had lost value and were emptying, much of their infrastructure was crumbling, with no money to maintain it, a veritable house of cards. Over 80 percent of the zip codes with the highest foreclosure rates were in the West.[5] Some were new kinds of ghost towns, places that had been built but in which no one would ever live.

Did any of the blame lay in the way in which the West had grown, the kinds of places we built, our well-known bet on the automobile? Much of the data said yes. Studies undertaken throughout the downturn linked auto dependency to higher rates of foreclosure.[6] Researchers found that rising gas prices in the late 2000s had dramatically increased the transportation costs of households with long commutes. For many of the communities where these households were located, the car was the only transportation option. These households had less flexibility in their budgets. This made communities with no other transportation options less desirable, lowering a home's value while overloading the transportation cost for the household owning it, helping to tip the nation toward mass foreclosures.[7]

Plus, the inflexibility with which suburban environments were built and the limited transportation options they presented prevented them from adapting to changes, an idea some coined "resiliency." Like single-crop monocultures, transportation systems dependent on one mode often had trouble adjusting to new demands or circumstances—à la the housing bust. And, as urbanist Christopher Leinberger put it, "Once large-lot, suburban residential landscapes are built, they are hard to unbuild."[8]

I also wondered what kinds of places existed in 89031 and what it felt like to walk around its streets and blocks. Before I did anything on this trip, I wanted to explore the heart of the West's crisis of the future.

I had ridden my bike here from the Stratosphere, up through the quiet streets of downtown and under the I-15 freeway. I took Martin Luther King Jr. Boulevard twelve miles up the valley to North Las Vegas. Arterial streets marked the miles—Vegas Drive, Lake Mead Boulevard, Carey Avenue—and for the first few, the riding wasn't bad. Traffic was light, drivers were deferential, and I rode on a nice shoulder at the side of the roadway. But somewhere north of Cheyenne, the sixth mile from downtown, walls appeared on either side of the roadway and the sidewalks shrank, turning a relatively democratic, if ugly, road into an auto-archy. The cars revved and pushed on the gas a little harder the farther north I went. I returned to riding on the sidewalks. The development on either side of me was becoming spotty too, like a checkerboard alternating stucco box houses with white dirt. By the time I turned into my destination shopping center, I had entered the upside-down world of North Las Vegas.

Carolin drove up in a silver compact sedan with the license plate "PLANR" wearing a tie-dye shirt, black slacks, and white Keds. She had driven from her house, near Tropicana and Pecos, east of the Strip; Las Vegans all seemed to describe their location as (a) relative to the nearest arterial road intersection and (b) relative to the Strip. She had come even farther than I had.

Carolin had never been to the particular place we were walking. But so what? It looked like a hundred other spots in the valley she had seen, fought over, and watched transform with despair. Her twenty years in the valley, ancient by Las Vegas standards, had attuned her to the depressing nuances of Vegas development. Like some ghastly form of geology, she could read the stories in each new blacktop road and stucco-slathered wall.

"Well," she said grimly, "let's go."

We walked through the strip mall parking lot up to a wide, empty street called Tropical Parkway and pressed the walk signal. I looked across the intersection and saw on the corner a grand monument to the subdivision behind it: a fountain, turf berms, and foliage that seemed to have been stolen from Florida. On either side, houses poked up above an artless white wall.

"Now," Carolin said. "If you lived in this subdivision and wanted to go shopping, even though that center with the Starbucks is right across the street, there's no way you could walk there."

There had been no entry to the subdivision at the corner, and the white wall ran unbroken toward the horizon as far as I could see. The walk signal came on and we crossed and began walking along the edge of the subdivision. It wasn't technically hot yet, but the wall, the concrete sidewalk, and the asphalt roadway sucked in the heat. Strolling quickly became trudging.

These adverse conditions weren't an accident but a formula. The street we were walking on, Carolin said, was exactly 100 feet wide. During the boom, the city grew in the 1-square-mile increments that had been the building blocks of the modern West since the 1785 Land Ordinance that effectively set the template for dividing the rest of the US frontier. A developer would develop a fraction, or aliquot, of that square mile. In many cases, the developer had to dedicate just 50 feet along the edge of the subdivision, which made half a street. And so even the public realm was a patchwork of half-streets—that always made Carolin mad.

Without looking down, she told me that the sidewalk was 5 1/2 feet wide—5 feet plus the curb. That was the minimum standard. The rest of the 89 feet was striped for vehicle lanes. There was no on-street parking and no requirements for marked pedestrian crossings of the street between the traffic signals a half mile or a mile apart. This wasn't a major link in the automobile network, yet it had been designed for cars to drive 50 miles an hour.

So you didn't want to walk along the street, you didn't want to cross the street, and, as Carolin was showing me, chances were you didn't have the gumption to be walking outside of your subdivision in the first place. It was a no-man's land. We had been walking for twenty minutes from the Starbucks, having gone nearly halfway around the wall's square circumference, and still had neither found a place to penetrate it nor saw another human.

"There's no way in," she said, "and no way out."

Walking with Carolin revealed something fundamental to the failure of the West. We had created places built for cars, not people. This may sound overly simple, but think about it: Cars are easy to please. They need only room and smooth pavement. They run best at relatively high speeds, without stopping. The operator of a car wants a simplified, consistent environment.

What people need is more complex. We are slower. We need shade and water. We like interesting things to look at and explore. We generally like to see the faces of other people. Walking, that basic unit of human movement, has a long list of demands that Clark County jurisdictions were in no mood to satisfy in the 1990s and 2000s. The city had a lot of money as it grew, but not a lot of time. Because developers and Clark County usually paid for their own infrastructure, they could ignore the environmental obligations that would have come with federal money. If it wasn't a traffic lane, the engineers didn't want to talk about it. There was no reason to accommodate people when they could expediently design to the vessels that carried them through the modern world.

They designed these aliquots for cars to move through in very narrow and specific ways. You usually had one way to get from your house out to a larger road and one way to move to an even larger road. From there you had your choice of identical six-lane walled arterial streets.

The homebuyers had little choice in the first place, Carolin explained. The blue-collar workers of the gaming industry sought to buy into this bonanza, and the houses here were cheap, for Vegas. The real estate machine that cranked out these subdivisions convinced itself and everyone else that people wanted walled subdivisions with traffic moats. Questioning the walls had become political taboo because they allegedly kept people safe. "When we drive the streets all we see are block walls," noted one *Las Vegas Sun* letter writer who was considering retiring to southern Nevada. "Why do all the houses have block walls around their property?"[9]

And so not only was the transportation choice here reduced to one option, residents also had few options to experience the city as humans. The West had always been built on the quick bucks of land speculation, but here and now it had been taken to a whole new level. This was quintessential cheapness, and the Great Recession of the late 2000s had exposed it in a spectacular way.[10]

A few minutes later we did reach an opening in the wall where a street led into the interior. Carolin was surprised that we could walk freely into the subdivision; gates protected most of the newer developments. Inside the walls, the houses didn't look as new as they should have and the sidewalks were starting to crumble. These private roads, where developers could get away with less right-of-way and no sidewalks, had no benefit of city maintenance.

After snaking through the empty streets, we emerged on the other side of the subdivision and traversed another 66-inch sidewalk on its far side. A person approached, and I had to walk in the gutter to let her pass. We walked to the next intersection and stood at the crossing of two collector streets completely sealed in by masonry walls. No traffic was in sight on this silent morning. The street we walked on ran out into the open desert past a dead end sign.

We could see the desert beyond. It was bright white and almost hurt my eyes. Carolin explained that most of the ground we had been standing on used to be publicly owned and federally managed, part of the American commons that had been auctioned off in the boom, the modus operandi for a lot of money and not a lot of time. There, beyond the Bruce Woodbury Beltway, was a theoretical limit to the auctioning of land for cheap subdivisions. And so, while some cities had an urban growth boundary, Las Vegas had a disposal boundary.

When Carolin and her husband moved to Las Vegas, they bought a house in a gated community. They tired of it and moved closer to an arterial street and commercial areas they could walk to. When the market tanked and her old neighborhood lost much of its value, her new house held.

"As we Baby Boomers retire, we'll really want to be where we can walk, because we won't be allowed to drive," she said. "I don't know what we're going to do here."

But there were other possibilities. The scene we saw at the end of the road in North Las Vegas was not the only option for the future of the West. I'd spend the rest of my trip looking for the other ones.

The Man behind the Double-decker Buses

Polly Carolin kept a glimmer of hope for the future because over the last decade a series of public works directors throughout the Las Vegas Valley had retired. Public works directors hold a lot of power in how a city is built. They set the city standards for its infrastructure. Engineers and their manual of the American Association of State Highway and Transportation Officials, *A Policy on Geometric Design of Highways and Streets*—commonly known as the "Green Book"—had long controlled how nearly every street in America was built. Those retiring engineers comprised the generation that had presided over the peak of automobility, when the stars of the transportation universe aligned to outfit the growing, thriving cities of the West with clean, simple roads that would continue the expansion.

In the Las Vegas Valley perhaps the most important changeover occurred when Jorge Cervantes became Las Vegas's public works director. Cervantes had come to the City of Las Vegas in the late 1990s as an assistant traffic engineer and rose through the ranks. He was beginning to change standards set in the 1970s, when Las Vegas was still a small city.

After I said goodbye to Carolin, I rode back downtown and met Cervantes at Las Vegas City Hall. The building was brand-new—a sharp civic monument that, in its crisp acoustics and prisms of crystal-refracting light, resembled Superman's Fortress of Solitude. There was something about the contrast between the modern, elegant space of the lobby and the fact that it was completely empty. Like Vegas itself, it felt at once world-class architectural object and one-horse town. Cervantes let me store my bike in one of the similarly empty, new-smelling conference rooms and then we were off on a walk through downtown.

Even before we left City Hall, Cervantes had launched into an enthusiastic summary of the city's plans to revitalize its downtown, beginning with the visions for the vacant block across the street.

"Wait a minute," I said.

He stopped and looked back.

"Aren't you the public works director?" I asked. "I mean, aren't you an engineer? You're talking like a city planner."

Cervantes smiled. "My wife is a planner," he said. "We are always having conversations about what a road is for."

As a traffic engineering student in the 1980s, Cervantes learned that a roadway primarily exists to move vehicles. But as he worked on projects as a young engineer in Texas, he realized that you couldn't eliminate congestion—the traffic engineer's primary charge in the modern world—simply by adding more lanes. Like some others throughout the profession, he realized that streets were for moving people, not cars. He developed the mindset that road designers need to accommodate all users.

The metrics to evaluate transportation systems are far too simplistic and auto-based, he said. Cervantes thought, for example, that transportation systems should be judged on travel time reliability instead of capacity. Once this mindset is adopted, he explained, the city looks a lot different to a traffic engineer.[11]

And yet, many in his profession, and in Las Vegas, did not share his view, favoring the solutions of the automobility monoculture. As Cervantes said, "I've got a lot of old school engineers in my shop."

It took the leadership of the Jorge Cervanteses to change the heavy book of street standards the engineers consulted religiously. Nothing would happen until cities changed the standards. So that's what Las Vegas had done. As we walked out of the City Hall forecourt, Cervantes gestured to the empty block across the street. "Look over there," he said. "You can see the old standard. A 5-foot sidewalk plus curb."

It was the same as the streets I had walked in North Las Vegas. The same everywhere in the valley. The bare minimum, little more than a buffer for fast-moving cars traveling along the walls on the side of the street. From where we stood, the sidewalk didn't read as a real sidewalk, just a ledge of concrete that happened to cling to the edge of the block.

"Five-foot sidewalks everywhere in the city," Cervantes said. "So you have these tunnels of roadway."

The new standard tripled the sidewalk's width, but it also recognized that a sidewalk served multiple purposes—as a place where people walked but also the place where people stopped to talk or sit, where trees softened the concrete jungle. In Las Vegas, as in most cities in the fast-growing West, these aspects of the sidewalk had been completely dismissed in the frenzy of the boom.

New downtown Las Vegas sidewalks would have 10 feet of walking room. That walking area would be separated from the roadway by a 5-foot area for street trees and shrubs and utilities. This area served as a buffer for pedestrians against the traffic in the roadway. It used to be common for the city to put a landscape strip on the outside of the sidewalk, along the building or parking lot, but Cervantes explained that it should have gone on the inside, buffering pedestrians from traffic and allowing the sidewalk to interact with the buildings alongside it. Now it would have to. The new standards also changed Las Vegas's tradition of planting shade trees on east-west streets and palm trees on north-south streets. Now all streets would have shade trees to attempt to cool the hot pavement.

To accommodate the increased width of the walking area, the city had shrunk the room given to motorists. There had been plenty to share. The previous standard for a typical collector street had been two 12-foot travel lanes and two 14-foot travel lanes. The average car is about 6 feet wide, so that means that a car had at least twice its width in room to maneuver. Now the lanes were 10 and 10 1/2 feet wide.[12]

We walked along a street that had been built with the new standard, and at once the environment appealed to my senses; it was cooler, quieter, more comfortable. I intuitively felt the balance evening between person space and vehicle space. You could start to build a city for people with these new streets.

⸻

At the same time that Jorge Cervantes was changing the Las Vegas street standards, the Regional Transportation Commission was trying to reshape the valley's transit system. In the field of alternatives to driving, transit is a crucial option. It is a way to move people long distances much more efficiently, and often much more affordably, than private cars. For example, considering the total costs of a trip per passenger mile, a light rail system moves people at about half the cost of a roadway in a medium-sized city.[13] Because it moves people rather than cars, transit produces fewer destructive impacts to cities and their public spaces. And there are perks to riding transit: You don't get road rage. You can read a book or your e-mail. You don't need to find a parking place. Every city needs a good transit system, and Las Vegas had a history of lacking one. At one point it had a privately run company running sixteen buses with up to one and a half hours between pickups. The Citizens Area Transit (CAT) had been created in the early 1990s by the RTC as a passable public alternative.[14] For many in the valley, the acronym stood for "Can't Afford Transportation."

RTC general manager Jacob Snow aimed to change that perception. Snow was a former airport planner from Boulder City, one of the small towns Las Vegas swallowed as it reached down the highway toward Hoover Dam. Unlike Polly Carolin or Jorge Cervantes, Snow was a southern Nevada native. His ancestors were southern Utah Mormons, descendants of Lorenzo and Erastus Snow, namesakes of the brilliant red rock Snow Canyon.

Snow had spent his whole life in the Las Vegas area except for two periods. One was during college and graduate school at Brigham Young University in Provo, where he also worked for a short time for the City of Provo Community Development Department.

The other was during his Church of Jesus Christ of Latter-day Saints mission, which he served in Hong Kong. In Hong Kong, Snow saw how efficient it was to get around, to move people quickly. He especially liked the double-decker buses. He used to ride those double-deckers and sit right up front on top and watch the streets roll by underneath.

After Hong Kong and BYU, Snow didn't necessarily want to return to Las Vegas. But a job at McCarran Airport was available, so he spent the next decade solving the growing airport's surface transportation issues and in 1999 began to manage the RTC.

Snow wasn't able to meet with me during my stay in Las Vegas; he had just taken another job as the city manager of Henderson, the Las Vegas suburb where he lived. But I had talked to him on the phone a few weeks earlier. Like Cervantes, the valley's growth made Snow uneasy, especially the dependence on the automobile. Perhaps, he thought, the valley's cities should be building a grid of streets instead of walling off every new subdivision. Snow was used to experiencing the city from outside a car—he had always been a cyclist. He said it kept him aware of his environment. Polly Carolin often ran into him in the RTC elevator wearing spandex, on the way in from his commute.

As a regional transportation agency manager in a town run by the development industry, Snow had a snowflake's chance in hell of changing how cities were building out in the short term. But he could create his own parallel world, one that would outline an alternate future for the valley. In the early 2000s, Snow learned that the Federal Transit Administration was looking for an agency to try out something that was becoming known as bus rapid transit. Bus rapid transit, or BRT, tries to mimic a rail system in its speed and streamlined experience, but at a much lower cost. It can have its own lanes, and traffic signals can give the buses priority. The vehicles can even look like trains, with covered wheel wells and aerodynamic designs. BRT systems are designed to save time. Riders buy tickets at machines outside the bus and board at bus level, which allows wheelchairs to get on quickly. These changes may seem small, but they add up; a BRT system can, in some cases, cut conventional bus travel times in half.[15]

Many transportation experts regard BRT as the future of transit for the world. Cities like Curitiba, Brazil, and Bogota, Colombia, had powered urban revitalization on the spines of bus rapid transit lines. Studying abroad in Ecuador during college introduced me to the pleasures of riding on a trolley-like bus that ran on its own little road. I could never figure it out—was it a bus or a train? I didn't know it at the time, but this was bus rapid transit.

Bus rapid transit was in its infancy in the United States. Only Cleveland, Boston, and Eugene, Oregon, had built real BRT lines, and they were short. Jacob Snow had no real familiarity with BRT, but he thought it could solve several problems that faced Las Vegas. Snow wanted to speed up the system and make it more competitive with driving. And even as the region's population exploded, the RTC finances struggled, an early crack in the financial solvency of the Las Vegas Valley. Snow thought a successful BRT system could get the agency back in the black.

The first BRT corridor the RTC chose to build was Las Vegas Boulevard, north of downtown. It was a blue-collar part of town with already high ridership from workers riding to the Strip. Snow convinced the state highway department to help him build the project with federal funding. The result was the MAX, a bus line that had many of bus rapid transit's most important elements—level boarding, off-bus ticket machines, dedicated lanes for part of the way, nice stations, and the train-like design of the buses. The barrel-shape of the bus shelters recalled Curitiba's BRT stations.

Jacob Snow was confident the MAX would work, and in many ways it did. The line's ridership increased by 40 percent after a few months. And it captured what transit planners called "choice riders," those who have the option to drive a car but choose to ride the bus. In the United States, attracting choice riders has been the utmost desire for many transit agencies because doing so reduces the stigma of riding transit and expands their markets. RTC surveys indicated that 10 percent of the line's riders had gotten out of their cars and began using the bus.

Recalling his days in Hong Kong, Snow replaced the older Strip buses with double-decker buses. Reducing the fleet of buses and having more tourists riding them brought the agency a profit. The RTC created a series of three commuter express buses whose goal was to bring workers living in distant corners of the valley to the employment core quickly and comfortably. It was on these routes that the RTC was most nakedly competing with the single-occupant automobile. Snow knew the system's ridership patterns had begun to change when he started noticing nicer vehicles parked in the park and ride lots.

Las Vegas's bus system began to resemble Curitiba's star-shaped pattern of buses running out from a center point.[16] When you look at the bus system maps of most western cities, you usually see an unintelligible rainbow grid of lines that don't seem to have any logic. When I look at those maps, I think of all the times I've had to take Bus X on a north-south street to an arterial intersection and then waited on the corner for Bus Y on an east-west street, an utterly painful journey. The RTC map has this rainbow grid too, but in the latest iteration, it's possible to make out a star-shaped pattern of express and BRT routes, and you can envision them efficiently pumping workers into the core at a point in the future. Like the city's new street standards, it set out a different vision of what a western city should look like.

Many in the City of Las Vegas welcomed Jacob Snow's vision. In the mid-2000s, Snow had made a presentation to the city on how bus rapid transit could help ignite its redevelopment plans. Jorge Cervantes sat in the audience and was intrigued by the project's mimicry of a light rail system at a fraction of the cost and the kinds of streets these new buses could inhabit.

A Different Kind of Street

Cervantes and I walked eastward along Clark Avenue until we came to what he wanted to show me: the confluence of the rapid transit renovation and the city's new street standards. We turned the corner onto a street that looked like a desert awash in Vegas neon, sweeping through downtown in an alternate vision of the future. In place of the listless black asphalt were red-painted bus lanes running down the center, islands of meadow grass, wide sidewalks and palm trees, and sleek metallic transit stations punctuated by repurposed neon signs. The auto lanes that usually dominated American streets were pinched to one each way.

This street, Casino Center Boulevard, had been built on more ruins of bad ideas. The Las Vegas Monorail, which I had watched from the top of the Stratosphere, was originally intended to run along the Strip but had been built behind the casinos after a casino-led lobbying effort. I had ridden it on past visits; it was not often a convenient way to get anywhere. In 2010 the monorail filed for bankruptcy.

The federal government had committed a chunk of funding for a $400 million extension of the monorail north to downtown but had pulled the money when the monorail's first phase didn't cover its operations or debt. Cervantes and the city swooped in and asked the Federal Transit Administration if they could salvage the money to do a bus rapid transit project on Casino Center Boulevard. This one would be a full rail emulation project, providing many of the benefits of light rail, with nice stations running down the center of the street, at a third of the cost. The RTC called it the Strip & Downtown Express—the SDX.

Its design was a revolt against a hundred twentieth-century engineering notions, each of which became a point of contention between Cervantes and the old school engineers in his shop. The project captured two traffic lanes—Robin Hood–style—from the car to give to the bus rapid transit system. This was engineer heresy; Cervantes was consciously creating more auto congestion.

But, he said, "even if we lost capacity it was worth the trade." In exchange for the lanes, Las Vegans received faster transit and a better walking environment.

Smaller design choices also shaped the street's character. The engineers designed the street corners with a smaller radius, which gave more space to pedestrians while forcing cars to slow down before they turned. They extended the sidewalks at the corners to make the crossings shorter. They colored the bus lane concrete a ruddy red to communicate that the space belonged to transit. They made the sidewalks as wide as the vehicle lanes, giving more total space to pedestrians than cars.

Each one of these details challenged entrenched practices. For example, Cervantes explained, there had been a long conversation with the fire department. Fire departments often constrain pedestrian-oriented projects like this one because they need to move large vehicles through streets in emergencies. But the city had negotiated with the fire chief for a certain curb radius to accommodate the smaller service trucks, and the massive outriggers did not need to get through the narrowed street.

I thought that the best thing about the street was that it looked and felt like Las Vegas. Casino Center showed that being a city street in an American desert doesn't necessarily mean a bleak tunnel of asphalt. The humanity and personality of this one street spun a different future for the West than the one cast in walls and monolithic blacktop. This street was a hint of what a future less focused on the automobile might look like.

I stood back and compared Casino Center to Tropical Parkway. They were exactly the same width. But where most streets in Las Vegas and the West felt like auto-ways that happened to allow people, Casino Center felt like a street for people that happened to allow buses and cars to move through. Where most western streets left people one option, this gave them many.

At the same time, the segment of Casino Center where we were now walking was next to vacant lots. It struck me that whereas the Tropical Parkways of the valley had been hastily crammed through new subdivisions during the good times, Casino Center had been crafted amid vacant lots in bad ones. The place didn't make sense today, but it would in the future. Unlike in the rest of the city, where the whims of the market dragged roads along, this street would lead the way forward—as streets in the West had done many times before.

Bus Number 11

Jacob Snow liked to tell a story from when he was a missionary in Hong Kong. He and his mission partner once met a woman at a park in the city, and at a point in the conversation, they asked her how she got to the park.

Bus number 11, she told Snow and his partner, in Cantonese.

Bus number 11? They wondered what bus that was. They knew the Hong Kong transit system and had never heard of bus route 11.

Bus number 11, she confirmed with a smirk. And then she took her hand, extended two fingers, planted their tips on the concrete picnic table, and began moving them along the table, like little legs going for a stroll.

"Bus number 11," Snow learned that day, was Cantonese slang for walking, which was often the easiest way to get anywhere in congested Hong Kong. It was the way anyone got to and from the bus, streetcar, or subway as well as around town. Everyone is a pedestrian; every trip is a walking trip at some point. Even auto travelers are pedestrians until they get in a car. Walking is a fundamentally human activity, the basic unit of movement. Places where you can't walk are inherently inhumane places. Any place that aspires to be a city of the future has to be a place for walking.

Snow, Cervantes, and others trying to change the transportation system were providing more options. That is rule number 1 for creating transportation for people rather than cars. Rule number two is bus number 11: the foundation for any good transportation system is walking.

When the real estate market busted in 2007, the City of Las Vegas cut its planning staff in half. With few applications left to attend to, the planners that remained at least had time to think about the city that was left in the wake of the housing bust and recession. They sifted through unfinished business from the last decade, finding in their city's dust-collecting master plan a clear directive from citizen input to improve walking in Las Vegas.

Now they had time to figure out what that meant. And they decided that hostility to walking was at the rotten core of what was wrong with their city. Planners knew that Las Vegas could not continue to be what it had been in the 1980s, 1990s, and 2000s. They winced at the city's poor air quality and massive use of water. The amount of raw acreage the city consumed for new development was hideous. But the planners recognized the common thread as the inability to walk in most of Las Vegas. Not walking meant that you traveled exclusively in a car, even for trips just around the corner or just outside the wall of your subdivision. That meant worse air quality or a sedentary lifestyle that ushered you into diabetes. It meant that people who couldn't afford a car were constantly exposed to the danger of being hit by one.

Streets like Casino Center and the public policy that guided them were a beginning—a kernel—toward a different future. As Jorge Cervantes and I continued to walk, I wanted him to guide me through the engineer-y details of the street design, but he was again speaking planner talk. He saw Casino Center as the spine of a district that would grow in the future. By now we were out of downtown, in what used to be a no-man's land between downtown and the Strip. During the boom, he explained, nearly three dozen projects were planned for Casino Center. Land was inexpensive and available. The engineer walked along the empty lots and dilapidated buildings like an ecologist exploring the scene of a wildfire. "In time, we're going to see development come back," he said. "It may take a while, and instead of high-rise you might see more mid-rise development. But it will come back."

Eventually we came to a collection of rehabbed buildings, where a group of men stood talking in a circle. Cervantes knew them.

"Jorge," one of the guys said. "How's it going?"

He introduced me. The men had founded an arts district that had taken hold in the area south of downtown. Cervantes cheerfully reported to them that he was trying to do something with a sliver of the median along the street so it wouldn't just be barren.

"Hey," he said. "Maybe someone could build a sculpture!"

We walked back to City Hall along 1st Street, along a nice new 18-foot-wide sidewalk adorned with rusted steel planters that the artists had designed. It was afternoon, and becoming hot. The cool desert morning was gone. Cervantes and I hightailed it back to the Superman fortress as fast as our legs would take us.

Greyhound I: Las Vegas to St. George

I planned to leave Las Vegas that night. I had a ticket for the 9:45 Greyhound bound for Salt Lake City—a city I'd get to eventually—but only after a detour through southwest Utah and northern Arizona. I'd get off the bus in St. George, the first town across the Utah border. The next morning I would meet my friend Jonny Wilde, and we'd ride into the Arizona Strip for a three-day bike tour.

After I said goodbye to Jorge Cervantes and retrieved my bike from City Hall, my phone rang and I saw it was Jonny. He was calling from near Fredonia, Arizona, where we'd pass by on our bikes. He'd just stashed a cache of water.

"Where are you staying?" he asked.

"The Stratosphere," I said.

"I stayed there once, it was pretty bad."

"It's the typical Strip thing. Big bed, small window."

"I was there ten years ago, and it was bad," Jonny said. "I can't imagine what it's like now."

I told him I'd ride over to his motel in the morning for breakfast and said goodbye. Talking to Jonny, I realized I still needed to buy some water bottles.

There would be no water along much of our route, and we needed to carry as much of it as we could. I had a Camelbak hydration pack but wanted bottles too. I had been riding with cheap plastic bottles from a drugstore. There was no telling what I'd find in St. George, so I had to buy them in Vegas. Google told me a few bike shops lay west of downtown, on the other side of the interstate.

By now I knew how to bicycle in Las Vegas. Rare were streets both lightly trafficked and long–distance, so you had to choose: either you wound your way through empty residential streets that you hoped kept going, and then dashed across the busy arterials or else you braved the arterials' sidewalks and hoped a car coming out of a parking lot didn't broadside you. Riding on the arterials in traffic was not an option.[17]

Somehow, coming out of downtown, I found a bike lane on a relatively pleasant street named Alta Drive. I rode west toward the Spring Mountains quavering in the heat, pausing under the freeway to appreciate the rare shade.

I turned down Valley View Boulevard into an industrial zone behind the Strip. Neither bike store was there. One had completely vanished and the other looked to be closed permanently. And from what I could see through the painted block letters on the dirty windows, it traded mostly in BMX. A waste of a half hour and another few miles sucked from my reserves of energy.

And now I had to either retrace my route or cross what Hal Rothman called the "Great Wall of Las Vegas"—the barrier created by I-15, the Union Pacific tracks, and the Strip—at a point I hadn't planned. Because I was the kind of traveler that avoided taking the same route twice, I headed into the Great Wall, turning left on Spring Mountain Road, which I knew intersected Las Vegas Boulevard at Treasure Island, where I had stayed once before.

I was also the kind of traveler who is prone to making choices without enough research, and that was how I ended up the most scared I had ever been on a bike. Spring Mountain was a nasty arterial road, which by now I was used to. But it rose up to pass over the railroad tracks and I-15, and once elevated, it joined a multilane off-ramp from I-15 coming in from the right. That meant that where I hugged the narrow right shoulder before the merge, I was now between two of the center lanes of a total of eleven lanes of traffic, with cars driving 70 miles per hour: I was riding in the middle of a freeway.

I am not sure this happens to other people, but when I get on a bike in a challenging environment, I become hyper-aware. Adrenaline pulses through me, and I feel like a different animal. I become more confident. Scientists call this "flow." My brain advised me that I was scared, but my nerves told me I was in control. I swiveled my head around at the cars switching lanes like in a video game. Then I looked straight ahead and pedaled hard.

And I got through it. When I landed on Las Vegas Boulevard a few long seconds later, it was a beautiful evening on the Strip. I felt like I had pushed through the membrane of a bubble and now breathed a different kind of air. The fleets of limos, taxis, and buses wound down between the city's greatest monuments as if in concerted movements. Coming onto the Strip this way was like coming into a theater from its backstage catacombs.

Like Manhattan, the Las Vegas Strip was one of the few completely man-made places I'd been where I experienced the sublimity of major landforms in the light of the evening. You had to be in the middle of it. From the outside, the Strip was a strange appendage to the city's modest skyline. Inside, it was its own dramatic landscape and, like mountains and canyons, its size and audacity had a serene power that you felt only at this time of day.

At the green light on Spring Mountain Road, I rode across Las Vegas Boulevard and right into the forecourt of the Wynn and was able to turn around and take a right onto the Strip. The night before, I had seen a few cyclists on the Strip and had wondered what they were thinking. But it couldn't be worse than what I'd just done. I stood at the exit of the Wynn for a few minutes and noticed that the Strip traffic platoons had large gaps, so at the right time I could ride out into the three northbound lanes of Las Vegas Boulevard and have it all to myself, for a little while.

I returned to the Stratosphere and walked my bike through the rows of slot machines to the elevator and packed up.

———————————————————————————

The Las Vegas Greyhound station was on Main Street, between Bridger and Carson Avenues. It seemed to fit right in with downtown, a fluorescent space that never slept and a convenient revolving door for street hustlers. The station's interior was a chaos of travel—lines of standing people, bags, and chairs crisscrossing the small room. I leaned my bike against one of the walls and someone loitering outside kept ramming into the wall, almost knocking my fully loaded touring rig over every few seconds.

When I planned this trip, attempting to map a route of carless transportation across the interior West, I quickly realized that Greyhound was my only option for many of the links I needed to make. Amtrak went fewer places than I had hoped, and I didn't have the time to cover most of the long distances on a bike. I'd heard all the negative things about Greyhound and had ridden a few over the years, but the relatively cheap tickets and the night runs that most buses made allowed me to make the most of my days. I worried about being able to take my bike on board, and I called Greyhound, where a woman assured me I'd be able to store my bike below. On paper, it was going to work out just fine.

Unfortunately, a lot of the Greyhound experience isn't on paper. I stood in line for a half hour to check my bag, and when the agent saw my bike, he scowled.

"You got a box for that?"

I shook my head. "The person I talked to didn't say anything about a box."

"Gotta have a box. We sell 'em. Fifteen bucks."

I checked my watch. After the wait in line, I had twenty minutes before the scheduled departure. I handed him $15 cash, and he gave me a new flat cardboard box, packing tape, and scissors, and then told me to get out of the way. I taped up the box and then broke my bike down as little as possible—I would have to put it back together two hours later when I arrived in St. George. I took the wheels off, then the seat, and tried to get the bike in, but the pedals wouldn't fit.

"You have to poke holes for the pedals," the agent shouted across the room. "That's what the scissors are for."

Once I stabbed in the incisions and arranged the pedals as he suggested, the bike slid in, and I fit the wheels in. The box bulged with the headset still attached, but it closed. For an uninterrupted two-hour ride, it would do.

I handed the tape and scissors back to the agent and then heaved the box onto the luggage scale along with the rest of my bike touring gear, which I placed into the large plastic bag I had used on the plane. The line for my bus was starting to move out the door.

He raised another eyebrow. "No plastic bags. They catch fire with all the heat down there. You gotta find something else."

I put one of the panniers on my back and wrapped my remaining pannier together with my tent and pad with a couple of bungee cords, which barely held it together. I showed the agent, who silently handed me a claim ticket. In this station you had to lug your bags with you to the bus, and I picked up my bundle of stuff and shuffled toward the gate. It was about three minutes before departure time, and the last person in line was filing through the door. I was dripping with sweat. Halfway across the room my bundle burst, and the tent and pad dropped to the floor. This was a shitshow among shitshows, in a theater where I suspected they occurred constantly.

When I got outside I told the baggage handler to please be careful with my bike, but he seemed not to care. I boarded the coach and took the one seat left, which was next to a sleeping, obese man. I sat.

Twenty minutes late, we pushed off onto I-15 north. The driver turned off the interior lights and most passengers sat quietly with their heads down. I had a fine view of the Las Vegas Strip—the one I was used to seeing, as if driving through on a regular road trip.

In walking, bicycling, and riding buses through Las Vegas, I experienced the illusion of the future that automobiles had provided the American West and saw it for what it is: a dead-end road. But I also saw other route choices that would create more options for moving around our cities and making them places to walk, to be human. The ways in which we get around, the character of our streets, and the places they define constitute a fundamental and primary choice about the future of the West and its place at the forefront of America.

Next, I'd step back to explore the most basic and recognizable aspect of the West: the land itself. This would allow me to see how our roads and streets treat the western landscape and create the very foundation for the way we move and the way we live.

Out of the city, the desert was dark. Time sped by, and at a certain moment I looked at my phone and saw the time change from 11:33 to 12:33. I was in Utah.

Ten minutes later, we exited the freeway and stopped in the parking lot of a McDonald's. Most passengers on the bus got off and pulled out cigarettes. Some went in to get food. I put my box on the little stoop of sidewalk in front of the McDonald's entrance and began cutting the tape with my Swiss Army knife. A short, stocky Latino guy had set up next to me to charge his phone in the electrical outlet and took an interest. The look on his face asked what in the hell was I doing. I told him.

I lifted out my bike, attached the seat, and then turned it upside-down to put on the wheels. The Latino guy watched, smoking, as I balanced my panniers on the rack and tied down the tent. He said he was traveling to Nampa, Idaho, where he lived, from Tijuana.

"Whoa," I said. "Long way."

"Yes," he said. "You too."

It was a beautiful, warm night. I found a dumpster in the corner of the parking lot, where I tossed my box. I got back on my bike and rode across the street to my motel.

Notes

1. John M. Findlay, *Magic Lands: Western Cityscapes and American Culture after 1940* (Berkeley: University of California Press, 1992); Kevin Starr in William G. Robbins, "In Search of Western Lands," in *Land in the American West: Private Claims and the Common Good*, ed. William G. Robbins and James C. Foster (Seattle: University of Washington Press, 2000) 6.

2. Although once all the groundwater was pumped out, the Southern Nevada Water Authority became a national model for water conservation. Las Vegas banned lawn in front yards and by 2013, the SNWA managed to cut the valley's water usage by two thirds of what it had been in 2003. Ian Lovett, "Arid Southwest Cities' Plea: Lose the Lawn," *New York Times*, last modified August 11, 2013, http://www.nytimes.com/2013/08/12/us/to-save-water-parched-southwest-cities-ask-homeowners-to-lose-their-lawns.html?pagewanted=all&_r=0.

3. Les Christie, "Foreclosures: America's Hardest Hit Neighborhoods," CNNMoney, last modified January 23, 2012, http://money.cnn.com/2012/01/23/real_estate/foreclosure_zip_codes/index.htm.

4. Lee Ross, "North Las Vegas City Leaders Declare State of Fiscal Emergency," FoxNews.com, last modified July 17, 2012, http://www.foxnews.com/politics/2012/07/17/las-vegas-city-leaders-declare-state-fiscal-emergency/.

5. Christie, "Foreclosures."

6. Stephanie Yates Rauterkus, Grant Thall, and Eric Hangen, "Location Efficiency and Mortgage Default," *Journal of Sustainable Real Estate* 2, no. 1(2010). As the National Resources Defense Council explains, "The 'Location Efficiency and Mortgage Default' study pulled highly detailed performance data on 40,000 mortgages in Chicago, Jacksonville, and San Francisco, as well as census data on neighborhood conditions, incomes, and automobile ownership. The study then modeled the factors influencing the likelihood that lenders would foreclose on homes in these cities. The average number of vehicles owned per household in the neighborhood, after controlling for income, was the key variable used as a proxy measure for location efficiency and was studied for its impact on mortgage foreclosure. Control variables also included the debt-to-income ratio at the time of mortgage origination for each borrower, borrower credit score, the home loan-to-value ratio at the time of origination, the age of the mortgage, whether the mortgage had fixed or adjustable rate interest, whether the property was owner-occupied, and variables on neighborhood racial composition, population growth, and unemployment. In all three cities, the study found statistically sound results that the probability of mortgage foreclosure increases as neighborhood vehicle ownership levels rise, after controlling for income." "Reducing Foreclosures and Environmental Impacts through Location-Efficient

Neighborhood Design," Natural Resources Defense Council, last modified January 2010, http://www.nrdc.org/energy/files/LocationEfficiency4pgr.pdf.

7. This study found that in 2008, transportation costs were, on average, 23 percent higher in the fifteen California cities with the most foreclosures. These high-foreclosure cities were, on average, sixteen miles farther from a core city and had half as many public transit riders per capita. As the authors write, "the calculus of suburban living changed. High commute costs made typical homes less valuable and mortgages less affordable for homeowners characterized by lower average incomes than urban counterparts. Some households could no longer meet mortgage obligations and others walked away from mortgage debt that exceeded the deflated market values of their homes." Steven Sexton, JunJie Wu, and David Zilberman, "How High Gas Prices Triggered the Housing Crisis: Theory and Empirical Evidence," University of California Center for Energy and Environmental Economics, last modified February 2012, http://www.uce3.berkeley.edu/WP_034.pdf.

8. Christopher S. Leinberger, "The Next Slum?," *The Atlantic*, last modified March 1, 2008, http://www.theatlantic.com/magazine/archive/2008/03/the-next-slum/306653/. The covenants, conditions, and restrictions that were the currency of North Las Vegas's subdivisions further prevented future flexibility.

9. "Ask Mr. Sun: Why Do All the Houses Have Block Walls around Their Property?," *Las Vegas Sun*, last modified March 24, 2010, http://www.lasvegassun.com/news/2010/mar/24/why-do-all-houses-have-block-walls-around-their-pr/. Mr. Sun's answers ranged from copycat developers to a lame way to provide privacy for bad subdivision layouts to the attraction of a cheap building material.

10. Researchers have also demonstrated the increasing value of places built for people rather than cars. The Partnership for Sustainable Communities explains that "Joe Cortright, founder of Portland-based Impresa, Inc., gathered the price information for 90,000 recently sold existing housing units in 15 metro areas across the country. Cortright then rated each property using the 100-point system created by WalkScore.com, which scores properties based on the number of amenities like schools, parks, or grocery stores that are within walking distance. He found that in 13 of 15 metro areas, a property's Walk Score adds $500 to $3,000 to the selling price compared a similar house in a less pedestrian-friendly place." Bendix Anderson, "Suburban Ghost Towns," Sustainable Communities, accessed July 17, 2014, http://www.p4sc.org/articles/all/suburban-ghost-towns.

11. "We go to enormous expense to save ourselves small increments of driving time," commented engineer Charles Marohn, calling the past half century of street engineering "professional malpractice." "Confessions of a Recovering Engineer," Strong Towns, last modified November 22, 2010, http://www.strongtowns.org/journal/2010/11/22/confessions-of-a-recovering-engineer.html#.U8gAo4BdXSE.

12. The largest hurdle, Cervantes said, was the development lobby. He found support for the new street standards because the city didn't increase the required right-of-way.

13. Considering vehicle, roadway, and parking, roughly $0.70 per passenger mile for light rail compared to $1.20 for driving per passenger mile. Todd Litman, "Rail Transit in America: A Comprehensive Evaluation of Benefits," Victoria Transport Policy Institute, last modified January 16, 2012, http://www.vtpi.org/railben.pdf. In nearly every city, the workings of transit agencies are the subject of intense scrutiny by the public and often the media over finances, service, and politics; the scope of this book does not include digging into these detailed and nuanced matters.

14. Geoff Schumacher, *Sun, Sin & Suburbia: An Essential History of Modern Las Vegas* (Las Vegas: Stephens Press, 2004), 226–29.

15. "Bus Rapid Transit: Bus System Design Features That Significantly Improve Service Quality And Cost Efficiency," TDM Encyclopedia, Victoria Transport Policy Institute, last modified June 11, 2014, http://www.vtpi.org/tdm/tdm120.htm.

16. This was made easier by Las Vegas's unique attribute of a very concentrated employment base in the service jobs of the Strip; and the commutes run twenty-four hours. When I rode the MAX into the Bonneville Transit Center in the early morning, there was a massive pulse of bus transfers between graveyard and day workers.

17. This is one of the toughest problems facing bicycle planners in western cities like Las Vegas that are built on the mile grid, because arterial connections occur only at the mile and possibly the half mile. One solution is to build wider protected and separated bike lanes on the arterials. Another is to build "bike boulevards" that run parallel to the arterials, offering the same connectivity through bike-activated signals crossing the arterial streets.

PART II

The Land

SALSIPUEDES

SAN BARTOLOMÉ

THE GRAND STAIRCASE, NEW SPAIN, 1776

FARNSWORTH PEAK

MOUNT OLYMPUS

JORDAN RIVER

INTERSTATE 15

TRAX

SALT LAKE VALLEY, UTAH, 2012

DOI: 10.7330/9780874219937.c002

Black Hill

When I was growing up, my family drove to St. George, Utah, every November to eat Thanksgiving dinner with my grandparents. During our visit, we'd always take a ride around town, and my grandmother, who we called Grammie, would point out all the new subdivisions pushing into the desert—like a colony of Las Vegas, all golf courses and red-tile-roofed faux-adobe houses. *I tell you,* Grammie said every time, with more than a hint of pride, *it's just changed so much.* My "Aunt" Ina, who had been Grammie's best friend since grade school in the 1910s, lived in a house on St. George Boulevard, and by the time I was a small child, in the 1980s, car dealerships and fast food franchises completely surrounded the house.

In the boom of the 1990s and 2000s, St. George, like Las Vegas, was one of the fastest growing cities in the United States. Grammie and Ina were both born there, little more than a decade after Utah had become a state and barely fifty years after the Mormons had settled it. When they were kids, a few thousand people lived in St. George.[1] During our drives, Grammie speculated that her town's population might in her lifetime reach 100,000, a projection that sounded absurd to my young ears. In 2003, the year she died, Washington

County's population hit 104,000.[2] My grandparents and their friends drove their Oldsmobiles around a Sunbelt retirement community that was a different world than the frontier town where they grew up.

The one change Grammie wasn't proud of was the Black Hill. This volcanic mesa rising to the west of St. George was a key part of the city's origin story. In 1861, believing the warm weather of what was beginning to be called Utah's Dixie would support cotton farming, Latter-day Saint church leader Brigham Young called a troop of Saints to settle along the Virgin River. They came into the St. George valley over the Black Hill, and, according to legend, a member of the party birthed a baby at the top of the hill before the troop descended to claim its land.

The Black Hill was also the most noticeable natural feature in a landscape that was the collision of three of the West's largest geographic provinces—to the southwest, the Mojave Desert, with its Joshua trees; to the south and east, the Colorado Plateau, with its sheer red rock; and to the northwest, the high sagebrush desert of the Great Basin. This varied geography gave St. George a stunning natural setting. A block of Moenave sandstone called the Sugarloaf—a giant "DIXIE" painted on its face—rose north of town (when, as a kid, I learned of the Sugarloaf in Rio de Janeiro, I thought they had copied St. George). The Pine Valley Mountains also climbed north, a Great Basin range of 10,000 feet. To the east, the towers of Zion National Park rose in a spectacular skyline. Within the St. George city limits one could find Kaibab limestone, Moenkopi mudstone, Chinle shale, Navajo sandstone, and a dozen other rocks that had weathered, pressed, and eroded for millions of years. The Black Hill, for its part, was formed by a million-year-old lava flow. Underneath the Mormon heritage and the banalities of suburban growth was another story told in geologic time, of one of the most radical landscapes on Earth.

In its rush to grow, St. George had trampled ecosystems, sucked aquifers, and polluted rivers. Short of mountaintop removal or strip mining, it was hard to screw up the bedrock of the city, yet St. George had managed to do this too. The Mormon founders of the city had quarried the Black Hill's rock for the foundation of the St. George Temple, and Dixie High School, like so many high schools in the rural West, had painted a giant "D" on the face of the hill. That was all fine with Grammie. But during the 1980s, someone began grading the Black Hill for condominiums, leaving long horizontal gashes where the underlying red clay soil had been turned up, so that from anywhere in St. George the Black Hill looked like it had giant razor cuts, in apparent recurring suicide attempts. Grammie, prone to superlatives, said each time we visited that it was the saddest thing she'd ever seen.

My view when I woke up at 6:00 the next morning told me St. George had continued to tread that same path. My second floor room faced the Black Hill, behind the pylon signs of Burger King and McDonald's and dying fronds of palm trees. (St. George, despite relentlessly billing itself as "Utah's Dixie" was just slightly too cold in the winter for palm trees to be completely happy, but that didn't stop people from planting them.) The early morning sun lit the Black Hill straight on. The top of it still had the marbled teal and black of desert shrub and volcanic rock, but almost the entire lower part had been scraped, the red dirt exposed like raw flesh. A few rows of condos had been built on the steep hillside, but mostly it was just pushed-around red dirt, someone's botched real estate dream.

I walked across the parking lot and around the pool to the lobby, where the clerk had checked me in the night before, a skinny hipster-type whose homely southern Utah accent gave him away. He mentioned that the room came with a large complimentary breakfast. I was supposed to eat at Jonny Wilde's motel with him and his family, but it couldn't hurt to have two breakfasts. Jonny and I planned on riding a long way today.

A tow truck driver with a lifting belt came over when he saw me making a mess of the waffle maker and walked me through the process. "I've been here for six weeks," I thought I heard him say to me. Fox News was on and a mom with three kids sat at the next table. I already felt a long way from Las Vegas.

After I finished my waffle, two bowls of granola with blueberries, a plate of sausage and bacon, and three glasses of orange juice, I walked back to my room, took a shower, and repacked my panniers. I rode up Main Street. It was a Tuesday morning. Sprinklers were on. Kids were walking to school.

Riding through St. George, I felt the Mormon grid. Like reaching the Tibetan Plateau and seeing the house compounds and prayer flags, you knew when you were in Mormon country by the settlement pattern—in this case, a large orderly grid of blocks and wide streets. When Wallace Stegner wrote *Mormon Country* in the 1940s, the telltale signs of Latter-day Saint communities had been the street grids and clumps of poplars in the desert. Now it was all about the cars and trucks that drove down those wide streets. The Latter-day Saint culture embraced cars. Utahns had traditionally owned more cars per household than residents of any other state.[3] In St. George, which had some of the widest streets in Mormondom, it seemed as if the directive existed to use the largest trucks one could find to fill the space from curb to curb.

This motel wasn't far from the one where I had stayed during my last visit here, almost a decade before, for Grammie's funeral. My grandfather had died ten years before that, and with no other immediate family left in St. George, I had no reason to return. It felt strange to be back, somehow divested in the place even with all the family history. I rode up to the St. George cemetery where we had buried Grammie and Grandpa. I had to call my dad for the exact location of their gravestone. As it turned out, he had just been down here to attend the funeral of a colleague who happened to be from a nearby town, and he was able to give me precise directions.

The grave was right near the maintenance shack, next to some juniper trees. I remembered when my grandparents had picked out this site and had shown it to my parents, my brother, and me. The day of Grammie's funeral, I was a pallbearer and helped the old Mormon men lift her out of the hearse that had driven from the ward building to the gravesite. We'd given Aunt Ina a ride back to her condo (she had since moved from the old house on St. George Boulevard). On the way she had given us Grammie's old "date book," a leather journal with all sorts of Grammie's appointments from the 1920s, the day-to-day life of a teenager in frontier Utah. Ina looked really good for a ninety-year-old woman, but she died a few months later and was buried here too.

The cemetery lay toward the head of the valley, where I could look south and see the geologic chaos in the blue mounds and towers in the distance. As a child, I based my opinion of St. George on swimming pools and trampolines and places to get hamburgers; even as a kid I recognized it as a second-rate backwater. Only abstract shapes surrounded the town. But at a certain point, I realized that the area outside St. George added up to something out of the ordinary. There were caves and creeks and buttes and arches, volcanoes and mountains, and deserts and cliffs. It was a first-rate landscape.

Before becoming St. George, it had just been a really spectacular valley in the desert. The first whites to see it were likely two weary Franciscan friars named Francisco Anastasio Dominguez and Silvestre Vélez de Escalante, who had trodden through the area in October 1776 looking for a way home to Santa Fe, New Mexico. The fathers left Santa Fe about three months earlier in search of an overland route to newly founded missions in Monterey, California.

They never made it. But in the process, they traveled a massive loop around the interior West—through New Mexico and what would become Colorado, Utah, and Arizona. Relying on Indian directions and guides, they found their way through some of the West's largest mountain ranges, around its largest canyons, along its deserts and lakes, and over its rivers. They blindly felt out the West's landscape for the Western world, and pieces of their route became major highways and population centers centuries later. In places such as the future St. George, they experienced the double thrill of both seeing the spectacular landscapes for the first time and assimilating them into the network of European expansion. As Escalante wrote, the expedition had "come to know such widespread provinces heretofore unknown" and that was "a greater reward and worth the longest journeys, the greatest hardships, and fatigues."[4]

These beginnings of European exploration of the West point the way to our first history lesson. From St. George, I'd pick up Escalante and Dominguez's trail southward into Arizona. I had seen the future of the West in Las Vegas; I wanted to understand how we got into our current position and how transportation had shaped it. So let's back up. America's frontier began with its land. The ways in which early European travelers like Dominguez and Escalante roughed it through the desert began the process that created the roads and places we have today.

A few hours after wandering the congestion of the Las Vegas Strip, I'd be in one of the most remote parts of the continent, tracing the paths that set the West in motion.

On the Trail of the Padres

The Wilde family was staying in a room in the Best Western Coral Hills, on St. George Boulevard, a few blocks from Aunt Ina's old house. It was a nice place, with swoopy modern buildings, a pool, and a few miraculously healthy palm trees. The two Wilde boys, August and Oliver, were bouncing around the room as Jonny packed up the bike trailer he'd be dragging into the desert on his cyclocross bike. He planned to bungee a giant yellow dry bag onto the trailer and was furiously trying to lighten his load.

Our plan was simple: ride south across the state line into Arizona into a region known as the Arizona Strip for a three-day tour that would roughly approximate a portion of the wanderings of Fathers Dominguez and Escalante. Jonny's family would meet us at Lee's Ferry, and I'd drive his car north to Salt Lake, one of two legs of the trip for which I could not find a non-auto substitute.

The Strip was a part of Arizona that had, for years, been an outlaw haven; it was out of the jurisdiction of Utah authorities, but the Grand Canyon prevented Arizona law enforcement from bothering anyone who wanted to hide out there.[5] Neither of us had been on a bike tour before, much less on dirt roads one hundred miles from the nearest town.

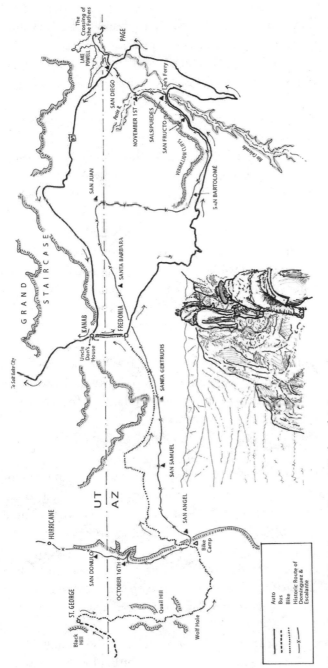

The Escalante and Dominguez Route, Utah and Arizona.

Today, you could hop in a Ford F-250 and rocket down the dirt roads of the Arizona Strip to the north rim of the Grand Canyon and be back by afternoon. But by choosing to move at 10 or 15 miles an hour, we ensured that our trip would take days, not hours. This speed would give us a much bigger appreciation for the immense distances these men traveled and the constant isolation and danger that the land presented.

Escalante's diary describes the distances they traveled in leagues; a league measured the distance covered by horse in one hour, generally about two-and-a-half miles. On a good day, they went about twelve leagues, or thirty miles. Although in such rough country, the fathers sometimes had to dismount and guide their animals on foot for leagues at a time. We hoped we wouldn't have to do the same with our bikes.

The padres traveled on Indian trails, and sometimes without trails altogether, but we needed decent dirt roads. Even with good roads, there was no guarantee that the spring wind wouldn't bring in a storm that would turn clay roads to glue. I had called the Bureau of Land Management (BLM) for information on the roads through the Strip. The person who answered in the St. George field office had never been there and had a ranger call me back. The ranger was not as certain-sounding as I hoped.

"Still an adventure going into that country," he said. There was no water. Getting lost in the web of logging and jeep roads was absolutely a possibility. He was just as confused as me about some of the conflicting names of roads and exactly what kind of condition they were in.

I asked if a lot of people did what I was about to do.

"Nope," he said.

Nevertheless, Jonny was on board. We'd grown up together and come of age hiking the Colorado Plateau canyons. Jonny was hungry to get to the Strip. He had fought some fires down in Wolf Hole and had always wanted to return. Like me, the more he explored the canyon country, the more he wanted to connect the remaining dots. The area between St. George and Zion and Grand Canyon National Parks was a part of the plateau he had not explored to his satisfaction. Was it scenic and spectacular? Maybe. But regardless, it was a piece of territory to lay eyes on and assimilate into the matrix of knowledge.

Our two main concerns became route finding and carrying enough water. I had painstakingly tried to erase almost all risk of getting lost by investing in a GPS and a full digital topographic map set. I drew the route in the map software then devised a clamp onto which I could mount the GPS so I could watch the dot click along the route as I rode, aware immediately if I took a wrong turn at any of the un-signed forks in the road I assumed lay ahead.

As for water, it was hard to picture how we could carry enough. There would be nothing even suggesting a stream or river for the three days. It was already nearing 80 degrees; by midday it would probably reach the mid-90s. We dumped some of our food to add more water.

We didn't start the ride until 11:00. We stopped in the BLM office for a paper map and then a building supplies warehouse to jury-rig Jonny's bike trailer hitch with some bolts. That was another huge difference between an auto road trip and a bike tour. When your car broke down, you found the nearest mechanic. When your bike broke down, you found some way to fix it yourself. The most common repair was a broken spoke, and I had taught myself how to change out a spoke before I left. As we were already repairing things at the outset, I figured we were in for some surprises down the road.

As we rode along the Virgin River out of St. George, I had that insidious feeling of being in the comfort and safety of familiar civilization but moving away from it to an unknown wilderness—the absurdity of climbing 3,000 vertical feet on bikes loaded with three days' gear and rations, riding into a people-less wilderness, starting at midday as the air temperature approached 80 degrees, and not really knowing what wild cards the roads would deal us.

The pavement ended at the Arizona line. We began climbing up the dirt road. It was steep and slow going at 6 miles an hour, and it didn't feel like we were getting anywhere.

Río Grande

Silvestre Vélez de Escalante was a twenty-six-year-old friar who had been wandering since boyhood. Escalante had been born in the mountains of northern Spain and while still an adolescent, came to the New World via Mexico City, where he took the Franciscan habit at age seventeen. He had lived in New Mexico for just two years, bouncing around assignments at two different pueblos—Laguna and Zuni—before the older Francisco Dominguez summoned him to Santa Fe.[6]

Dominguez had been sent to Santa Fe to evaluate the New Mexico missions, and as part of this work, he and others decided to look for an overland route to Monterey, on the California coast. The Franciscans were intent on creating a network of missions and Spanish civilization in the New World. Earlier that year, Fray Francisco Garcés had successfully found his way from Mission San Gabriel, near present-day Pasadena, California, to the Hopi pueblos. The Spanish now wanted to become familiar with the lands further north, in present-day Utah, and wanted to explore and connect to other European settlement and potential Indian converts.[7] In these days, western North America was not a network but a puzzle, the pieces scattered in the minds of Europeans and Indians.

Escalante had been in Santa Fe for scarcely a month before leaving with Dominguez's Monterey-bound party on July 29. They started by moving north from town to town through the familiar northern New Mexico country. As they reached into present-day Colorado, the towns petered out and the question became how to cross the Rocky Mountains. The party recruited two Utes to guide them across the mountains, and following these Indian guides, they emerged on the other side of the mountains near present-day Provo, Utah, where they encountered their second obstacle: the Great Basin Desert. The Ute and Paiute Indians they met were not familiar with the desert beyond the plateau country of the Wasatch Mountains and refused to guide them across it. So the party moved south, traversing the edge of the Wasatch and looking for a passage across the desert. The expedition struggled to find water and pasture for its animals. With winter approaching the men worried they would not be able to cross the mountain passes ahead. They were almost out of food. Near present-day Milford, Utah, the fathers "cast lots" to determine if they would continue or turn around. They turned around.

But the key part of the fathers' route wasn't their failed way toward Monterey but how they managed to get back home. Trying to turn the journey's lemons into lemonade, they were intrigued by the prospect of finding a new route between Santa Fe and present-day Utah, with its wide snowmelt-fed valleys fit for civilization and Ute tribes ripe for Catholic conversion.

"Weighing all this, therefore, and that continuing south from Santa Brigada we could discover a shorter and better route than that of the Sabuaganas [Utes] to go from Santa Fe to Laguna de los Timpanois [Utah Lake] and to these other full-bearded Indians," Escalante wrote, "we thereupon decided to continue south for as much as the terrain permitted as far as El Río Colorado [the Colorado River], and from here point our way toward Cosnina, Moqui, and Zuni"—the pueblos of New Mexico.[8] The fathers knew that the biggest challenge of this return trip was crossing el Río Colorado, which Escalante also referred to as el Río Grande, a name the Spanish gave to any big river. We now recognize the Colorado River country as the essence of the western landscape—an immense barrier to travel, a spectacular scenic draw, a fulcrum of ecosystems, and endless pockets of adventure. As a rule of thumb, the canyon country becomes more complex and interesting the closer you get to the Colorado. Even today, for the roughly five hundred miles of the river between its mellow stretches in the Grand Valley in Colorado and the

Hoover Dam in Nevada, there are exactly five bridges over it, many of them feats of engineering to span the deep canyons.

The Arizona Strip in particular was a fitting theater for the drama of the padres figuring out how to cross the river. It was a patch of high desert criss-crossed by bands of cliffs and confusing patterns of washes. Grammie used to tell me stories of trips she and my grandpa took into the Strip in their camper trailer with friends. They would just circle around the bleak roads for several days. The Strip remained almost as rugged and isolated as it was back then or, for that matter, in 1776. Today, the only decent vehicular route through the Strip was a graded dirt road that twisted up a canyon toward a mountain pass that would then give way to a series of long valleys with abandoned cattle ranches, where it became known as "Main Street."

Our first challenge was to get up this canyon, and Jonny was kicking my behind. Prior to heading into the canyon country, Jonny always pretended he was out of shape, saying things like, "Sure, let's go, but I just hope I can keep up." No. Jonny was a fireman. He had kept wildfires at bay for a decade, running up slopes with fifty-pound backpacks and digging firebreaks for hours on end. As we started riding, he casually mentioned that he had a marathon to run the week we got back. He was a speck in the distance as I struggled up the hill.

After difficult climbing up the road for a few hours, Jonny stopped for lunch on a rock at the side of the road. When I caught up, I looked at my GPS elevation reading. We were just shy of 3,700 feet—1,000 feet above our starting point in St. George. It was clear now that we were on the right road, the GPS locator clicking along the route I had drawn, and I was happy with the progress. We could see the folds and buckles where the West collided with itself; St. George was a blotch of green amid this turbulent landscape.

It occurred to me that in gaining all this elevation we were moving between geographic zones, rising up onto the high-elevation Colorado Plateau from the edge of the Mojave Desert. Negotiating this kind of transition in a car on a modern highway is barely noticeable—say, driving from Denver on Interstate 70 to the Loveland Pass tunnel at the crest of the Rockies. With an automatic transmission, a six-cylinder engine, and music on the stereo, you may not notice the change in elevation or steep climb. But being on a bike, you felt every foot of elevation gain. The land below became less abstract. I understood what every climb and twist inflicted on the human body. In trying to cover long distances in this country on a bike, I felt like an ant on a log, a dog in a tornado—a vulnerable being under a force of nature. Likewise, from this vantage I saw St. George not as an obscene growth of sprawl but as a toehold of human civilization only scarcely less vulnerable than it had been when my ancestors had settled it 150 years before. Around the small patch of green, gnarls of black and red rose up, themselves subservient to the supreme mound of the Pine Valley Mountains thousands of feet above.

Following Escalante and Dominguez through canyon country, to me, represented the essence of the early western transportation network: small groups of humans maneuvering through big nature. It was a sobering contrast to Las Vegas, which had so forcefully hammered its nature into the background. While a basic tenet of the modern environmental movement is respecting natural systems—the opposite of what cities like Las Vegas had done—Escalante and Dominguez had no choice in the matter.

And neither did we. We got back on our bikes, and as we rode we saw the scrub turn to piñon and juniper as the amphitheater of the pass closed in, blocky pale sandstone escarpments on either side. These were the blurry blue forms I had seen from the St. George cemetery; it always amazed me how, up close, the western landscape was so much bigger and tough and blunt than it looked from far away, as if to say that it just did not care about you.

I ate another Snickers. A friend who had done several bike tours gave me one piece of advice: bring an unlimited pile of Snickers. The climb became a rhythm of unwrapping Snickers and checking the GPS altimeter every thirty seconds.

By the time we summited the pass—benignly named Quail Hill—it was 4:00 in the afternoon. The temperature had reached 90 degrees and we had gone through about two quarts of water each, making a major dent in our reserves. We still needed to ride another thirty miles to stay on track for the trip. But plenty of daylight remained.

From Quail Hill the country opened up into softer contours of valleys rimmed by low ridges. We saw a new series of hazy blue lumps in the distance and speculated whether one of them might be the famous Mount Trumbull, where the Mormon settlers had cut timber for the St. George Temple. We rode into Wolf Hole, near where Jonny had fought wildfires, whizzing by an abandoned ranch and a waterless lakebed covered in purple flowers.

It was fun to be moving downhill. It was beautiful weather. Up the canyon, over the pass, we were locked into making it through this remote place on our obsolete two-wheeled machines.

At the point where we joined their trail, Dominguez and Escalante were not as enthusiastic. They had come into the explosion of landscape that surrounded the future site of St. George after weeks of wandering along the toe of the Wasatch Mountains, a slog that had been covered in early October snow. Just a little over a week before, they made the gut-wrenching decision to turn back to Santa Fe and give up on reaching Monterey.

Like us, they felt the transition between geographies. The party had descended down the canyon of Ash Creek from the Great Basin to the Mojave Desert, encountering the Virgin River where Ash Creek flowed into it near modern-day Hurricane. They called it Río Sulfureo (Sulfur River) because of the smelly hot springs they found there.

Escalante struggled to describe the changing land, interpreting it through the places he was familiar with and the goals of the Spanish crown and the church. Escalante characterized the country as "mesa-strewn land, and it shows signs of having many minerals," such as gypsum and mica. He and Dominguez analogized the ubiquitous sagebrush to the heather they remembered from Spain. From the Virgin River, they continued south to the wide valley that the Mormons later named Hurricane Wash. Above them, the Hurricane Cliffs rose a thousand feet into the October sky.[9]

They knew they were headed for the Colorado River and that the river was likely their major obstacle to returning to Santa Fe. They began to hear more details about this river and its canyon. Setting off in the morning, the padres encountered a group of Paiute Indians who offered to trade strings of turquoise and small pink conch shells. The fathers had nothing to trade in return; their provisions, except for two blocks of chocolate, had run out at the camp they called San Donulo, just north of the modern Utah-Arizona border. The Paiutes walked with them anyway to meet up with the rest of the party, which had more items of interest. Along the way the Paiutes told them that the Colorado was two days away, but they could not go by the route they intended because it had no water sources and the river was contained in a deep canyon that was, Escalante wrote, "very much boxed in" and had "extremely tall rocks and cliffs on both sides."[10]

A century later, this landform would become known as the Grand Canyon, celebrated by an entire nation of modern Americans. But on that day, the news of a deep canyon did not please the padres. Yet in exchange for two large all-purpose knives, strings of white glass beads, and additional pay, the group of Paiutes agreed to show the Spaniards a side canyon that would lead them to a river crossing. The Indians could not go farther, Escalante wrote, because they did not have shoes.

The party continued to move down Hurricane Wash, along the cliffs, and when they arrived at the small canyon where the Paiutes told them they could climb up onto the mesa, they walked up a league and a half before the steep rocky inclines became too much for the horses. They spent a half hour at a time trying to move the animals through narrow passages in the sandstone. They turned around, back to the wash. They had burned a whole day and had made no progress homeward.

That night they killed and ate one of their horses. "Tonight we were in direst need," Escalante wrote, "with nothing by way of food, so we decided to deprive a horse of its life so as not to forfeit our own." They were so discouraged, they didn't even name the campsite.[11]

Jonny and I likewise made our way south. We were making great time. The roads continued to stay in good condition through the shallow valleys of the Arizona Strip. We hadn't seen anyone—in a car, on a bike, or otherwise.

Then I felt the sickening feeling of instability on my back wheel. I slowly pressed down on my brakes and came to a stop. The desert was completely quiet and windless. Jonny was, as usual, way ahead. I looked down at what I knew was a flat back tire. A pain, since I'd have to remove all my gear to fix the flat. It was annoying but entirely expected, given the riding with camping gear on a dirt road. I replaced the tube and was soon rolling again.

Soon we were at the junction for Route 30, which the BLM had named the Navajo Trail. County Route 5 continued down to Mount Trumbull. Even a BLM sign was comforting in such a desolate place, an assurance that someone had been here before and that the place we were standing was within the human network.

We were now covering ground quickly. We'd gone forty miles, with twenty left for the day. We thought we could be on top of the Hurricane Cliffs by nightfall.

The Navajo Trail climbed quickly, then topped out on a ridge and descended down to Hurricane Wash. It was a rocky, bumpy ride, and partway down I had another sickening feeling, but even more this time. Another flat. We stopped, and wanting to conserve my extra tubes, I patched the flat as daylight leaked away. We kept riding down.

Then, just when we were almost out of the canyon into the valley, it happened again. The same wheel, immediately flat—a blowout—almost tossing me off my bike. If I'd been going a little faster, I'd have wrecked off the road. I wanted to change this one quickly, so I just put in a new tube and rode out into the expanse of the valley.

The evening light on the Hurricane Cliffs became more golden and the challenge of the situation kept ratcheting up. We had adjusted our goal for the day. Now we just hoped to get to the base of the cliffs.

The sun set and we were still riding, ants marching in the giant shape of the shadow. Jonny was out of sight. A few miles later, my front tire went flat. But it was a slow leak, so I could pump up my tire periodically until I caught Jonny at the base of the cliffs. Our day was done.

"How far have we come?" Jonny asked.

"About fifty miles," I said.

"That's pretty good," he said.

The valley was endless to the north and south, a channel of transportation since the days of the padres. The Mormons used Hurricane Wash for their Temple Road, to haul lumber from Mount Trumbull to St. George to build their temple. The view was flecked with occasional yucca plants and cows. There was no wind. The scenery lacked the obvious drama of other canyon country places; it had no spires or arches and the dominant color was a muted beige. But the constant line of the cliffs and valley heading to the horizon gave the place a sublimity I had rarely seen. Geologic time was bluntly exposed, its power writ on the barren land.

The place where we'd stopped was very close to where Dominguez and Escalante camped on the night of October 17, 1776. They'd had a better day from the unnamed campsite, coming nine leagues—about twenty-three miles—though Hurricane Wash. They had made it up the cliffs to a campsite they called San Angel. I loved the Spanish names of the camps; they created an alternate geography of the same land that the Mormons named a hundred years later and conjured in my mind an alternate future of Spanish rule and Spanish cities in these endless valleys. The party's mapmaker, Don Bernardo Miera y Pacheco, also saw this vision of Spanish civilization. As they traversed the canyon country, their minds tried to wrap around how it could be employed to make the necessary roads and routes.

It was here that Dominguez and Escalante decided they wouldn't be able to cross the Grand Canyon and turned east. An advance scouting group of the party had climbed up on top of the Hurricane Cliffs and reported that the ground was level and there was likely plenty of water. The party agreed to follow them.

But they only knew that they didn't know what they were doing. "We well knew they were fooling themselves," Escalante wrote about the scouts. "Toward the south we had a great deal of good level land in sight, and today we had found so much water in contrast to the Indians' story . . . so that our aforementioned suspicion kept growing. But since we now found ourselves without provisions, and the water could be far away . . . we told them (for our sake) to choose the way that suited them best." The next three weeks of their trip would be exclusively dedicated to the task of crossing the Colorado River canyon.[12]

Jonny made noodles with canned chicken, bacon, and red sauce. We talked about whether to pronounce Hurricane Wash like the town of the same name—"Hurrakin." We wondered why the Mormons had come all the way down to Mount Trumbull for their lumber and had not tapped the much-closer Pine Valley Mountains. Once it was dark, Jonny pointed out the glow to the northwest coming from St. George, and when we looked to the left, we saw a much bigger glow: Las Vegas.

In the tent, I lay awake, discouraged. When we arrived in camp, the adrenaline made me feel like I could ride another twenty miles, but now I felt the miles on my body. Two days into my trip and so far to go.

Casting Lots

The morning was as still as the night, and almost as clear, but a few clouds had drifted in. We were all business when we got up. I started right out fixing my front flat, which I had not been able to look at the night before because I was so frustrated and, frankly, spooked. Now I wanted to change the sad look of the deflated tire as fast as I could. I patched the tube that had deflated the quickest—a "snake bite" that comes from the tire being pinched by a rock. It seemed to hold.

We ate bagels and Nutella for breakfast and then were on the trail. We hoped to reach the highway by lunch by way of the town of Colorado City, where we'd ride on to the Pipe Springs Indian Reservation and then to the Arizona town of Fredonia before turning off on another dirt road—the so-called Winter Road—that would lead us to House Rock Valley, where our day would mercifully end.

First, though, were the Hurricane Cliffs. This morning's challenge had silently loomed over us the previous evening. Just past our camp the road cut a diagonal up a gap in the cliffs, climbing almost 1,000 feet and onto the Uinkaret Plateau. The climb was steep, but the cool morning made it bearable. Once again, I watched my GPS tick upward past 5,000 feet. We'd climbed a total of almost 4,000 feet since leaving St. George.

On top was a new view. Where for the past day we had been groping through the Strip's maze of thin valleys, we were now high enough to decipher our place on the Colorado Plateau: the middle step of what geologists called the Grand Staircase (the namesake of Grand Staircase National Monument that President Bill Clinton designated in 1996). The Staircase referred to the stepping down of the land from the peaks of the plateaus in central Utah down successive bands of cliffs and older geologic layers to the depths of the Grand Canyon and the silvery schist that formed its innermost walls. In between, the Pink Cliffs, the White Cliffs, the Gray Cliffs, the Vermillion Cliffs, and finally, the Chocolate Cliffs terraced down, down, down, down, and down to the Colorado. Underneath the ground, the rocks tilted and weathered, exposing glimpses of the range of layers created during the time of the dinosaurs. Escalante and Dominguez, of course, did not have this information. They had no idea of the geologic mayhem that awaited them between here and the Colorado.

The roads up here—the ones the ranger had warned me about—were clay. For now, they were great to ride on, hard and smooth. In a rainstorm, though, clay roads turn into paste. You can barely walk on them or drive with a monster truck, much less ride a fully loaded bike touring outfit on them. By committing to our route, we had effectively put our fate in the hands of the weather. And as we rode north toward Colorado City, we saw that rain had intruded into corners of the sky. A black cloud was an inconvenience in a car; on a bike it could be a disaster.

The rain held off until we reached Colorado City and the highway. As we turned onto the blacktop of Arizona Route 389, it began to sprinkle. We were riding fully into the wind. Then the rain picked up, and so did the wind. The road hit a large hill. We rode most of the twenty miles from Colorado City to Pipe Springs at about 6 miles an hour with a headwind in the pounding rain. I shuddered to think about those clay roads. We stopped at a Pipe Springs gas station, ravenous and dripping on the floor, and tried to eat everything in sight. An older couple came out of the store to where we were sitting in front. They looked at us as if to say, *What are you doing?*

We didn't know. When we rolled into Fredonia, at sixty-three miles for the day, the sun had come out and we had regained optimism. But we were twenty miles behind our pace. We didn't know the Winter Road or House Rock Valley. If we set out and it rained on the clay roads, we could be stuck for days.

Jonny checked the weather, and more rain was forecast. It would be unwise to take touring rigs onto eighty more miles of dirt roads without knowing their condition and with rain in the forecast. Our lots had been cast. Jonny called his family.

The Crossing of the Fathers

We met the other Wildes at a restaurant in Fredonia, ate, then turned north toward Jonny's Uncle Don's house, seven miles away in Kanab, Utah. The next morning we woke up to snow. I was up early, and Don had already made coffee and was watching the weather report. It was 36 degrees.

We spent the morning walking in the red rock around Don's house, and I left for Salt Lake at midday. Jonny handed me the keys to what he called his "Subarrari." I had accepted driving this stretch because there was no good alternative. I'd have to return to St. George to catch the Greyhound. I found a shuttle service that moved people between national parks and Lake Powell, but it was expensive, slow, and infrequent. To get around in the heart of canyon country you had to rely on yourself and whatever vehicle you might have, be it horse, bike, or car.

I also wanted to follow the rest of the fathers' route over the Colorado River. I took the Subarrari to Jacob Lake at 8,500 feet, then down into House Rock Valley, around the Vermilion Cliffs. I found the marker for San Bartolome, the camp Dominguez and Escalante had made after they emerged from House Rock Valley.

As I closed in on Lee's Ferry, the land dropped all forms of pretense. The air seemed clearer, the forms sharper. The cliffs were taller and redder, the sky bluer. At Lee's Ferry, I caught my first glimpse of the Colorado. It was busy with boaters putting in for the Grand Canyon downriver and jet boats whizzing toward Glen Canyon Dam upriver. This was one of those rare places where the Colorado could be accessed by a road.

Dominguez and Escalante had arrived here thinking it was the spot to cross—the point where the river that became known as the Paria (but was called Santa Teresa by the fathers) entered the Colorado. Escalante described how two members of the party who knew how to swim entered the river naked, carrying their clothes above their heads. The river was so swift and deep, though, that when they dropped their clothes midway across, they never saw them again. The nude scouts barely reached the other side. Exhausted from flailing in the current, they had no energy to explore. Once they caught their breath, they swam back.

The party tried to build a raft and ferry across the river but retreated three times. They sent another scout up the Paria canyon to look for a route to a better crossing of the Colorado, but he found nothing. They camped here for a week. "Not knowing when we would be able to get out of here," Escalante wrote on October 29, "we ordered another horse killed."[13]

The river was so small here, it was hard to believe this was an unsuccessful crossing. Today, with motorized boats idling in the eddies and dashing up and down, the river seemed to be a playground.[14] But to the padres, with little idea of where they were, the walls and the muddy river were a prison. The sheer canyon prevented them from walking along the river. They could only explore potential crossings through an exhausting game of trial and error.

Mockingly, they named the place where they camped at the mouth of the Paria San Benito de Salsipuedes. San Benito referred to a white cassock worn by Franciscan monks as a mark of punishment. Salsipuedes was Spanish for "get out if you can."

But they were very close to solving the puzzle. When the fathers' scouts returned with an idea of a way out of the canyon, the party packed up and left San Benito de Salsipuedes. They humped up a few miles of the canyon along the route found by the scouts to the top of the mesa. They made a steep push up the escarpment on its east side to what is now called Dominguez Pass, a notch that helped them gain the canyon rim. They then walked through the Navajo sandstone bluffs across the plateau, where they were still about two miles from Salsipuedes but 1,700 vertical feet above it.

They had heard from Paiutes about a place where the river was wide and shallow, and so in the first days of November, they wound their way along the rim of the Colorado chasm, looking for a route down, across, and out. Their scout went without rations for three days—and without pants, when he tried to cross the river on top of the horse as it swam. The horses found descending and ascending the Navajo sandstone bluffs difficult, and they often lost their footing, tumbling down the slickrock. The meat from the last horse they killed had run out, so they breakfasted on prickly pear and gruel made from hackberries. Then they killed another horse.

On November 6, a thunderstorm of rain and hail swept in and sent a flash flood careening down the canyon below them. They recited the Blessed Virgin Mary's litany.

The next morning, Escalante thought they found the ford, and they began to descend again to it, praying against another Salsipuedes. With their axes, they cut holds into the sandstone slopes for the horses. When they reached the river, they went downstream to where it appeared to be widest, and hence shallowest. The fathers crossed on horseback, their animals' hooves touching bottom the whole way. They were finally across the West's mightiest barrier.

"[We] finished crossing the river at five in the afternoon, praising God our Lord and firing off some muskets in demonstration of the great joy we felt in overcoming such a great problem, one which had caused us so much labor and delay," Escalante wrote.[15]

"And now that we had undergone all this we got to know the best and most direct route," he continued. Now, he reflected, they knew the way "to the ford without any special inconvenience while evading many detours, inclines, and bad stretches."[16] He recounted in detail just where they should have gone, beginning way back in Hurricane Wash—the passage read like Google directions for riding on horseback. The white man's battle against the West had begun, and this kernel of a transportation network would grow to be his biggest weapon. The western land had beaten the Western world, but it was more or less the last time.

I had originally wanted to trace the padres' path over Dominguez Pass. This was the origin of my interest in their trek; I had first learned the details of their adventure while backpacking in Paria Canyon. But even today, Dominguez Pass is a ridiculously hard cross-country hike, up loose sand and rock, with exposure. There was no way I was taking a bike up it; it's tough to fathom how the horses made it. I had spent a lot of time driving the sandy back roads around Page, Arizona, looking for slot canyons, and they did not seem like ideal bike touring byways. To give an idea of how severe this country is, from Lee's Ferry to where the fathers' trail crosses US Highway 89 near Dominguez Pass, is an as-the-crow-flies distance of about ten miles. But even now, the only way to drive between these two points meant driving south to access the top of the mesa then back north through Page—four times as much mileage. This was the route that I drove as the sun began to dip.

An hour later I was on top of the mesa, staring at the place where the padres had finally crossed the river and began the two-month but straight-forward trip back to Santa Fe. I had crossed at Glen Canyon Dam, just above Lee's Ferry, which now held back the Colorado in Lake Powell.

The ford, which had become known as the Crossing of the Fathers, had been buried under 550 feet of Lake Powell water and silt for almost half a century. Now it was late in the day, and the huge reservoir shone its unnatural blue. The blobs of metallic cobalt between the domes of Glen Canyon were always a shock, but particularly so today, as I had been tracing the antique route of the fathers since St. George.

They completed their journey through the pueblos of northern Arizona and New Mexico, arriving back in Santa Fe just after New Year's Day 1777, having gone some 1,700 miles. Escalante died less than four years later from a kidney ailment he had contracted at Taos before the expedition. He was thirty years old.

The fathers' expedition, as it was technically unsuccessful, remained relatively unknown, serving mainly to help trappers negotiate the wilderness. Then, in the mid-1800s, German geographer Alexander von Humboldt came across Escalante's journal. Von Humboldt published references to the route and drew a map based on Escalante and Dominguez's. John C. Frémont followed von Humboldt's instructions, and, in turn, the Mormon settlers took cues from Frémont's report.[17] The network of the American West had spread from this hellish trek, but the padres would never know it.

"God doubtless disposed that we obtained no guide," Escalante reflected, "either as merciful chastisement for our faults or so that we could acquire some knowledge of the people living hereabouts. May His most holy will be done in all things, and may His holy name be glorified."[18]

The Network and the Frame

So what does the Dominguez-Escalante expedition tell us about our reclamation of the West from the auto? This route represented the beginnings of the first iteration of the Anglo West—a network that connected and framed the land in a (necessarily) respectful way. Due to a lack of technology and information, the early Spanish explorers had to learn the nuances of canyon country and adhere to the contours of the landscape.

At the same time, many of the intentions of the Spanish and other Europeans set the West on a path that would undermine those very qualities. That the place where the fathers finally forded the Colorado River was now submerged underwater and overtaken with jetboats and water skiers succinctly told the story of the West in the two centuries that followed their journey. The expedition began a two-hundred-year public works project to tame the rugged and arid western landscape into a piece of the modern world. Glen Canyon Dam, the reservoir it created, and the roads that led to it represented the West's two biggest engineering challenges: transportation and water. Overcoming these challenges reached an apex in the 1960s with the completion of the dam and the Interstate Highway System, which became the hyperlinks for western cities. The dam's bulk and the roads' reach matched the scale of the western landscape ton for ton. Once having dwarfed the ambitions of the Spanish priests and their horses, the West's land now seemed under the calm command of man.

We had fused a giant network, a connected web of roads and pipes that made the West a habitable place for millions of humans, so much so that most Americans now thought little of it. The speed at which this network now allowed us to consume the West's space, scenery, and resources was staggering.

Even more than its utility of throughput, though, was how the network changed our view of the West. My parents remembered the West before freeways. My grandparents remembered the West before roads. The West of my own childhood was mapped through the thick blue lines of the interstates, the places where they crossed, and the yellow of the metro areas around them. As much as I hated to admit it, much of the way I thought about the West involved car windows and freeway exits.

A parade of intentions created this network—some noble, some not—all struggling to get a grip on a wild landscape, laden with potential. The padres and their contemporaries, and the fur traders from the East Coast and England and France that came on their heels, wanted to connect the dots for connections' sake, for the basic human desire for habitation and comfort and orientation. But they also worked for their respective institutions, most of them powerful: the Catholic Church, the Spanish crown, East Coast corporations. The money thrown at these costly explorations sought an even bigger return in mineral extraction, animal pelts, and souls. The connection of the West was an exploration, but it was also exploitation and extraction from the get-go. The young Silvestre Vélez de Escalante had appreciated the expanses of the Arizona Strip, perhaps recalling his boyhood home of northern Spain, but would other denizens of New Spain and New England and New France really deign to settle in the desert without a damn good reason?

The Euro-American West as a place of habitation was never a humble vision. From the very beginning, Don Bernardo Miera y Pacheco, the padres' cartographer, envisioned the largest public works project the world had ever seen. The extraction of natural resources, the production of crops and livestock, fur trading outposts, stagecoach stops, mine supply stations, quarter-section homesteads, speculative railroad gridiron city plans, and weapons testing facilities accumulated; and the power of these ventures dictated the coarse way in which the West was divided up. In essence, the master-planned developments connected by freeways were always on the boards, but it took two centuries to accumulate the technology and infrastructure to execute them.

The building of the West became a constant ante against the house. By the twentieth century, the region's constraints of isolation and aridity were in clear focus, and much of the century was spent overcoming these obstacles with industrial infrastructure. As technological innovation picked up speed, the US government and the states, along with private entities, engineered the West into what we see today. They plumbed the West's rivers and built roads through its deserts and mountain ranges. The junctions in these networks became cities of millions of people, accessible from one another in a day's drive. The networks were powered by hidden engines like Glen Canyon Dam that pumped out livelihood to cities. This was the machinery of the modern West.

I drove the Subarrari north toward Salt Lake City as far as I could while I still had daylight. By the time I got to Panguitch it was dark and I was nearly out of gas, having burned almost a whole tank driving the circle from Kanab to Page and back.

I called my parents in Salt Lake to let them know where I was.

"Panguitch?!" my mom said. "Why don't you get a motel?"

I filled up the tank and continued driving, now heading west over the Parowan Gap. I was now back in my road trip comfort zone. I played one of Jonny's CDs on the car stereo. If there had been a McDonald's in Panguitch, I would have gone there.

Working my way down the winding road, I saw the lights of Interstate 15. Having spent three days in places where control of destiny seemed in the hands of nature, I was back in the network where man appeared to be in charge.

━━━ ━ ━ ━ ━ ━ ━ ━ ━ ━ ━━━

Did these very impressive transportation networks produced by five hundred years of exploration, enterprise, and engineering address the greatest needs of America today? For most of the time we'd lived in the West, our goal was to conquer it. We'd done that. We figured out how to extract resources at an industrial scale. We figured out how to use the West's isolation to make and test weapons of mass destruction. We figured out how to pipe water across hundreds of miles of desert. I could drive from the heart of the Colorado River's geologic maze, which had taken Dominguez and Escalante weeks to untangle, three hundred miles to Salt Lake City in five easy hours.

Now we had to figure out how to live here. This was a much harder task. We had to ask ourselves: Did the crossroads where these freeways and pipes intersected make for good places for people to live?

The transportation network, as much as moving people, is also a frame for the land. The network frames the land by turning it into a place and giving it its essential character. It defines how you get to places and how you perceive where you live. Cities are nothing if not networks of public streets that frame the lives of their citizens. The majority of older cities throughout the United States, such as Boston, New York, New Orleans, and St. Louis, were built around ports on seas or rivers, and their streets radiated to their hinterlands, creating a neat economic, cultural, and geographic network. The ancient cities built for worship were patterns of roads arranged in tribute.

The general frame given to the interior West focused on allowing its vast expanses to be surveyed, cataloged, and sold as efficiently as possible. In 1785 Thomas Jefferson drafted the National Land Ordinance, which decreed that the American West would be divided up according to a grid of parcels measuring six miles by six miles. These pieces of land would be called townships. Townships could be divided into 36-square-mile sections. Townships and sections formed the basis for all land sold by the United States in the West. Jefferson believed that this township and range system would be the most efficient and equitable way to distribute western land. But it also became the de facto transportation network for many new American communities, including the one we had seen in action—or inaction—in North Las Vegas.

But what network and frame both regards and highlights a landscape? One interesting example of the tension between the desire to use the western grid to profit and the desire to highlight a spectacular landscape can be found in one of the most prototypically western cities of all: San Francisco. The city's famous street network derived from an 1847 plan of dividing land that engineer Jasper O'Farrell applied to the community emerging on the geographically advantageous tip of the peninsula jutting between the San Francisco Bay and the Pacific Ocean. Landowners expressed suspicion at any attempt to depart from the orthogonal grid, believing it to be the fairest, most equal way to divide property. This grid of closely and uniformly connected streets also happened to be great for pedestrians, yielding a variety of options for a walk to any destination in the city. Within a few years, though, it was clear that the grid had trouble reaching over the hills, and so a city committee proposed maximum slopes for streets. But when city planners realized that to qualify under the maximum slopes, Telegraph Hill, Russian Hill, and Nob Hill would have to be flattened, the city reconsidered. Another committee of engineers convened in 1854 and reversed this approach. They instead wanted to see how the city and its streets could leverage the hills as an asset for people to enjoy the city.

"Why are the hills to be cut down? Are they deformities? Are they nuisances?" the engineers wrote. "The hills are certainly not deformities. The stranger, on his first approach to San Francisco, as he ascends the Bay and doubles Telegraph Hill, cannot fail to be struck with the singular and peculiar beauties of the site."[19]

And so the grid of streets ran steeply over the tops of the hills and provided a frame for the city that gave it both drama and accessibility for walkers. "The traditional urban grid used on flat land," wrote Florence Lipsky in *San Francisco: The Grid Meets the Hills*, "in this case met with a rebellious and as-yet untamed environment." But the effect, as Lipsky wrote, was "to be made perpetually aware of the human scale with respect to the scale of the landscape." By acknowledging the value and character of the land, the builders of San Francisco transformed their frame into one that appealed to people. This is still true today.[20]

And when the automobile came to prominence and wrapped freeways around the city, San Francisco resisted, fearing it would destroy its frame of grid and hills. With help from the Loma Prieta earthquake, the city cleared the rubble of the Embarcadero Freeway and instead built a surface street that reconnected the city to the waterfront, restoring its frame and the way its citizens saw and experienced it amid its landscape.

John Wesley Powell, the first white man to take a boat down Glen Canyon and whose name was lofted onto the reservoir that covered it, had an idea for a completely different frame for the West, which he pitched in his *Report on the Lands of the Arid Region of the United States*. Powell wanted to scrap the township and range system. He believed that it was a bad idea to impose an eastern United States frame on a landscape that was completely different than the eastern United States. Instead, Powell reasoned that access to water would be the defining resource for the settling of the arid West, and so land management units should be organized around watersheds. Nested inside the largest watersheds (like the entire Colorado River) would be smaller watersheds (like the Paria River), and perhaps inside them still smaller watersheds, until you had a pattern at the scale of the community. This is the essence of network theory: that small things should connect to bigger things through networks and that all networks should be designed to connect to both bigger and smaller networks. San Francisco's network did that in connecting a person to the landscape. Powell's system could do that.[21]

Powell also recommended a system of irrigation based not on individual enterprise but on community-managed watershed collectives. In this way, the landscape could be woven into the settlement of the West. Its frame would be something that worked for both the long-term management of the land and the lives of the people.

"The division of these lands should be controlled by topographic features to give water fronts," Powell wrote. "Residences of the pasturage lands should be grouped; the pasturage farms cannot be fenced—they must be occupied in common."[22] This was perhaps the first call in the Anglo West for smart growth and its principles of compact settlement, ecological respect, and public space.

These ideas were buried like Glen Canyon. And, in fact, most western city builders—eastern capitalists or investors as they were—simply abdicated the decision of choosing a transportation network in balance with the land, as the San Francisco engineers had done. They opted to frame their cities by the convenient township and range system, by selling off mile and quarter mile chunks surrounded by roads. Does this sound familiar? It wasn't just Las Vegas. Today, in almost any western city, the streets we drive and try to walk and bike are remnants of this disposal of the land, rampant speculation, and the caging of the landscape into the mile grid—in this way, Las Vegas' "disposal boundary" is historically appropriate. The metros of the West are a sad brand of capitalism, an example of city building as pure conquest.

And American civilization was racing forward on the back of the automobile. When the western city departed from infilling the township and range with gridirons, it was not for something better, but worse. The mile grid might have been heavy-handed, inhumane, and boring, but at least it was connected. The networks of the twentieth century made a point of fracturing all connections except for those made by a car.

The builders of today's transportation system obliterated the natural network that had challenged the early explorers, but they also failed to provide a network that worked for people in the long run. Our roads consolidated options to one or a few, congested easily, and disconnected people from one another. And the more our streets congested, the more streets we built, and the more they continued to disconnect us.

In the end, the million-person behemoths that the cities of the American West became were not built as frames for individual lives, communities, and landscapes but for mass production. They are good for the big scale of cars, agribusiness, and the defense industry. But people still live lives at human scales, and the large networks of the West do not connect to the smaller systems sized for people, they overwhelm them. They are not good networks; they do not connect big things to small things.

Growing up, I accepted the West as it had been rendered in freeways, walls, and McDonald's restaurants, not thinking that it could be anything different. But let's consider what else could have happened. Salt Lake City, my hometown, toward which I was hurtling at 80 miles an hour, was built in a deep valley bounded on two sides by mountains rising 7,000 feet above the valley floor. The gently sloped aprons of land below the mountains were treeless expanses covered in bunchgrass, angling down to the Great Basin Desert, each spring inundated by snowmelt from the awesome peaks. The creeks from the mountains took the snowmelt to a river running down the center of the valley. To the immediate north was a salty remnant of an ancient megalake pinching the arable land to a thin strip. To the south was another valley with another shallow and swampy lake. When Dominguez and Escalante came into Utah Valley, where they camped with a band of Ute Indians, their cartographer wrote to the King of Spain, "This is the most pleasing, beautiful and fertile site in all New Spain. It alone is capable of maintaining a settlement with as many people as Mexico City, and of affording its inhabitants many conveniences, for it has everything necessary for the support of human life."[23] This was, to borrow the term of San Francisco's savior engineers, a site with a singular and peculiar beauty.

What would Salt Lake have looked like if, for its 150-year history, it had followed Powell's ethos of building according to watersheds rather than over them?[24] Allow me to speculate. Reverence would have been given to the clearly defined network of streams that transported runoff to the river in the center of the valley, which Mormon settlers had named the Jordan. The streams of City Creek, Mill Creek, and Red Butte, Emigration, Parley's, and Big and Little Cottonwood Creeks all emptied into it. Respecting the watershed would have meant allowing the streams to flood, stepping back from the oxbows and groves of cottonwood trees. These green corridors could have been the centers of resource management as well as great urban public spaces. And while Powell was interested in an efficient and sustainable distribution of resources, wouldn't his watershed idea have made a very nice basis for a transportation network too? Streets could have been woven into the stream corridors, and people would have been connected to the things they needed, and to each other, in a diverse range of ways. Most people in the valley would live within a mile or so of one of these verdant linear corridors, making the centers of community life within biking and walking distance. Community-oriented water use and transportation would have defined neighborhoods around each of these waterway public spaces.

This was the furthest thing from what actually happened. Now, 2 million people live in three linked valleys between the mountains and lakes. Interstate 15, which connects most of the region, has been widened to a dozen lanes to handle the peak traffic at commute times and joins mostly belt route freeways and large arterial streets. If you look at a map of the Wasatch Front, as this linear region is called now, you'd find it very hard to tell where the creeks are because they have been covered and culverted and now existed, if at all, mostly in people's backyards. The Jordan River, the valley's seam, was forced to exist alongside the freeway and industrial yards. And the Wasatch Front's poor air quality has become an increasingly noticeable symptom of our development pattern and dependence on autos and fossil fuels. Like Mexico City, the deep valleys of the Great Basin trap air, and the growing fleets of autos cough out soot, metals, hydrocarbons, and oxides into 4 million lungs. The problem is exacerbated in winter when the trapped air, now cold, sinks into a dense layer on the valley bottoms, creating a heinous smog in the city as the powdery Utah snow sparkles on peaks above the mess.

But Utah had begun to change. As in other cities throughout the West and America, people now experienced the city on trains, on bikes, and on foot. Most notably, a new network was growing along the Wasatch Front.

I drove to Salt Lake to find this new network, asking how my hometown could reconnect its city and its land. In Salt Lake I would talk to people who were, as in Las Vegas, rebuilding the city by fixing its network, creating a different frame.

These were questions I had never asked as a kid. We don't question what we know. Now, without a car, I would experience my city through new eyes.

The Wasatch Front begins in the small Mormon farming town of Nephi. The concentrations of lights every fifty miles—a day's carriage ride apart on the old Latter-day Saint road—began to blend together in a procession of freeway exits. Just past midnight, I pulled into my parents' driveway. The house was dark.

The Inheritance

In the morning, my mom was shaking her head.

"You should have got a motel in Panguitch," she said.

I told her my plans for the day.

"Do you want a ride?" she asked.

Whenever I returned to Salt Lake, people were always trying to give me rides. When I wanted to walk somewhere or take the train, my family members and friends acted like it was the last resort. Like, anything but walking, or even worse, taking public transit.

I liked to walk when I went back to Salt Lake. It slowed the day and gave me a chance to think. I left my parents' house and walked west toward downtown. The unpredictable weather had followed me from down south. It was the ultimate spring day in northern Utah, with young leaves and snow in the foothills. Clouds still hung around the Wasatch peaks, but clear blue sky showed in patches.

The mountains watched over Salt Lake Valley like a deity. It was no wonder the Wasatch Front suited the Latter-day Saints so well; it constantly reminded you that you were not in charge. Unlike Las Vegas, which managed to create

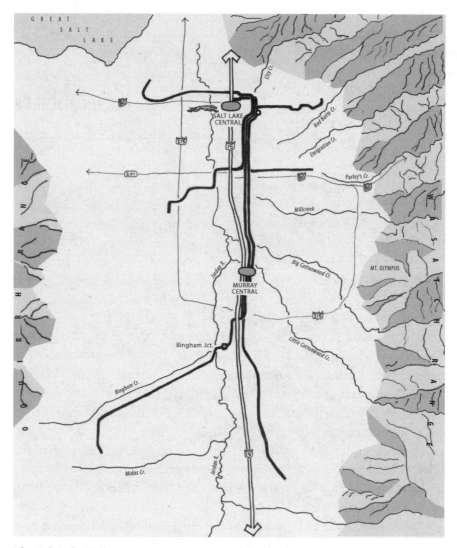

The Salt Lake Valley.

a cityscape that pushed its mountains into the background, Utah city builders had to acknowledge that they had not completely overtaken the nature of
Salt Lake's Great Basin Desert valley.

Which isn't to say they didn't try. Perhaps no metropolis in America was
more delineated by non-oceanic natural features. Yet once in the valley, the
streams and canyons born of the mountains disappeared under a blanket

of asphalt roads and cul-de-sacs. The result, as I came to know as I grew up in the 1980s and 1990s, was a city that hardly seemed to know the land around it.

Adding to this sense of displacement were the otherworldly origins of the city's street network. The frame of the original city was a throwback to the world's ancient cities of worship rather than township and range. Salt Lake's street network was the quirky result of a plan drawn up by Mormon Church founder Joseph Smith Jr. in the 1830s called the City of Zion. Almost all Utah towns, from St. George in the south to Brigham City in the north, sprung from this layout, as were a string of Midwestern towns founded and abandoned by the Saints in the church's early years. Salt Lake City was the master stroke. Like other western cities, Salt Lake had been stamped with a coarse network of outsized streets. But instead of being a city made for selling, it was a city made for waiting for the second coming. The City of Zion was not so much a plan predicated on living in the Great Basin—or really anywhere— but a prefabricated theological kit that had been assembled in a place with a lot of space and not very many people.

The DNA of the City of Zion was a street grid of 10-acre blocks and streets with rights-of-way spanning 132 feet. While originally intended for horse-drawn carriages, this grid had become a wonderland for the cars that Mormons grew to love. The large streets and blocks proved in step with the auto age. Lanes were plenty, intersections were few, and all turns could be made. In a sense, the Mormon planners were ahead of their time.

For the pedestrian, though, the large blocks made routes indirect and crossings long and scary. The streets seemed to stretch the city out like chewing gum, dead stretches of asphalt that did little to connect the city blocks to one another. At transportation planning conferences, walking experts trotted out Salt Lake as the ultimate example of an unwalkable street network because of its massive blocks and streets. The streets took so long to cross that the city installed bright orange flags for pedestrians to carry across the street, like a defeated warrior making a truce.[25] Somehow, the Latter-day Saints had managed to build the one unwalkable pre-auto city.

Salt Lake's streets, like its freeways, were very good at connecting vehicles but failed at connecting people. Today, I would be talking to people who were making these connections—at the smaller scale of the street and neighborhood, the larger scale of cities and the region, and back to the land.

In the lobby of Salt Lake City Hall, I met Robin Hutcheson, the city's new transportation director. She wanted to show me that the city's large streets were actually an asset for reconnecting the city for walkers and bicyclists.

We walked eastward through the massive block of Washington Park—supposedly modeled after Philadelphia's Center Square but would have fit nine of them—into the old residential area east of downtown. It wasn't only the major streets that were as wide as a football field—it was all of them. And, at least today, most of these streets were empty. I could walk straight down the center of streets without much fear. This had not gone unnoticed at Salt Lake City Hall. Hutcheson led me right on 300 East, another completely empty 132-foot-wide street.

She walked out into a traffic lane. There wasn't a car in sight.

"I think we have room to do other things here," she said.

Here, the city was in the process of removing the vehicle lane where Hutcheson stood. In its place, the city would stripe what had come to be known as a cycle track. A cycle track is a type of bike lane in which cyclists ride on the inside of the parking lane next to the sidewalk, so they are buffered from moving traffic by the parked cars. The European idea had been adopted by American cities such as New York City. Three months after my visit, the lane removal and cycle track striping would be carried out, with both motorists and residents noticing more cyclists and traffic on 300 East, proving it to be calmer and slower with the cycle track. A few years later, the city would build another mile-long cycle track on another street.

"This is not hard," Hutcheson said. "It's fast. It's just a resurface. It's just paint."

As we learned in Las Vegas, good transportation means options—most importantly, choosing how you get around. To understand a good urban transportation network, you actually have to pull it apart into different strands, like cooked spaghetti, so that you understand the different experiences of different kinds of travelers. For example, a bicyclist has a completely different experience than a driver, and a pedestrian has a different experience than either, and so on. These various networks must all occupy the same space. In a built-out city, the challenge is fitting all of them within existing streets without each mode of transportation getting in one another's way.

So for planners, designers, engineers, and politicians, street rights-of-way had become negotiations of space. From this perspective, Smith's Zion streets were an asset, not a burden. Filling in the space of the streets with walking, bike, and bus routes was a way to relieve traffic congestion, but more importantly, it was a way to reconnect the city for people, to frame it for pedestrians, bicyclists, and transit riders in addition to motorists. The city was thinking bigger about what people wanted in their rights-of-way, a new way to see the city and the landscape surrounding it. Salt Lake City had inherited a street network, this antique Latter-day Saint frame for the city, and its planners were intent on retrofitting it for the new century.

So transportation planners had been following the city's paver all over town, restriping streets with more bike lanes. Planners saw pressure mounting for better biking and walking conditions; a survey they conducted found that two-thirds of residents wanted more places to bike and walk. So they had doubled the bike lane miles in two years and had documented a 30 percent increase in cycling on city streets.

The 10-acre blocks were also troubling for the transportation network. Research by some colleagues had concluded that the highest risk of fatal or severe car crashes occurred with very low street network density, while safety outcomes improved as the intersection density increased.[26] In the 1960s and 1970s, the city had exacerbated this condition, like the rest of America, aggregating the Zion blocks into superblocks for convention centers and malls.

We came to State Street. The crosswalk button failed to produce a walk signal, so we each took an orange flag.

Safely across, we walked to City Creek Center, a downtown mixed-use development with retail and apartments and condos that the LDS Church recently built next to Temple Square. We approached it from 100 South, using a nice crossing the city had built in the middle of the long block to line up with a street the church put though the block. It lined up with Regent Street, a commercial alley across the street.

"Look at this crossing," Hutcheson said. "Compared to what we just did on State Street, I want to walk here. This is welcoming."

From the crossing, we walked onto what was known as a shared street, which was technically open to vehicles but belonged to pedestrians. If pedestrians were guests grudgingly accommodated on most streets built in the last half century, cars were guests on shared streets now being conceived around the world. A critical part of shared streets is that cars are allowed. While the pedestrian malls of the late twentieth century stressed separation of people and cars, shared streets are part of a vision where the foot network and the car network can safely share space and activate a city's public streets together.

This shared street had no curbs, just one level of concrete pavers, with silver bollards directing cars where to go. It was people space, a plaza, until a car came by; it would not sit as idle asphalt, wasted space like the rest of the city streets. If every Zion block had two or three of these, then Salt Lake would begin to feel like a much more energetic, connected place. Here, the Church of Jesus Christ of Latter-day Saints had begun cutting up the same blocks it had designed 150 years earlier.

Journey to the Center

As in every other city in America, Salt Lake's historic core had become a precious relic. Brigham Young wanted to replicate the City of Zion over and over, out into the space of the Great Basin valleys, but the builders of the twentieth century had other plans. Having grown up amid the order of the Zion grid, I was always unnerved when my friends and I drove out into the southern end of the valley. We had trouble navigating the suburban streets and their disconnected stubs and cul-de-sacs, often driving in circles.

But the Mormon cooperative ethic had extended out beyond the Zion grid and into the new millennium and a new network. The Utah Transit Authority (UTA) and its burgeoning rail system, which worked alongside the region's freeway building and road widening, was one of the fastest growing in the United States and now ran along a nearly ninety-mile stretch of the Wasatch Front.

UTA was itself a kind of back-door regional planning.[27] It had emerged in 1970 as automobility hit fever pitch across America. The bus and railway companies that had provided Salt Lake's waning public transit had shut down service, and in order to keep transit on life support, five Salt Lake

County cities salvaged a fleet of buses from the 1950s and formed UTA. The fledgling agency found success by attracting riders with low fares; it created momentum as other metro area counties—and even ski resorts—joined and chipped in money. UTA became one of the only entities to match the sinuous shape and scale of the entire Wasatch Front metro region, growing to serve seventy-five cities and 80 percent of Utah's population. Into the 1980s and 1990s, Utah's explosive growth, while unarguably auto-fueled, was quietly mirrored by UTA such that by the turn of the twenty-first century, Utah's first modern light rail line was ready to open.

Mass transit had drawn skepticism in Utah for a long time. In elementary school in the 1980s, I had been assigned to argue against light rail in a debate. My main argument (supplied by my dad) was that the Salt Lake Valley was too spread out to benefit from a mass transit system. It was a persuasive point.

But from the start, the new light rail—named TRAX—was a smash. The initial fifteen-mile starter line, from downtown Salt Lake to the southern suburb of Sandy, was ridden by over 50 percent more people than the agency predicted. UTA started to run longer trains more frequently to handle the demand. The agency built the project millions of dollars under budget.[28] And the trains saved the agency operating costs over buses.[29]

The growth of the system over the last fifteen years had been stunning. A year after trains began running, in 2000, voters approved an additional quarter-cent sales tax to fund more train lines. From its hub downtown, UTA built TRAX extensions east to the University of Utah, west to the airport and West Valley City, and south to South Jordan and Draper. It built a commuter rail named FrontRunner north to Ogden and south to Provo. Now, people in most corners of the Salt Lake Valley who worked in downtown Salt Lake or in other major employment centers had a real choice as to how to commute to work or school.

By the end of 2013, UTA had built eighty-five rail stations on 148 miles of track, about 90 percent of the mileage of the Wasatch Front's freeway network.[30] It built five new rail extensions several years ahead of schedule, and its diligence and thrift in coming in ahead of schedule and under budget snowballed into increasing trust with federal funders. Each weekday, 68,000 people rode TRAX, making it ninth out of twenty-eight systems nationwide, twice as many as systems in larger cities like Seattle, Minneapolis, and

Baltimore.[31] The stigma of transit had vanished with the clean trains; every city along the Wasatch Front seemingly wanted TRAX.

Most importantly, UTA's rail network was reframing the entire Wasatch Front. Many other light rail systems in the United States were conceived as single lines. But, with an aggressive and skilled acquisition of federal funding, UTA had created a whole regional network to compete with the freeways. The new transit network along the Wasatch Front was like a hub-and-spoke pattern typical to many transit systems but elongated, so it looked like a long insect. The natural constraints of the Wasatch Front—its mountains and lakes—made it easier for mass transit to serve the region. The thin line of settlement along the mountains was perfect for the main line and its spurs. Fortunately, I had been wrong in my elementary school debate.

In many ways, mass transit provided a better regional network than highways. Sure, roads gave individual travelers more customized routes and were often faster outside rush hour. But in the long run, with the entire community taken into consideration, mass transit was a better frame. It carried more people in less space. It brought people together rather than isolating them. It polluted less. Transit also connected big things to small things, seamlessly bridging long distances across metros to small, walkable blocks. Freeways did none of these things.

I walked onto a platform on Main Street. After a few minutes, a TRAX train came by headed south. I boarded it.

I sat across from three kids traveling to see their grandma in Sandy. At first, the train ran through the downtown streets, barely making a dent in their width, but after we left downtown we hooked into an old Union Pacific right-of-way behind warehouses and truck yards. We picked up speed and moved quickly. I looked around at the other passengers. They appeared to be students and families, singles and couples, all ages, many ethnicities. High school girls, sports club bros, grungy urban cyclists, chaperones and kids, starched middle-aged men on tablet computers. With every stop and opening of doors, a mosaic of people boarded and alighted, the alternating pulses of stops and smooth gliding in between forming the rhythm of our trip through the valley.

By now, TRAX had been around long enough and reached enough places that it was no longer a novelty or an urban non sequitur but an established, working part of the Wasatch Front. The first TRAX phase, known now as the Blue Line, was conceived, like a freeway, as a way to move residents of the southern Salt Lake County suburbs into downtown Salt Lake City. But increasingly, the areas around the stations along it had begun to fill with housing and had become destinations in their own right. And so travel along the line began to more closely resemble that of an urban metro, with shorter trips as well as longer ones.

I was not used to traveling this way through the Salt Lake Valley. The freeways formed the rhythm of my home when I was growing up. The structure of the valley in my mind was the line of I-15 and its numbered exits, looped by the belt route of I-215. Traveling behind industrial warehouses gave me a different sense of the valley. Some of them had interesting graffiti. The whirred views of the mountains in between the buildings and cottonwood trees were different than the ones on the freeway. The elevated I-15 roadway gave you an omniscient view of the valley, like you weren't even in it; down here, each view was more personalized. Perhaps most importantly, I shared space not with cars but humans. Driving with faceless cars on the freeway mostly made me resent the other users of the road; sitting on the train with other people, their faces in view, steered me more toward trying to understand my fellow Utahns.

The center of the UTA rail map featured a wide black oval labeled "Murray Central," the colorful lines of three TRAX and FrontRunner routes running through it. The suburb of Murray had been the valley's second settlement after Salt Lake City, an industrial helper to the church's headquarters. But it had become largely indistinguishable from the rest of the urbanization of the valley—just another suburb in a line heading south on I-15. I knew this area mainly through my childhood trips down the freeway and its exits and places right off the freeway. The only place I remembered out here, the 49th Street Galleria, was the venue for any good birthday party. It was a majestic palace of glassy towers, miniature golf, and arcades. It had been the only reason, in my mind, to get off the interstate that far south. You exited the freeway, parked in the big lot, walked through the big doors, and the rest was a sequence of magic: the large atrium, tokens, the arcade, miniature golf. Then it was back to the car and back to the orderly grid of Salt Lake.

Murray's roadways widened as its smokestacks and brickyards came down, and the city had increasingly become a transportation juncture for regional travel. In fact, Murray was in the exact center of the Salt Lake Valley, which was why I was going there. I had made plans to meet a transportation planner named Ned Hacker at Murray Central station. Hacker worked for the Wasatch Front Regional Council, the agency responsible for writing transportation plans for the region. In its latest plan, known as Wasatch Choice for 2040, it had drawn a big thick circle around the Murray Central station, indicating its intention to make it an urban center—that this unassuming spot in the middle of the valley would one day be a regional hub.

I met Hacker at the station platform. It was afternoon, and the Wasatch were covered in storm clouds and snow. We stood on the highest point in the valley, a subtle hill noticeable for its views. Because the adjacent parking lot was so big, I could see the storms whirling around the mountains. The shield-like face of Mount Olympus projected out of the clouds, its quartzite cliffs dusted with snow. Hacker wore a green Mountain Hardware winter shell, his gray hair under a hat. He nibbled on beef jerky as we began walking through the parking lot.

We were in the guts of the valley's transportation network. Like Glen Canyon Dam or Lee's Ferry, it was a place made of the concrete bones that supported civilization but was itself a little unnerving to hang around. We could see where construction for the FrontRunner station was underway next to the TRAX station, the industrial yard of a vinyl fence company beyond. Next to the station was a massive hospital that had been built five years earlier. A parking lot the size of twenty-five football fields sat between it and the train station. Surrounding it all was the auto traffic flung from the big roads that crisscrossed here. It was not yet a place to live, or even do anything but move through briskly.

To regional planners, it seemed wrong that the center of the valley would be such an arbitrary place. And so on the backs of TRAX and FrontRunner, planners were radically redrawing the map of the valley's network. Around the oval icon of the train station, planners wanted to make a walkable, intense human place, a focal point where none had existed.

The Regional Council wanted to put 30 percent of new Wasatch Front growth in 3 percent of the land, and Murray Central station was a critical platoon of that 3 percent army. Even with the multitude of freeways here, little traffic capacity remained to serve new growth. But the wealth of new rail transit made way for more growth. From the perspective of a transit rider, it was a very advantageous place to be. You could be in downtown Salt Lake, at the north end of the valley, in twenty minutes, and in downtown Sandy, at the other end of the valley, in fifteen. You had direct connections to three of the four corners of the valley.

The biggest problem with that vision was the reality of what happened when you got off the train. This was the major challenge of dropping a new transit network in a twentieth-century suburban valley: the human-scale network wasn't there to support the transit. You got off the big thing, and there was no small thing to connect to. So it wasn't a good network, yet. The early TRAX lines had succeeded in part due to their ability to funnel drivers or riders from all over the built-out valley to the centrally located new stations— transit needs density, and TRAX attracted a density of trips converging on the stations rather than a density of the immediate community surrounding a station. The newer lines had less low-hanging fruit to pick and thus had to rely more on the largely suburban communities immediately surrounding them, which could not yet fully support the transit.[32]

Regional planners had very little actual power to fix any of this, or to direct 30 percent of the valley's new growth to places like Murray Central station and their 3 percent of land area. But they were good at collaborating. Like many western metros, the Salt Lake Valley was a dizzying network of agencies: state highways, transit, and local government. All had come to understand that network *was* collaboration; along with auto dependence, the transportation network failed due to fractured jurisdictions and competing interests. Building the new network involved a network of people and command lines as well as physical roads, sidewalks, and tracks. The auto network was so problematic in part because it was the product of an isolated engineering profession building roads for an isolated city or state government.

Utahns were beginning to discover urbanism as collaboration. They had created a groundbreaking model for voluntary regional planning called Envision Utah that had been founded in the 1990s by some of the state's power brokers who wanted to preserve Utah's quality of life. It was all-inclusive but completely voluntary. In the conservative political climate of Utah, planners were not going to dictate to the Wasatch Front's nearly one hundred cities how they should grow. Envision Utah spent much of a decade holding meetings and public workshops building a vision for the Wasatch Front decades into the future that was as close of a consensus as it could get. At the same time, creating a new frame for the entire region in a top-down manner actually held appeal in Utah, where, for many, looking to a higher authority for guidance is a central cultural value.

A key part of the consensus vision was TRAX, which had been conceived at about the same time as Envision Utah and was now part of a major regional rail network that also included Front Runner and the first of a series of street-cars. The rail network enabled much of the compact growth sketched by the vision; it was in many ways the new frame. This new frame was a work in progress. Some cities had embraced the vision while some had not. But the frame and the vision to fill it were on the table, a new form of regional cooperation tying the disparate parts of the metro area together. As the light rail stations had opened, the cities they were located in—many of them sub-urban-as-it-gets suburbs like Sandy and Draper—took interest in the new regional frame and vision. They looked at the economic growth beginning to emerge in Utah out of the recession and developed ambitious plans for often-dense and often-walkable places around the new rail stations. Despite its huge parking lot, the new Intermountain Health Care hospital looming above Murray Central Station packed the trains that ran by it.

In some ways, it was better just to close your eyes here. Murray Central didn't look the part, but the networks were in place the train connections, the government structure, the personal relationships, the emerging centers of human activity. There were new bones, a new frame. The city could grow now, however slowly. As resources become scarcer for the West's growing population, the old auto network will become less useful. When, as climate scientists predict, the West's assault on air quality succumbs it to drought, and as fossil fuels run dry, concentration and public space akin to John Wesley Powell's vision will become necessary. In the Wasatch Front, I was seeing the beginning of this new, necessary network and frame.

Near the end of our walk, Hacker told me that he actually lived less than a half mile from the Murray Central station, in a neighborhood across this Great Wall of the Salt Lake Valley. He described the route, located past the looping, indirect streets of his subdivision, along the arterial through the spartan industrial areas, across the freeway and the railroad tracks. He didn't make the walk too often.

On Ned Hacker's recommendation, I reboarded TRAX and rode one stop north, to a station called Fireclay, a reference to the brickyards of days past. Brickmaking was just part of the milieu of industry here, which included canning, flour mills, and silver smelting from the ore of the Wasatch. Scandinavian Latter-day Saint converts had come here to work in the smelters and settled villages on Big and Little Cottonwood Creeks. Joe Hill, the famous Swedish-born labor activist, was arrested not far from here for a double homicide in 1914.

Alighting at Fireclay was one of the Alice-in-Wonderland experiences of riding urban rail. It wasn't located at a crossroads of major thoroughfares but rather plopped at a smaller local street. So stepping off the train put you in something of a miniature world—for Utah, at least. Unlike driving somewhere, you could get off a train and then, bam, you were in a place built for people, whether it was Central Park, Trafalgar Square, or this interesting spot in the middle of the Salt Lake Valley. Even though I knew the freeway was nearby, I couldn't see it. I didn't know how I'd ever come upon this place had I driven to Murray.

A partially built scene stood here that was not quite of the present. This was one of the places where Envision Utah had drawn up fanciful visions of urban transit-oriented development fifteen years ago, before TRAX had been built. Now the train was here, and things were starting to happen. Many of the blocks around the station were empty, but they had the bones of good streets. And the skeleton here had both arm and hand bones, the fine metacarpals and phalanges that brought people from train stations to their doors. This frame of small streets expanded from the station, and I walked east on the small namesake street of Fireclay Avenue. One of the streets with a small center island already had parking spots striped and acorn-shaped pedestrian streetlights but no buildings.

Fireclay Avenue led not to the highway of State Street but to its more civic parallel, Main Street, where new buildings had been built where doors opened optimistically onto well-apportioned streetscapes. In the distance, cranes rose over the wood structure of a nearly completed four-story building. The Wasatch Front had reframed itself, and now it was time to build onto that frame.

This was not a vibrant urban place by any stretch, yet. Like most TRAX stations, the Fireclay Station was relentlessly abutted by a surface parking lot that, no doubt, helped deliver many of its riders. But a place was in process, the right ingredients mixing slowly: the train, the views, the streets, the new construction, the density. It was like being at an archaeological site, but I was reading the future instead of the past.

Restoration

I wanted to explore one more network. Throughout the Salt Lake Valley, a hidden system ran under the streets and highways and newly laid train tracks: the watershed and its buried vision of John Wesley Powell. When Spanish explorers entered Great Basin valleys like this one, they first tried to navigate the waterways. Once they found that rivers such as the Jordan and the Provo went nowhere and were often too dry to float a canoe, much less the giant ships of trade, they gave up on making a city and got back on their horses.

The rivers had been pushed away ever since. I knew that the clear mountain streams of the Wasatch plunged down the canyons that bore their names. The meter of these checkpoints is branded into the mind of every Salt Laker. But what happened to them once they crossed into civilization? I didn't know.

I had glimpsed Big and Little Cottonwood Creeks when I walked around Murray. At the edge of the area around Fireclay station, Big Cottonwood Creek ran in ice blue raging water. The sound of the creek nearly drowned out the construction noise.

Now I would take a river trip down the main channel, the notoriously gross Jordan River. The Jordan was another strand of the corridor running through the center of the valley, like I-15, TRAX, and State Street. While the light rail was the valley's brand new network, the watershed was its ancient one, the Jordan its forgotten artery.

The next morning, I awoke to more anxiety about the weather. I was sure it would be a cold day on the river.

My mother asked who was boating with me.

"Bob Thompson," I said. Thompson, a scientist who worked for Salt Lake County, was working toward restoring the valley's watershed.

"I knew some Thompsons," she said. "They played football and basketball. Those Thompson boys were big."

The sky swam with gray clouds, but no rain had dropped. I walked over to the university football stadium and took the train south once again, branching off just beyond Murray Central onto the Mid-Jordan Line. I got off at the next stop.

I walked across the vast muddy lot between the station and the river. Bob Thompson was skeptical of my plan to do a carless river trip in the middle of the Salt Lake Valley. But I was confident it would be easy enough. When we took out of the river, I'd just have to wind my way through some streets for about a mile and find Murray Central station.

When I reached the river, I found a paved recreational trail running through willows along it, and I turned right to follow the river northward. The Jordan was not like the great navigable urban rivers of North America—the Mississippi in St. Louis, the Ohio in Pittsburgh, even the Willamette in Portland. It was a desert stream, creeping through the valley. Yet it caught the runoff of the massive Wasatch snowpack, emptied the rivers that carved the mountain canyons, and connected two large lakes. That it served such an essential function should have been more celebrated in the overall scheme of the city.

Walking along the Jordan today was in many ways the opposite of what Dominguez and Escalante had done. Their goal was to cross a river that formed a ferocious obstacle to the West's transportation network. I walked along a river that had nearly been killed. The city backed onto it like it was a rubble heap. The networks of cities throughout the world had been oriented to rivers and bays, celebrating the natural contours that sustained them: New Orleans, Paris, Venice. Utah had simply steamrolled its rivers. One Utah river advocate had gone so far as to say that "rivers in Utah don't have a legal right to exist."[33] Indeed, the Wasatch Front's creeks and rivers had been piped, diverted, and dammed—whatever was necessary for the West's growth. Powell wanted watersheds to organize politics and roads in the West, but roads and politics had subjugated many western watersheds nearly out of existence.

When I reached the 6400 South bridge about twenty minutes later, Thompson was sitting on the riverbank on one of the kayaks he had brought. He was indeed tall and athletic. But instead of football and basketball, he had gone for the outdoor life, doing things like running up Utah's highest mountains.

When I had contacted Thompson about taking a river trip, he said it depended on the level of the river. At the time I talked to him, the Jordan was running too high to kayak safely. It wasn't because of spring runoff from the Wasatch or any other natural reason. The river was artificially controlled by the water master at Utah Lake. A few days before, Thompson had sent me an e-mail informing me that the water master had reduced the flow. Today it was flowing at a nice 377 cubic feet per second (cfs), a pleasant day's float.

Before the modern transportation network altered it, the Jordan was a magnificent waterway—fifty miles of oxbows and wetlands running between Utah's two biggest lakes, the centerpiece of the Salt Lake Valley. A meander corridor over a half mile wide, supporting lines of majestic cottonwood trees marking the corridor of water through the desert.

Mormon pioneers began altering the Jordan watershed two days after arriving in the valley, diverting water to irrigate otherwise-doomed crops. Within a few decades they had built a dam for diversion, and droughts from the dam's impact led to the turn-of-the-century construction of a pumping station, then the largest in the United States. In the 1950s, the river was straightened and dredged for more efficient high flows.

These alterations also made it easier for cars to move around the valley. A straight river was easier and cheaper to bridge and had a narrower floodplain that opened more land to suburban development. The bridge just upstream from us, which spanned the Jordan at 6400 South, was a good example. It was built in the 1950s, when a whole section of the river was straightened to save money on the bridge and connecting roads. Water resources usually received the blame for wiping away the vitality of the West's waterways, especially in urban areas, but the modern road and highway network was another major culprit.[34] While demand for drinking water puts pressure on river systems, demand for roads fundamentally alters the shape of river channels and the water they carry.

In this way, the Jordan and its tributaries—the glorious mountain streams that carried snowmelt into the Great Basin—were considered a plumbing system rather than the centerpiece of an ecosystem and a civilization. The plumbing worked; it transported flows from the headwaters to the Great Salt Lake quickly and efficiently. That is, until a major flood. Because the river was now disconnected from the floodplains, it had no room for error, relying on levies to keep the water back. When the plumbing failed, the system had no backup, and the raging river would rip the bank off, inundate the closest subdivisions, and leach pollution from farms and industry into the water. Exactly such a flood occurred in the early 1980s causing millions of dollars in damage.

The plumbing of the Jordan also wiped away the ecology that depended on the river. It became a near-vertical bank covered with invasive plant species. The watershed had been changed to mirror the network of highways: concise, efficient, controlled, sterile, and lined by weeds.

Now boaters can float only three stretches of the Jordan. We stood at the beginning of the middle stretch, bracketed by a weir above us, below 6400 South. Thompson explained that the weir had almost killed two people last year who floated down on two mattresses tied together, using brooms as paddles.

We pulled our boats into the water. It was still overcast but not raining yet. After pushing off we began paddling down the flat water. A red-winged blackbird perched on a nearby tree. I hadn't been in a kayak since my one attempt at whitewater boating when I was sixteen, which was a debacle. Thompson assured me that the low flow would guarantee a smooth float.

"No one's going in the water today," he said.

After a few bends, though, a giant mass of concrete came into view: the belt route of Interstate 215, which we had to pass underneath. In the pleasant, miniature world we traveled in, the bulk of freeway seemed to be an object from space. Its legs were girth-y to support the one hundred thousand vehicles that drove over it every day. As we paddled into the darkness, the river quickened for a few seconds and then spat us out on the other side.

Thompson used to shun the Jordan, preferring the more far-afield rivers in and beyond the mountains. In the 1990s, the Jordan's banks were notorious places for drug dealers and gangs. It stank. Women were raped along it.

Bodies were routinely discovered in it. Intuitively, even beneath the urban detritus, Thompson knew something was fundamentally not quite right about the river.

Later, as a watershed scientist, he was able to put that intuition into words. With the straightening of the river came a loss of the life that the floodplains and oxbows and natural banks supported. A trifecta of invasive species—phragmites, Russian olive, and tamarisk—competed with natives for sun, soil, and water. They didn't stabilize the bank. They crowded out the mighty cottonwoods, which needed to survive in large clusters.

Still, Thompson had come to love the Jordan along with the potential to help it reclaim its former glory. A former high school science teacher, he had joined the county's watershed group about five years before. He did the slow work of rebuilding its natural system, trading the straight channels for meanders, invasives for natives, and plumbing for floodplains.

I saw it too. Kayaking down the Jordan gave you that timeless perspective on the valley, before the establishment of the subdivisions I knew were just on the other side of the brush. The Jordan had no polish but it did have soul. The freeways could carry us out to the urban fringe, but this river brought us inward. It remained where the Wasatch snowmelt coalesced, the true center of the grand theater of the valley.

A few more minutes downriver, we pulled into an eddy and got out of our boats to see one of Thompson's restoration projects. The bank had been a junk pile of steep mud, eroding into the water with each flood. Thompson had started simply by planting willows and cottonwoods and dressing the bank with rocks. It wasn't perfect; it directed water to a golf course, which acted as a floodplain. And in restoration circles, using rock was bad form, a Band-Aid.

"It's natural-ish, but it's not a natural system," Thompson said. He paused to pull a plastic bag out of the water.

But he continued to innovate. Where we had stopped, he and other restorers had completely rebuilt the bank as a more relaxed slope, with a flat area that could act as a mini-floodplain. They planted a wider variety of native plants: cottonwoods, Woods' rose, boxelders, willows, golden currant, bunchgrasses. He fenced the cottonwoods to protect them.

As it was Saturday, a smattering of people were walking and jogging on the trail. In the 1980s, you wouldn't see many people here, maybe a few homeless. But Murray had sunk millions of dollars into building parks along the river. Just as the plumbing of western watersheds had proceeded hand-in-hand with the drive for automobility, the restoration of urban watersheds was helping to reverse the harm of auto dependence.

"Murray can be great if it continues on its current development course," Thompson was saying as we got back in our boats. "But it can't fall into the trap of wanting growth at all costs."

I had never given suburbs like this a second thought. I'd just seen them for how they looked on the edges of I-15. But a lot was going on here. Walking through the Salt Lake suburbs between the corridors of the Jordan River and the light rail, this transportation spine had taken hold in my mind as the multiple threads of river, light rail, freeway, and the streets in between. Where before I thought of this neck of the woods as bland suburbia, I now saw it filled with the rich possibilities that come with rivers, parks, and mass transit. In a car, these places were not so interesting. On foot, on the train, and in a boat, they were intriguing.

We had oversimplified the system. Just like I had oversimplified the picture of my hometown valley in my head. The industrial age had stripped the world of its rich depth and complex connections. Now we were reintroducing the complexity nature possessed in the first place. Many things that had taken hold in America since the dawn of the millennium—heirloom vegetables, local business, ecological restoration—rested on reintroducing complexity to the way we do things. Connecting the watershed, transportation, and open space was complex, but so was nature.

In mucking through the Jordan, I saw that the same network principles I'd been mulling on foot, on my bike, and on the train held true on our waterways. The river is a means of accommodating our movement, giving us options, connecting big things to little things, and connecting people to one another. As my trips through the Salt Lake Valley were beginning to suggest, a community frame in the modern West is most likely based on cars; but transit, walking, biking, and nature can together comprise a legitimate alternative community frame to the point of creating a parallel reality that can, perhaps one day, become a replacement. Conversely, if you opt for cars, you sacrifice just about everything else. And as the last hundred years had shown, that is not an even trade.

Thompson had one more place to show me. We paddled down the river aways and as we approached our take-out spot, he asked, "Do you want to see Little Cottonwood Creek?"

The name brought images of a sparkling mountain stream and its headwaters in some of the most spectacular Wasatch high country. I never considered that these streams actually reached through the valley to the Jordan. In a sense, they didn't.

"The Cottonwoods below the canyons are wastelands," Thompson said.

"I never even noticed them before," I said.

"They're not noticeable," he said, "Until they flood."

I could smell what he was talking about. We took a right at the confluence of a small creek into the Jordan and paddled up through the still black water. This was the end of Little Cottonwood Creek. As Big and Little Cottonwood Creeks ran through the valley, they existed mostly in backyards. Property owners dumped oil and grass clippings in them. They were a distant horizon for restoration, a problem for another day.

There was no point in going very far, so we turned around, ferried across the riffles in the Jordan, and took out on the opposite bank. Once the boats were up on the bank, Thompson fished out a brown sack of beers from his truck.

We drank and stared across the river at what ought to be one of the holiest places in the valley: where Little Cottonwood Creek met the Jordan, the Big Cottonwood Creek confluence just downstream. As holy as the Wasatch peaks above us.

Even with the clouds, the chill, and the stink of Little Cottonwood Creek, it had been a great day on the river. It was always a great day on the river.

"That was so mellow," Thompson said. "Imagine commuting to work like that every day. There would be no road rage!"

Recapitulation

I walked back to the train through the winding streets and their clumps of randomly placed land uses—a patchwork of apartments, warehouses, subdivisions, and a barbecue restaurant in an old convenience store. On the way I saw something familiar. It was a large industrial shed, but over the top peeked three shiny cylinders, their mirror glass refracting the gray sky. An empty parking lot was beside it and the rush of Interstate 15 beyond.

It was the 49th Street Galleria. I walked down the driveway and up to the grand entrance. The place was vacant. I could tell that a long time had elapsed since the last birthday party, and the sign in the parking lot announced its bank ownership. Grass grew through the cracks in the parking lot. The neighbors probably hated this place when it generated traffic jams and hated it even more as a blighted eyesore.

I looked through the locked doors at the inside; the curved stairways and open atrium were still visible but worn and empty. I saw a high density of garbage and broken windows. I looked down into the basement to what must have been an office, where desks and papers were still piled and scattered on dirty green carpet.

I kept walking. Murray Central station was just beyond the abandoned Galleria, the hospital tower imposing in the day's gloom. A northbound train came quickly, and I took it. The train was nearly full; many passengers were families out and about on this ominous Saturday.

I planned on leaving Salt Lake that night for Wyoming, and I needed to do a few errands for the trip. I needed to shop for food, get some more bike inner tubes, and visit my grandma.

My mom's side of the family was from all over the place, everywhere but Utah. My maternal grandmother, my only living grandparent, was a product of the Bronx and had a different life than Grammie in just about every way imaginable. She was raised by a strict Catholic single mother and took the train to school in Manhattan. She began modeling for magazines when she was fifteen. She and my grandpa met during World War II when she was on a modeling shoot in Phoenix and he was an Air Force pilot stationed at nearby Williams Air Force Base. They married two weeks later, and a few months after that he had a job in Salt Lake selling Cadillacs. Grandma and her Episcopal husband and five kids were planted in a house in the Mormon capital of the world.

My mom had just recently moved my grandma from the senior apartments where she had lived in the decade since my grandpa died to a place with a higher level of care. It was only a few long Zion blocks from one of downtown's TRAX stations, and I picked up some groceries on the way over.

Grandma was eighty-seven years old and still sharp, and even though she had just been declared legally blind, she managed to make out the grocery sack I was carrying. I asked her if she had been to the new downtown Harmon's, Salt Lake's first downtown grocery store in decades, just down the street. No, the center's staff had told her that the urban supermarket's aisles were too narrow for the walker she used.

She was surprised I had been able to walk and take the train all over town. Coming from New York City, my grandma had never driven when she moved to Salt Lake; she had always taken the train. When she moved to Utah, she resisted obtaining a driver's license or learning how to drive. My grandpa always drove her places in whatever Cadillac he happened to be driving at the time.

"I used to take your mother on the bus downtown to go shopping," she said. "But mostly I had the kids drive me around."

I told her that in a few hours I was getting on a bus to Rock Springs, the small town where my grandpa had grown up. It was a coincidence of the trip, the place where the Greyhound happened to stop closest to where I wanted to start my bike ride on the Oregon Trail.

"When he took me there for the first time," Grandma said, "I thought it was the biggest dump in the world. I saw that sign, Rock Springs Coal, or something like that, and I wanted to cry."

Outside the rain was coming down in sheets. I walked up 500 East to South Temple. This was a grand part of Salt Lake, with apartment buildings and the wide sidewalks and treelawns of the City of Zion plan. I had walked and driven these streets hundreds of times but had never thought about how they could be any different.

Now I wondered how they could stay the same. I had seen how, especially in the rugged and singular landscapes of the American West, the transportation networks we chose created powerful frames for the cities we lived in. The frames we had been using had evolved out of hundreds of years of exploration, enterprise, and engineering. But they came to be dominated by high-speed roads good for driving and little else, disconnecting the places we lived from one another and from the land around and within them. By experiencing a different transportation network in the city where I'd grown up, I'd seen the possibilities of a new frame for the city that connected rather than disconnected.

Next I would shift my focus to the engine of the West, the reason why Euro-Americans had come here in the first place: opportunity. What were the economics of getting out of our cars?

Greyhound II: Salt Lake to Rock Springs

I was in a hurry when I returned to my parents' house. My Greyhound left in two hours, and after my experience in Las Vegas, I wanted to leave plenty of time to box up my bike and wait in any unforeseen lines.

"Do you want us to drive you to the bus station?" my dad asked.

But it was an easy bike ride, all downhill. I did borrow a duffel bag, to consolidate my stuff in the storage space at the bottom of the bus. I packed up my bike with my touring gear, said goodbye, and rode westward. The Greyhound station was located in Salt Lake's new Intermodal Hub, where TRAX and FrontRunner trains met near downtown, in what Salt Lake City had dubbed its Depot District. Locating the Greyhound terminal in the same station as the light rail and commuter rail made so much sense it almost seemed wrong.

It promised to be a better experience than the one in Las Vegas. The terminal was larger and less crowded, and instead of abrasive middle-aged attendants, a pleasant girl checked me in. I did have to pack up the bike and consolidate my panniers, tent, and sleeping pad into the duffel bag, but it only cost $10 for the bike box and $10 to check the extra bag.

The bus boarded, and I found a seat across from a man wearing work boots and a camo jacket who looked like he had just gotten in a fight; he had a moon-shaped gash under his eye. In front of him was a good-looking young guy, also in a ranch-hand getup, who immediately started reading a Book of Mormon by flashlight as the bus pulled out of the station. It was almost dark, and all the skyscrapers in downtown reflected the remains of the last sunlight.

"I ain't never coming this goddamn way again!" shouted someone sitting in front of me.

The guy with the gash pulled out something from his jacket pocket. "Jerky man?" he said with a twang, extending a stick across the aisle to me.

The ride through the dark went quickly. After a stop in Evanston, only an hour passed before we pulled into a McDonald's next to a freeway interchange outside Rock Springs.

Everyone got off to smoke and buy food and I collected my bag and box from the bottom compartments. Once again I reassembled my bike next to a McDonald's in the middle of the night while a bunch of strangers smoked and watched.

It was Saturday night in Wyoming—12:15 a.m. and a line of pickup trucks in the drive through. The Book of Mormon guy walked up and asked me if I was going to bike the rest of the way.

I said I was, to Casper at least.

He pulled a $10 bill from his pocket to give to me.

"No, no, I'll be all right," I said. "I'm doing this for fun. I'm going on a bike tour." He seemed to half-understand. I put my box in the McDonald's dumpster and rode off.

The Motel 6 where I had made a reservation was on the other side of Interstate 80 from the McDonald's. The front office was locked, so I had to conduct business through a slit in what looked like bulletproof glass.

The clerk, an overweight woman with painted eyebrows, gave me my key. As I walked my bike over to my room, it began to snow.

Notes

1. "Population of Washington County Utah by Minor Civil Divisions, 1890–1940," rootsweb.com, accessed July 17, 2014, http://www.rootsweb.ancestry.com/~utwashin/wpa/census.html. Even in the 1980s, Washington County had a population of less than 30,000.

2. And by 2012, the US Census Bureau estimated that the county had grown by almost half again, reaching a population of 144,809. "Washington County, Utah," US Census Bureau, accessed July 17, 2014, http://quickfacts.census.gov/qfd/states/49/49053.html.

3. In 2000 the Salt Lake City Metropolitan Statistical Area led the nation in households with three or more cars available and was last in households with one or zero cars. "Census Transportation Planning Products: Chapter 5. Vehicle Availability," US Department of Transportation, Federal Highway Administration, last modified April 28, 2011, http://www.fhwa.dot.gov/planning/census_issues/ctpp/data_products/journey_to_work/jtw5.cfm.

4. The narrative of Dominguez and Escalante's trip is primarily based on Escalante's journal, edited by Ted J. Warner and translated by Fray Angélico Chavez, *The Dominguez-Escalante Journal: Their Expedition through Colorado, Utah, Arizona, and New Mexico in 1776* (Salt Lake City: University of Utah Press, 1995), 87.

5. Or, as the case has been, practice polygamy.

6. Warner, *Dominguez-Escalante Journal*.

7. Thomas G. Alexander, *Utah, The Right Place: The Official Centennial History* (Layton, UT: Gibbs Smith, 2003).

8. Warner, *Dominguez-Escalante Journal*, 85.

9. Ibid., 94.

10. Ibid., 98.

11. Ibid., 99.

12. Ibid., 100

13. Ibid., 114.

14. Glen Canyon Dam, just upstream, had even created a completely different river than the one that was here two hundred years ago. The river wasn't controlled by snowmelt but by the air conditioning and irrigation needs of Las Vegas and Phoenix.

15. Warner, *Dominguez-Escalante Journal*, 120.

16. Ibid., 120.

17. Thomas G. Alexander, "Utah, the Right Place," Utah History to Go, accessed July 17, 2014, http://historytogo.utah.gov/utah_chapters/trappers,_traders,_and_explorers/dominguez-escalanteexpedition.html.

18. Warner, *Dominguez-Escalante Journal*, 121.

19. Florence Lipsky, *The Grid Meets the Hills* (Marseilles: Parentheses, 1999), 62. While one might think that a network following the contours of the hills—think leafy streets softly running along curved hillsides—would honor the hills more, the grid actually accentuates the hills while providing dramatic views of the larger Bay Area.

20. Ibid, 12.

21. J. W. Powell, *Report on the Lands of the Arid Region of the United States: With a More Detailed Account of the Lands of Utah* (Washington, DC: Government Printing Office, 1879), 27–28.

22. Ibid., 28.

23. Terry B. Ball and Jack D. Brotherson, "Environmental Lessons from Our Pioneer Heritage," *BYU Studies* 38, no. 3 (1999): 63–82.

24. After all, didn't Powell have just as much experience designing cities as Joseph Smith?

25. My four-year-old daughter loves to grab these flags and wave them around as she crosses a street, like she is in a parade.

26. Wesley Earl Marshall and Norman W. Garrick, "Does Street Network Design Affect Traffic Safety?," *Accident Analysis & Prevention* 43 (May 2011): 769–81, http://www.sciencedirect.com/science/article/pii/S0001457510003179.

27. "UTA History," Utah Transit Authority, accessed July 17, 2014, http://www.rideuta.com/uploads/FactSheet_History_2012new.pdf and Lynn Arave, "Utah Transit Authority Has Long, Winding Road of History," *Deseret News*, last modified September 26, 2010, http://www.deseretnews.com/article/700068895/Utah-Transit-Authority-has-long-winding-road-of-history.html?pg=all.

28. The total project cost of $300 million was about $22.8 million per mile.

29. For the full first year of operation in 2000, operating cost per passenger-mile by TRAX plunged to $0.15, compared with $1.04 for UTA's bus operations. "Salt Lake City: Light Rail's a Hit," Light Rail Now Project, last modified December 19, 2003, http://www.lightrailnow.org/features/f_slc001.htm.

30. Interstates 15, 80, 215, and 84 and State Routes 201 and 67 comprise approximately 170 miles of freeway in the Salt Lake Valley.

31. "Public Transportation Ridership Report: Fourth Quarter 2013," American Public Transport Association, last modified February 26, 2014, http://www.apta.com/resources/statistics/Documents/Ridership/2013-q4-ridership-APTA.pdf.

32. Some colleagues and I did a quick study to see if even the planned 2040 growth for the half mile radius around each TRAX station in Salt Lake Valley would, on paper, have a density to support light rail, about thirty housing units to the acre or fifty jobs per acre. Very few of them did.

33. Stephen Dark, "River Rats," *Salt Lake City Weekly*, last modified June 10, 2009, http://www.cityweekly.net/utah/river-rats/Content?oid=2138468.

34. The wide-ranging effects of roads on watersheds and their ecology include sedimentation, stream temperature change, channelization and floodplain diversion, habitat fragmentation, increased peak flow, and accelerated delivery of chemicals to streams. See Chris Frissel, "The Ecological Impacts of Forest Roads in an Era of Climate Change," Pacific Rivers Council, presentation at Watershed Restoration and Forest Roads Symposium, Tacoma, WA, April 4, 2008, http://pacificrivers.org/files/roads/Frissell-Symposium-Presentation.pdf.

PART III

Opportunity

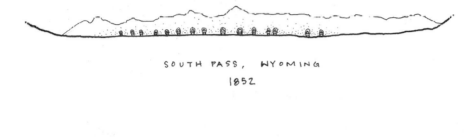

SOUTH PASS, WYOMING
1852

DENVER TECHNOLOGY CENTER, COLORADO
2012

DOI: 10.7330/9780874219937.c003

Home of Rock Springs Coal

The morning sky was a miracle of blue. I pushed aside the vinyl curtains of the Motel 6 room and stared into the blinding sun.

It was still winter, though. As I had moved further north, the seasons moved backward, from the burning heat of Las Vegas to the wet spring of Salt Lake and now to frozen Wyoming. Snow from the night before dusted the bare beige hills. At the truck stop across the street, men in parkas buried their faces as they emerged from their truck cabs. I returned to bed, wanting to enjoy the warmth and mental comfort of a heated room for as long as I could before venturing into the bleakness of Wyoming for four days. I was as unfamiliar with Wyoming as I was familiar with the state I had come from. I was headed out into a freezing mystery.

I took a shower and dressed in Lycra tights, a Capilene shirt, and a hat. I tried to fill up my water bottles and Camelbak, but no cold water came out of the faucet. I went to get help. Working the front desk was a twelve-year-old boy with a brown pompadour and a gold chain necklace.

"In the winter, when the AC isn't on, we don't have cold water" was the explanation he gave, taking my water bottles to fill them up himself.

I checked out at 8:30, and with most of my skin covered against the cold, I rode into the heart of town, which was several miles away, most of the national chain motels had clustered around the Interstate 80 exit.

Rock Springs, despite the slow national economic recovery, was in the throes of an energy boom. Wyoming had the nation's second-largest natural gas reserves, and in a pattern of resource extraction that had been playing out for centuries, national companies had descended on the state's Red Desert in the 1990s to drill, pump, and transport fuel to places all over the world. Jobs attracted workers from as far away as Florida. Houses seemed to be either gaudy mansions on the hill or trailers parked in the desert. Shifts were as long as sixteen hours, but some gas field operators made six figures.[1] As one reporter observed, there wasn't much else to do in Rock Springs but work.[2]

I figured that was why every service job in town seemed to be staffed by a kid; the able-bodied men and women must have been working in the gas fields. At a Kum & Go I bought a lighter from a ten-year-old. He confirmed my theory.

"It's a weird town," he said.

The center of Rock Springs was a grid of streets bisected by the railroad. The downtown church bells chimed 9:00 as I rode through. I didn't know what to make of it. I caught a whiff of the New West gentry here—a bike shop, a microbrewery—but in between were the decrepit remnants of the town's glory years as a train stop. And the streets were empty early on this Sunday morning. I had been here once, as a teenager on the way to the Wind River Mountains for a camping trip, and, having never poked into one of the bleak little western towns off the freeway, was awed by the ruins.

Sure enough, right at the train station I saw the "Home of Rock Springs Coal" sign my grandma had remembered. My mom told stories about Rock Springs; she spent summers here in the 1950s while she was growing up. These were her paternal grandparents, who she called Mom and Pop. Mom and Pop lived in a big white house on Bridger Avenue, where they operated— believe it or not—a guesthouse for Greyhound bus drivers. My mom helped Mom make beds in the house and had pretend tea parties with the grizzled drivers. Each evening my mom would sit right between Mom and Pop in the front seat of the family's Pontiac on their nightly ride. They picked a section of town and drove around all of its streets, always ending up on Front Street, where they parked and watched the town go by.

My mom shared my grandma's negative impression of the town; she remembered coal dust coating everything. It was always windy, usually cold, and, apart from equally small Green River, one hundred miles separated Rock Springs from the nearest city.

In those days, the arc of the natural gas industry was just beginning to rise, ratcheting up toward the boom of the 1970s. My mom's perception of the magnitude of her grandparents was skewed by her young age, and as she grew older she began to realize the economic realities of their lives. My mom thought the house on Bridger Avenue was the biggest one in town, but it was the same size as the ones across the street. She had always thought her grandfather owned the grocery store where he went to work. But once, toward the end of her summer trips, she happened into the store and saw him bagging groceries. She realized he was only an employee there.

Rock Springs was just a tough town on the Wyoming steppe that rose out of the necessity of transport. Founded in 1862 as a stop on the Overland Stage route, it became a train town when Union Pacific built the first transcontinental railroad. Now, in addition to being a natural gas capital, Rock Springs was one of the world's largest producers of soda ash, which is used to make plastic bottles. Each generation was just another iteration of the same process of pure economics consuming the land. The boys my mom saw strolling down Front Street had become boys in pickups rolling into the McDonald's drive-through at midnight.

For the next few hundred miles through Wyoming and Colorado, I would be following this scent of opportunity carried on the winds of transport. If nothing else, the American West always signified opportunity for the rest of America. Western historian William G. Robbins called the West an "investment arena for surplus capital . . . a seemingly vast vacant lot to enter and occupy."[3] Rock Springs was one version of investment in this arena, but what were others? How did transportation create opportunity in the West? How did automobiles compromise opportunity? And how are transportation alternatives reclaiming opportunity?

I looked for the old house on Bridger Avenue and found it quickly, just outside downtown. It was still a big white house, with a red sedan parked in the driveway. I knocked on the door, but no one answered.

Anyway, it was time to leave, as many had from Rock Springs. My route pointed north, to the trail that opened the West's opportunity, and I began to ride.

Crosswinds

The Oregon Trail was America's first superhighway, the Conestoga wagons that beat down its ruts the first moving vans. It brought almost a half million people across the United States to settle the West in the middle of the nineteenth century. They looked for homesteads in the Willamette Valley and gold in the foothills of the California Sierra. The crux of this route involved crossing dry, rugged Wyoming and the surmounting of the Continental Divide.

Like the Dominguez-Escalante route, this trail's toughest stretch threaded through a maze of mountains and rivers. In the years since the padres' journey, Thomas Jefferson had made the Louisiana Purchase, gaining control of an 828,000-square-mile diagonal swath of land in the middle of the continent. The US government wanted to exploit the new land, but it had to figure out to get there first. Jefferson sent Meriwether Lewis and William Clark to explore the commercial possibilities of the new territory and the land beyond.

At the same time, merchants had begun operating along the rivers on both sides of what Americans were beginning to understand as the Continental Divide—the mountainous separation between waterways that ran into the Atlantic Ocean and Gulf of Mexico on one side and those that ran to the

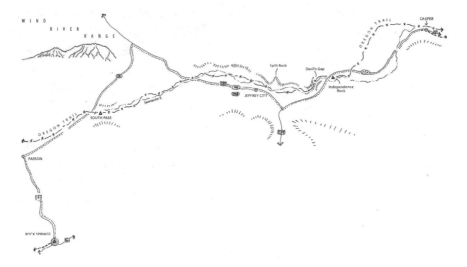

The Oregon Trail, Wyoming.

Pacific Ocean on the other. Traders explored the Mississippi and its tributaries on the east side and the Columbia on the west, and problems arose on both sides. The most convenient Mississippi tributaries had muddy waters that were too shallow and crooked to employ for water transport. Upstream, the Columbia fractured into small mountain rivers and creeks.

Jefferson and others soon realized that the yellow brick road to western expansion would be less a navigable river than a route over the mountains that common wagons could handle. And so American trailblazers worked into the interior from either end. The way east, initially, was clear-cut. Fur trappers followed the route west from St. Louis along the Missouri River through Independence, Missouri, along the flat country of the Platte River into Wyoming. The western end, likewise, was simply a trip up the Columbia River, a trek over the Blue Mountains of eastern Oregon, and a trudge up the Snake River in present-day Idaho, also an incipient fur trading route.

That left a terra incognita between the Snake and the Platte that consisted mainly of modern-day Wyoming, within which rose the Continental Divide. Lewis and Clark had reached the Pacific coast via the Missouri River, but the routes they took were unprofitably sinuous and brutal. There had to be a better way.

It took the raw desires of capitalism to find a route through. In 1810 the industrialist John Jacob Astor decided to enter the fur market when he heard about Lewis and Clark's journey and the subsequent profits of foreign fur trading outfits. Astor organized the Pacific Fur Company to compete in this new trading space. He envisioned a "widespread commercial conquest," with company trading posts up and down the Pacific coast and the rivers that emptied into it.[4]

Astor sent two parties to found a settlement in Oregon, one by sea and one by land. The sea expedition sailed from New York down the Atlantic coast, around Cape Horn, and up the Pacific coast to the mouth of the Columbia River in six months, losing eight crew members when it sailed over the windswept sandbar at the mouth of the Columbia. It took them two months to clear an acre of Pacific coast rainforest, during which they constantly remained vigilant of Indians, with "an axe in one hand and a gun in the other." They named the settlement Astoria after their patron on the other side of the continent.

The overland expedition, meanwhile, slowly wound through the terrain of the interior West. It took the overland travelers three times as long as their seafaring colleagues to arrive at the mouth of the Columbia. The party, led by Wilson Price Hunt, initially followed Lewis and Clark's route up the Missouri. Then it cut up the Grand River on horse and foot through present-day South Dakota and across the Teton Mountains to the ostensibly clear path of the Snake, where it transferred to canoes and subsequently wrecked in rapids, lost rations, and fractured into several disoriented parties that wandered through the mountains of Idaho and Oregon and, in early 1812, began to straggle into Astoria.

Hunt's party failed to accomplish what Astor wanted. Like Lewis and Clark's trail, its route was too indirect and rugged. It hardly constituted the desired corridor of transport and trade. Six months later, though, in the summer of 1812, a party led by an Astor partner named Robert Stuart set off eastward to deliver an update to Astor in New York. Stuart would cross the Continental Divide so easily as to not know it, a broad opening in the mountains that would become the key to westward expansion for the next half century, eighty miles northeast of present-day Rock Springs.

———————————————

I rode in a valley alongside a ridge that rose to the west. It was still sunny, but clouds hung in the sky in every direction and the thin coat of snow on the buttes had not melted. The gas well and mobile home sprawl of Rock Springs had thinned out, and now I was riding along the fenced range, with not a tree in sight. It had not warmed up much. My constant physical activity and the thin clothing covering my whole body kept out the cold.

When you're driving long distances, a road is just a road. You think in the big picture: how many hundreds of miles to your destination. To my wife's distaste, my mind tends to wander. Driving almost becomes like sitting in a movie or listening to background music—and yes, I am a terrible driver. On a bike, though, every nuance is apparent. I was aware, for example, that the shoulder of Route 191 varied between a smooth asphalt lane and a washed-out, cracked concrete edge, and my speed and safety depended on which one it happened to be.

I was also increasingly aware that the wind would be my companion for the trip through Wyoming. I hoped it would blow at my back. The difference between a headwind and a tailwind could mean going 10 miles an hour versus going 30 miles an hour. For now, I had a crosswind coming from the northwest. I hoped that as soon as I turned east, it would push me along the Oregon Trail.

Elevation became my obsession. Twenty miles north of Rock Springs I began climbing to gain the ridge that had been on my left. I had changed the readout on my GPS to show me my elevation in big digits. I was rolling. Distance wasn't the problem; it was climbing toward the elevation I needed to reach, especially with the crosswind. I started out at 6,200 feet at Rock Springs and had to climb to 7,000 feet on the ridge, then descend down to the valley floor and the town of Farson at 6,600 feet.

Being on a bike also forced me to spend time looking at what I would otherwise consider an ugly, boring landscape. The more I looked at the expanses of sagebrush, the more my eyes could pick out the green of spring coming through below the silver shrubs, the geologic patterns etched by the snow dusting the buttes. As soon as I reached the crest of the ridge, I pulled over and had my first Snickers of the day.

At noon, I rode into Farson, the place where mountain man Jim Bridger had encountered Brigham Young and told him about the Salt Lake Valley. In exchange for the information, Young gave Bridger a free pass across the Mormons' Green River ferry. The trade turned out to be a great deal for the Latter-day Saints.[5]

But like some places along the West's routes of transport, Farson had remained a crossroads, a mere junction in the business of the West. I arrived there just as a dark black cloud towered over the plains on the flat northwest horizon, exactly the direction where the wind was coming from.

One corner of Farson's highway crossroads contained the Farson Mercantile, housed in a brick storefront. I hoped that it would be open on Sunday because without it, I would be sitting in a gas station to wait out the storm. It was. Two kids staffed the place, and they were mildly surprised by my mode of travel.

I watched the storm come in with a fury. Hail hammered on the building and ground, eventually turning to rain. At 3:00 the sun came back out. I turned east from here, with thirty miles to go.

South Pass

I began to see the Oregon Trail. My first glimpse of it was a dormant imprint on the sagebrush scrub alongside the highway, but eventually I saw pairs of sandy paths that had been made by wagon wheels. While researching my route through Wyoming, I had assumed that the Oregon Trail had simply evolved into auto roads the way an old highway might have been widened. But like old civilizations that sat amid modern life, the trail sat through history as a set of parallel tracks that no one had bothered to wipe away. This was the most powerful kind of history, the kind that had simply been left to exist and weather without any care. It gave an authentic and eerie sense of connection between now and before.

In some ways, the Oregon Trail was a misnomer because for much of its distance it consisted of a collection of different trails overlapping and separating, like a braided river, up to several miles wide. But in some places, out of geographic necessity, the lanes of the trail converged—at a major fort or where natural geography created only one option. In some of these places the trail ruts were gouged so deeply they resembled 5-foot-deep railway cuttings.

One such place of geographic necessity had come to be known as South Pass and was the key to the whole cross-country route. South Pass allowed American migrants a relatively flat route all the way to Oregon and California.

Before Robert Stuart pushed his way through the interior West in the fall of 1812, no whites had crossed South Pass. Stuart, a twenty-seven-year-old Scot, had been a passenger aboard Astor's sea expedition two years earlier alongside his father. He hoped to reach New York in six months, a third of the time it had taken Wilson Price Hunt. He started from Astoria in June 1812 and more or less followed Hunt's route in reverse (now the present-day course of Interstate 84) along the Columbia, over the Blue Mountains, and into the wide smile of the Snake in present-day Idaho. The party encountered a Snake Indian on horseback who had been hired by the Hunt party to care for its horses. The man told Stuart that Hunt's route was far too circuitous. He knew of a route more direct and less arduous.

With this information, Stuart's party entered present-day Wyoming. This was the toughest country for mountain men, and for the emigrants that followed their trails, because they could not follow the simple path of a long, wide river like the Columbia, Platte, or Snake. The top of the West was a confusing maze of headwaters, passes, peaks, and ridges. Here, like Escalante and Dominguez, they had to navigate from point to point on scant trails and along small creeks, using mountains and ridges as their beacons.

At this point, the members of Stuart's party, like the Spanish fathers, were starving. But Stuart remained an iron-nerved leader. For his job, as one trapper described, "courage was an indispensable qualification, not merely for the casual encounters with the Indians, but to intimidate any competitor in trade with whom he might come in collision." Aboard the Astor ship on its journey from New York to Oregon, Stuart had stood up to the ship's bully of a captain, who threatened to maroon his passengers. He had seized several pistols from the ship and demanded that the captain wait for everyone to board.[6]

One of the Canadians in the group approached Stuart and proposed to cast lots to kill one member of the party so to "preserve" the rest. Stuart looked him in the eye and, much as he had done to the captain, stuck a gun in his face. "I snatched up my Rifle cocked and leveled it at him with the firm resolution to fire if he persisted, and . . . he fell upon his knees and asked the whole party's pardon," Stuart wrote. "I felt so agitated and weak that I could scarcely crawl to bed."[7]

Then, on September 19, a group of Crow Indians robbed the party of all of its horses. They continued on foot, spending weeks looping in indirect courses up and down various rivers. At the headwaters of the Green River on October 16, moving eastward in the northern part of what would become Wyoming, Stuart decided to turn abruptly to the south into uncharted wilderness. "Having thus lost the intended track by which we crossed the Rocky Mountains knowing it must be to the South, and the great probability of falling in again with the Crows," Stuart wrote, "we at once concluded that our best, safest, and most certain way would be to follow this river down." In essence, they decided to skirt the peaks of the Wind Rivers to the south rather than to the north, as Hunt and Lewis and Clark had done. This was terra incognita, but Stuart did not want to see any more Crow Indians.[8]

On October 19, the party reached the bank of Big Sandy Creek. The Wind River Range was the most imposing geographical feature in sight, pinching their course to the southeast. The Wind Rivers' namesake waterway was coined for the constant breeze that came from the gap between the two mountain ranges through which it flowed. By now, Stuart was well aware of the existence of a depression between the Wind Rivers on the north and the "considerably elevated ridge" to the south. "We therefore made our way for a gape [*sic*] discernable in the mountains in a S.E. direction," Stuart wrote. It was a "beautifully undulating country."[9]

Stuart's party spent the next day traversing the toe of the Wind Rivers to a camp at Dry Sandy Creek, which he called "a little drain on the bare prairie." They killed a buffalo and used "an indifferent" sagebrush to start a fire that the ragged wind kept putting out, so the men retired early to their tents.[10]

Once I left Farson, having crossed Big Sandy Creek, I saw the Wind Rivers. They were the first real mountain range I had seen today, a long strip of snowy peaks in the northern horizon.

It was still cold. Even in midafternoon I wore a hat under my bike helmet and long underwear under my jacket.

But now I had the hoped-for tailwind. A steady breeze continued to blow from the northwest as I rode. Uphill at 20 miles an hour was no problem—that's how you knew you had a tailwind. I gobbled up the miles as the straight road rose and fell with the topography. The Oregon Trail ruts were still there, my parallel companion on the other side of a livestock fence.

As the altimeter on my GPS rose toward 7,000, I recognized the landforms that hemmed in the low point that Stuart had picked out. The sloped top of Pacific Butte was alternately covered with rain clouds and blinding sunlight.

At around 5:00, I arrived where my GPS indicated I was overlooking Pacific Springs, which snaked up to the Continental Divide across the meadow.

Stuart had been forced to camp across the small valley of Pacific Creek on October 21, when the party encountered snow after traveling fifteen miles.

I was now in South Pass. Like the Crossing of the Fathers, South Pass was one of the hidden, hallowed places of the West and, fortunately, no one had built a reservoir here. These soft hills were a respite in the mostly jagged Continental Divide that ran the width of the whole young nation. In the postscript to his journal, Stuart called what lay immediately ahead "a handsome low gap." Two miles after leaving the party's camp on Pacific Butte, he encountered the headwaters of the Sweetwater River, after which it was all, more or less, downhill to St. Louis.[11]

Stuart thought he might be at the top of the West, the place that held the headwaters of the Columbia, Missouri, and Colorado Rivers, all bound for different seas and oceans. "The ridge of mountains which divides the Wind River from the Columbia and Spanish waters ends here abruptly," he wrote, "and winding to the north of East becomes the separator of a branch of Big Horn and Cheyenne Rivers from the other water courses which add their tributary waves to the Missouri below the Sioux Country."[12]

The revelation that that this was actually the key to cross-continental expansion and enterprise, though, came later. In reference to the Stuart party, the *Missouri Gazette*, on May 8, 1813, under the headline "American Enterprize," wrote, "By information received from these gentlemen, it appears that a journey across the continent of N. America might be performed with a waggon, there being no obstruction in the whole route that any person would dare to call a mountain in addition to its being much the most direct and short one to go from this place to the mouth of the Columbia river."[13]

It was getting dark, and I had to make camp. I saw a small knoll below the dirt road, smooth of any vegetation, where the ridge above would protect me from the wind, still blowing from the northwest. I put down my bike there and quickly began to set up my tent. I had come eighty miles today.

The landscape at South Pass was unremarkable. The mighty Wind Rivers to the north would capture the eye of the average visitor. Oregon Butte was nearly treeless and barren. Emigrants would be practically disappointed when they did not get to squeeze through a "narrow defile in the Rocky Mountains walled in by perpendicular rocks hundreds of feet high," as one emigrant envisioned the pass.[14] John C. Frémont, traveling through South Pass with Kit Carson in 1842, noted that he and Carson had to "watch very closely to find the place at which we had reached the culminating point."[15]

But some understood the importance of this portal to the West—that from this point westward, the rivers would be running toward their new home as opposed to back toward the one they had come from.

And the anticlimax of South Pass was entirely the point. Capitalists and boosters of American enterprise admired the wide corridor through which a whole nation could move and expand. It was one of the most beautiful places they had ever seen.

The Biggest Bust of Them All

When I woke up, I could see ice crystals on the orange nylon of my tent. I also saw from the way the fabric glowed that the sun was out. I had slept in three layers, and it was a good half hour before I dared to leave my sleeping bag and emerge into the morning. The ground was frozen. It was indeed sunny, but a lenticular cloud hung over the mountains. My phone showed a temperature of 24 degrees.

The road ahead followed the Sweetwater River, which began just over South Pass and emptied into the Platte near Casper. I had wanted to ride the web of dirt roads that followed the river from its headwaters, but with the leftovers of winter lurking around every bend, that was a bad idea. Plus, in the weeks I spent trying to track a route through this region on Google Maps, I could never figure out how I'd actually navigate it on the ground while carrying fifty pounds of gear on my bike. I took to the highway.

After the pass, the highway rejoined the Sweetwater at Sweetwater Station, a Mormon outpost. The Sweetwater Valley, the heart of the Oregon Trail in Wyoming, turned out to be a gravy train of flat riding. Compared to the country around Rock Springs, it was a Shangri-La of mountains and lush valleys. The river gave ample pasture to the wagon trains' animals, and the rock spires and far-off mountains provided a constantly changing set of landmarks to guide the emigrants. It provided a break between the difficult route finding from the Platte to the Sweetwater and the ruggedness that lay ahead in Idaho.

With the tailwind, I was rolling along at 20 miles an hour through the Sweetwater country. I began to see signs for a place called Jeffrey City, though it was spelled "Jeffery City" on half of the signs I saw. I had no illusions about what Jeffrey City was. In Wyoming, the only places named "City" were usually either very small or extinct. As I drew closer to where Jeffrey City was supposed to be, I looked hard for the clump of green marking its distant appearance. In dry country like this, you could usually see any sort of town for several miles. I didn't see anything.

That was because Jeffrey City was not a normal town, or really a town at all. When I rode past the "JEFFREY CITY, ELEV. 6324" sign, I began to see scattered cinderblock and tin sheds. I rode further, toward what I figured was the middle of town. But instead of a nucleus of a few charming storefronts around a crossroads, like in Farson, I saw only more tin sheds. Behind them were the type of stout, rectangular modernist buildings that I remembered from old pictures of the Soviet Union. The way they had been plunked on the plains reminded me of the grim, treeless oil camps of the Patagonian steppe, which was also the only place I could remember being windier than here. I turned off on a cross street and rode through a neat grid of streets that was mostly empty; several blocks were just squares of weeds. It looked as if someone planned a town that was never built.

It was lunchtime, so I found what had once been the town park. I recognized it as a park only because of a rusty swing set and bench rising from a field of cheatgrass and what appeared to have been a tennis court on another corner. The wind blew incessantly. I ate a sandwich on the lone bench.

After lunch, I biked through town to the only open business I could find, the Split Rock Café. I was looking for double-A batteries for my GPS, which had announced it was low on power. Inside were four people: a woman standing behind the bar, two men sitting at one of the tables working on laptops, and a blond hippie who sat at the bar. These were perhaps the only people in Jeffrey City.

They were making use of just a part of the expansive space. Behind them the room faded back into crumbling walls and old stuff, dark corners where probably no one had set foot for years.

"You want some lunch?" the woman asked. She was a sturdy woman, maybe about my age, wearing a Split Rock Café T-shirt.

"I'm looking for batteries," I said. "Double A."

"Nope," she said.

"I'll sell you some," the hippieish guy said. "Let's go over to my studio across the street."

I had seen the pottery studio across the highway.

"That's all right," I said.

The woman identified herself as the new owner of the café. She had just purchased it. She had grown up in Jeffrey City. I got the rest of the story.

A uranium mining company built Jeffrey City in the 1950s for the sole purpose of housing mine workers. The company had constructed it over a small ranching community named Home on the Range after a prospector discovered uranium nearby in 1954. He named it Jeffrey City after his biggest financial backer. The company went through several iterations—Lost Creek Oil, Western Nuclear—before finally merging with the giant Phelps Dodge Corporation during the second uranium boom in the 1970s. Phelps Dodge built up the town even more, adding more housing, streets, and parks.

At its peak in 1980, 4,000 people lived in Jeffrey City. It contained a school with 600 students and an Olympic-sized swimming pool, several bars and restaurants, a grocery store, and a bowling alley.

Then the uranium market began to move overseas. The price of uranium dropped steeply. The company laid off its workers and made them move their trailers off the lots. Hence, the empty blocks.

"And then there were the environmentalists," the café owner sighed.

By 1982, only two years after its peak, Jeffrey City had fewer than 1,000 residents. Today it had less than 100. And I suspected the number was closer to 4. A sign on the way out of town identified Jeffrey City as "the biggest bust of them all."

"And there's the wind," I said.

"Natural population control," the potter said proudly.

"I've had a tailwind mostly," I said.

"It's not windy today," the owner said. "Not even blowing."

She looked at my bicycle, which I had brought into the bar, and said that the old owners of the café would have chased me out with a shovel.

"And the people over to Muddy Gap would still chase you out with a shovel," she added. Herself, she had put out a "Bicyclists Welcome" sign to emphasize the new policy.

Independence Rock

The creations of capitalists like John Jacob Astor and Phelps Dodge were spewed all over the West, the ideas of outside money men having framed what counted for settlement here. But the individual families who risked everything to move across the continent and fill and flesh out these new cities were the West's more muscular creator. Transportation directly created their opportunity. Astor could pay for a circumnavigation of the Americas, but families wishing to move West needed a good road.

After Robert Stuart found South Pass in 1812, the secret of the route remained dormant for almost thirty years until, in the late 1830s, an economic depression cast a shadow over America, primarily an agricultural nation at that time. Farmers and merchants struggled with depressed prices and poor transportation to markets. Oregon materialized as an agricultural paradise with greener grasses, its picture painted by missionaries and government reports. The route along the Missouri, Platte, and Sweetwater, through South Pass, and up to the Columbia became the Oregon Trail.

Each year in the 1840s saw more and more parties leave their midwestern towns for Oregon. Travel along the Oregon Trail reached its crescendo in

1852, when over 50,000 people were estimated to have traveled along its thick spine before splitting off to Oregon, Utah, and California.[16]

The Scott family provides one vivid example. A company consisting of John Tucker Scott and twenty-five of his family and friends left Tazewell County, Illinois, for Oregon in the peak year of 1852. "Oregon Fever" had overtaken Scott for over a decade. His uncle was an Illinois agent of the Oregon Provisional Emigration Society, and Scott himself had known some of the men in the first party organized for settlement in Oregon Country in 1839. He was familiar with the descriptions of the country and the climate of the Willamette Valley.[17]

In 1852 a minister in the Scotts' community left for Oregon, and the Scott family was financially able to make the move with him. And so, in the winter and early spring of that year, Scott assembled a party of twenty-six people—most relatives but not all—sold all the party's belongings that they could not carry and headed west with a team of oxen.

We know about the Scotts' journey—and hundreds of other individual emigrations—because many of the parties assigned one member, usually a child, to document the life-altering trip. This was a big deal for each of these individual families. Compared with frontiersmen like Robert Stuart or Silvestre Vélez de Escalante, the migrants were making a much bigger commitment to the trail. They would likely never return to the home and family they left behind, so they documented the trip carefully.

The Scott party's primary journal writer was seventeen-year-old Abigail, John Tucker's daughter, but Abigail's sisters Fanny and Kit also took turns. The teenage girls were both young enough to be optimistic and wide-eyed about the adventure but old enough to reflect and lay down shrewd observations about the rapidly transforming American frontier they drove through. And they minded the details. Thirteen-year-old Kit described that on the early April morning when the party left, they were still sewing clothes and blankets. Kit remarked of "the tears that fell upon these garments, fashioned by these trembling fingers by the flaring light of tallow candles."[18]

The Scotts' five wagons were painted green with yellow bows made of hickory. They carried bacon, flour, rice, coffee, brown sugar, and hard tack. Two to five yokes of oxen pulled each wagon. A rifle hung from leather straps between the bows on one side. They rigged their wagons to carry boxes during the day, which they would move aside to reveal a feather bed on which to sleep.

When the wagons pulled up to the house on the scheduled morning of departure, it was snowing lightly. "The word was given, the sluggish oxen started, and the journey of more than two thousand miles was begun," Kit wrote. Her grandfather was standing at the gate, his words drowned by the creaking of the wagons and the shouts of the drivers.[19]

At the beginning of the journal Abigail commented, "to me, it was a great trial to leave the home of my childhood, the place where, when care to me was a stranger I . . . loved to wander alone to the sequestered grove, to hold communion unseen by the mortal eye with the works of nature and God."[20]

Abigail's older sister Fanny remembered that several miles from the family home, their dog, Watch, followed the party until it crossed the Illinois River on a ferry. The dog stood on the distant shore howling. "After we reached Oregon," Fanny wrote, "we had a letter to the effect of the poor Canine went back . . . to the Family Home & refused food & in a short time he died!"[21]

By now the route was well established. The Scott party followed a book called Platt's Guide, a sort of Michelin guide for Oregon Trail emigrants written in 1848.[22] They shipped supplies to places down the road like St. Joseph, Missouri. The early part of the route was somewhat familiar but plagued by late winter storms that dropped up to four inches of snow. They traveled as much as twenty miles a day if the roads were not too muddy or snow-covered, which, in April they often were. They drove through mud up to two feet deep and often had to ask local residents for shelter from storms. The boys killed dozens of pheasants and squirrels, and occasionally a turkey, at one time for dinner. They held preaching in their camp on the Sabbath days.

After two weeks of traveling, the Scott party crossed the Mississippi on a large steam ferryboat that chugged them seven miles up and across the river. Once in Missouri, Abigail noted a major difference. In Illinois, she was used to seeing the mostly white farmers work, while here she noticed that black men did it, and the "contrast was so great, she could think of little else all day." She called slavery a "withering blight upon the prospects [of] happiness and freedom of our Nation."[23]

They reached St. Joseph, on the Missouri, on May 4, after little over a month and kept going because the rush of emigrants had crowded the town beyond its capacity. They were behind; they should have been on the plains by May at the latest. After crossing the Missouri, they "took a farewell view of St. Joe and the United States." Even though the United States now owned the western territories, the Scotts literally felt like they were leaving the country.[24]

On the plains, they were often in the midst of Indians. They met a French-Indian "half breed" hauling a wagon of buffalo robes. They killed a buffalo, which "tastes almost exactly like beef but has a considerably coarser grain." They followed the Blue River to the Platte and then passed through Fort Kearney ("a rather shabby looking concern").[25]

Abigail became increasingly taken with the passing landscape. She saw the "wildest and most romantic scenery" that she had ever seen: columns of sandstone formed in massive bluffs that reminded her of "renowned ruins of the magnificent structures of the Old World." Mountains began coming into the picture. "To me who had never seen a mountain, they seemed to be one continued chain," Abigail's sister Maggie wrote during a time while Abigail was sick.[26]

Before ending her entry for the day, Abigail often noted how many graves the party had passed. The deaths were mostly due to colds and diarrhea brought on by exposure and fatigue. Abigail thought it was mostly imprudence in eating and drinking, though in one instance, two of the graves belonged to a murdered man and his killer, who had been hanged by the party.

Graves became more meaningful to Abigail. Her own mother died on June 20 when "a violent diarrhea attended with cramping" occurred through the night, but she did not wake anyone. By morning, no one could do anything, and she died that afternoon. The family buried her next to another woman who died the same day, on a small hill overlooking a ravine with small groves of pine and cedar, a fitting final resting place, Abigail thought, for such a "lover of rural scenery." They were near the border of present-day Wyoming, looking west at Laramie Peak in the distance.[27]

East of Jeffrey City I enjoyed a pleasant afternoon's ride in improving weather. The temperature had risen to 55 degrees. When I turned around I could still see the white tops of the Wind Rivers, an important guiding beacon for travelers along the Oregon Trail.

The geography of the Sweetwater Valley held a lore of intriguingly named landmarks: The Ice Slough was a marsh that hid ice floes that emigrants harvested to chill their meat. Split Rock was a notch in the Rattlesnake Range visible far to the east and west. Devil's Gate was a short, narrow canyon through the rocks of the Rattlesnake Range, which the Sweetwater actually passed through.

The trail still ran along the highway, rolling and dipping with the land, without the smooth grade of the highway at its disposal. Having ridden sixty miles for the day, I felt the trail's pain.

The most celebrated landmark of the Sweetwater Valley was a mound of granite named Independence Rock. At almost half a mile long and 700 feet wide, the outcropping was named after a party of trappers who celebrated Independence Day here in 1824, though it helped that many parties reached the landmark right around the Fourth of July.[28] Independence Rock became a bulletin board for travelers, called by Jesuit missionary Pierre Jean de Smet "the great register of the desert." Travelers often stopped here for several days, taking the time to climb the rock and inscribe their names in it. They let their oxen rest and gave birth. Later travelers happily found the names of explorers or emigrants they used to know who had passed by years or decades before.

I rode through Muddy Gap, across the valley and around Devil's Gate, and then saw the lump of Independence Rock. Having ridden so far today, I hoped for a visitor center, with drinking fountains and bathrooms, interpretive trails, maybe a snack bar, an impressive museum, and helpful rangers.

Disappointingly, Independence Rock was mostly a truck stop. There were bathrooms, but of the industrial rest stop genre. An interpretive trail with a meager display left from the edge of the parking lot. If I had been driving, I would never have known this place was anything more than a highway rest area.

I looked for a camping spot. I had seen enough drawings of the wagons encircling the rock, grazing oxen in the distance, that in my head I had envisioned Independence Rock as a great meeting place on the Wyoming desert, where perhaps I'd run into other travelers who could advise me of conditions further down the road. A BLM ranger I spoke with on the phone told me I could find campsites on BLM land near enough to the landmark. Now, looking around, I was unclear where to go. I sat back down on my saddle to look for the next dirt road into the American commons but then I saw the gate of the caretaker's grounds open and a battered pickup drive out into the truck stop parking lot. I rode over to intercept the truck. Its driver was a middle-aged guy with a weathered face, sunglasses, and a ponytail sneaking out of a ball cap.

"Hello!" I said. "I'm on a bike tour and looking for a place to pitch my tent for the night. Know any spots around here?"

The man winced and thought. "No," he said finally. "But . . . "

I waited.

"You can stay next to my place."

I looked over at his grounds, which were right next to the rock, separated by a quaint log fence. There was a nice grassy area in the corner.

"You sure?" I said. And without giving him time to reconsider, I thanked him and walked my bike into the gate.

I unloaded my bike, leaned it against the log fence, and set up my tent with a perfect view of the rock. At least I had this whole place to myself—not a tourist or trucker in sight, much less another bike tourer.

I walked over to the short trail to Independence Rock itself and then found a place to ascend it. I walked up the mellow slope to the top, where I could see my route. To the west was the braiding of the highway and the Sweetwater. The Oregon Trail here was deep enough that it beat a clear path across the plains to the horizon.

I looked for names on the rock. Travelers had used materials as varied as wagon tar, buffalo grease, and black powder to write their names. Some simply carved them with tools they brought to fix their wagons. An enterprising group of Mormons had set up a "professional" engraver to inscribe names for a few dollars apiece.

The Scott party arrived at Independence Rock on June 29, 1852, just over a week after they buried Abigail's mother. They found their way to the Sweetwater at 2:00 and an hour later had emerged at the "immense mass" that Abigail estimated to cover 10 acres and rise 300 feet (it really took up about three times as much area but was about half as tall). Unlike many parties who traveled the trail that summer, the Scotts did not stop to camp at Independence Rock. They decided to continue on another five miles up the Sweetwater to Devil's Gate.[29]

But when the party passed the rock, Abigail and her sisters could not resist trying to climb it. They ascended thirty feet before the arrival of a hailstorm forced them to, as Abigail wrote, "desist." They ran to catch up with the wagons as the party moved on, catching the last wagon before it crossed the Sweetwater.[30]

There was no time in this wagon company for sightseeing. "They had intended to let us wade (it was waist deep) to learn us not to get so far behind the team," Abigail wrote. "I would have liked the fun of wading well enough but did not like to get joked about being left."[31] The party pushed on to Devil's Gate before camping for the night a mile off the trail. Abigail noticed that names were written on Devil's Gate too, some from as early as "'38"; many were from "'50 and '51," but most had been scrawled that summer of 1852.

A week and a half later, on July 6, the party traveled through South Pass. Like Frémont, Abigail noted that "the ascent and descent is very gradual it being impossible to exactly determine where the culminating point is." Three months later they arrived in Oregon.[32]

Abigail met her future husband at the end of the trail, becoming Abigail Scott Duniway, a name that would become famous throughout America's Northwest, where most of the family stayed for the rest of their lives. She became an activist, a teacher, a poet, a novelist, and the publisher of the Portland newspaper the *New Northwest*. She died in 1915, a hero of the Oregon women's suffrage movement. Her life had been enabled by her family's risky trip on the Oregon Trail.

When I returned to my campsite, the caretaker's truck was back next to his trailer. After a while I saw him emerge and light up his gas barbecue. I walked over. His sunglasses were off now, and I noticed his kind eyes.

His wife's grandparents had been the caretakers until they left to live on a nephew's ranch. Out of work, he and his wife took the gig. He loved it. Each summer, busloads of people flooded the site, especially Mormons from Utah.

A gorgeous Conestoga wagon sat in the corner of the yard. It was painted blue and red, reminding me that the black and white photos and drawings from the overland trails obscured how brightly the emigrants painted their vehicles. This one had a baby blue hull with bright cherry red applied to the wheels and the small mailbox-like attachment on the side.

I asked the caretaker if the wagon was left over from someone's trip. He said it was. I told him that I couldn't believe how they all did it.

"Can you imagine?" he said. "Coming over a hill and seeing another one. It's like, 'Where are we going again?'"

Colonies

The next day I hit the road after drinking some hot chocolate powder emptied into a cup of boiling water. It was sunny and warmer than the day before, but the wind was still blowing eastward.

The fifty miles to Casper was a long descent down almost 1,000 vertical feet. Just outside of town, I noticed that my bike was making a *thwap-whap-thwap* sound in rhythm with my wheels. I thought it was my brakes, as bike brakes often become misaligned, and reluctantly I stopped.

The sound was coming from my brakes, but it wasn't because anything was wrong with them. What I saw horrified me: a bulge in the rim of the tire was rubbing against the brake pads. The metal of the rim was beginning to tear.

I had brought equipment to patch tubes, replace tires, switch out broken spokes, and adjust my drivetrain if it wasn't working right. But nowhere did I envision my rim ripping apart. No way could I have slung an extra wheel over my shoulder. I unhooked my brake and kept pedaling, hoping for a bike shop in Casper.

Casper was rougher than I imagined. It sprawled out over the plains like an oil camp, in some ways a larger version of Rock Springs. With its 55,000 people, it jostled with Cheyenne, the state capital, for the honor of Wyoming's largest city. Casper was named for Fort Caspar, which had been a toll bridge across the Platte for westward emigrants in the 1800s, but by the turn of the century shifted its economy to energy, and there it had stayed since. Casper's first oil refinery appeared in 1895, and by the 1980s, it had three of them.

The refineries, though, were fading, like logging mills or silver mines. Only Sinclair's remained. British Petroleum had just torn down its refinery and built a golf course on top of it next to downtown Casper. On the old Texaco Casper Works refinery, which had closed in 1982, Chevron had built an eleven-turbine wind farm in 2009, enough to power about 5,000 houses. Wind was increasingly big business in a city that thought of itself as an energy capital. Earlier this year, Denver-based Anschutz Corp. announced plans for the largest wind farm in the country in Carbon County, the next county to the south. The news was an encouraging sign for those who envisioned a New West of renewable resources, and the 1,200 jobs were encouraging to a county otherwise reliant on natural gas, with its continually sinking price.[33]

I found a bike shop near downtown. I couldn't tell if my wrecked rim impressed the mechanic, a short twenty-something redhead. When I told him about the bit of the trip on dirt roads in Arizona, he wasn't surprised. I didn't have time for him to rebuild a wheel with my hub, but he offered to sell me a new wheel.

It was strange to be suddenly wandering among racks of activewear as the mechanic switched my cassette onto the new wheel. In marketing its products, the outdoor industry had managed to equate the experience of the wild with the experience of shopping surrounded by victorious images, ego appeal, and the new smells of rubber and polypropylene. Over the last week, my world had veered more toward fear, questions of self-worth, and body odor, and I had suddenly popped into the sanitized parallel world of the gear store.

In anticipation of my Greyhound trip that night, I asked a store employee if they had any leftover bike boxes—which they did—and I said I'd come back for the box before they closed.

I spent much of the overcast afternoon in a bar in downtown Casper. Having eaten meals of backpacking food the last few nights, I ordered up a burger. The bartender, a young, bland-looking guy whose pleasant looks belied his cynicism, shrugged when I asked him about the new wind farm.

"I knew a few kids who got jobs, but mostly it was outsiders," he said.

The television in the bar was tuned to a Colorado Rockies game. Seeing the baseball teams in the stadium and being aware that Interstate 25 was just a few blocks away made me feel that I had been reinserted into the urban matrix, the Sweetwater Valley having been a dreamland outside of it. I felt as though we were a dot dangling on the outer reaches of the Denver metro area. I asked the bartender if Wyoming fans rooted for Colorado teams.

"Wyoming fans root for whoever they want," he said. "Colorado teams are the closest, it's where we can drive to see games. I drive to Coors Field with my son to see the Rockies. We don't root for 'em though."

I headed back to the bike store to pick up my bike box and then walked through downtown to the Greyhound station. It was a miserable walk. The Wyoming wind made no exception for Casper and seemed to scour the streets of any people. I held my bike with one hand and the box with the other, and gusts of wind caught the box like a sail, almost knocking me down several times.

I passed the Dick Cheney Federal Building. It was a sad image: the veep sitting in Washington among oil company friends while the wind blew through Casper's empty streets. Even Wyoming's biggest city felt like the province of somewhere else—a colony of global energy companies and Colorado sports teams. Another elbow on the route to somewhere else. Wyoming and its history gave the impression that the West had no economic determinism, whether it was people moving through or energy moving out. Someone else was pulling the strings.

Looking for a more compelling picture of opportunity in today's West— and the routes that were creating it—I headed south to the megapolitan capital of the new Rocky Mountain West.

Greyhound III: Casper to Longmont

The Greyhound station was at the end of downtown, between the railroad tracks and the freeway, and actually calling it a "station" would be generous. It looked like a former convenience store that had been selected for its location adjacent to the freeway and half assedly repurposed. It was empty except for one clerk, a rotund man who worked at a computer at the front of the room. When I asked about the plotter in the corner, he said he did architectural drafting while watching the bus station. Ambient New Age music played in the background.

The bike shop had given me an especially small box, so I had to use a Coors box I found in a corner of the station to complete the bike packaging. Luckily the clerk couldn't have cared less.

A few people showed up in the office, peeving the clerk with requests to change tickets or check luggage, and they waited in idling cars outside. I could see the moving headlights of southbound traffic that would be in Colorado a lot faster than I would.

At just past midnight, the clerk announced that the bus would arrive in five minutes. Boarding a bus in the middle of the night is always a chaotic experience. People are waking up, lights turn on violently. When I asked the bus driver to be careful with my bike, he spat back, "Well, you can put it in yourself!" and walked away.

One stop into the trip, just as I was starting to pretend I was asleep, the police came aboard and arrested a haggard senior citizen. Compared to some of the characters I had already seen on the Greyhound circuit, the man appeared completely harmless. Nevertheless, the two officers handcuffed the graybeard and put him in the car in front of the quickie mart we had stopped at. The process took a half hour, and when it was over, the driver apologized over the loudspeaker as if it was a routine delay, then kept driving south.

The Most Important Trip of the Day

Denver was built on a spur of the Oregon Trail a few decades after the trail was established as America's go-to cross-country route. In 1858 a party of California gold rush veterans and Cherokee Indians found twenty ounces of gold in Dry Creek, a tributary of the South Platte River, in what are now the southern Denver suburbs. The discovery touched off the Pike's Peak gold rush that blanketed the Front Range of the Rockies with prospectors for a decade. After the rush ended, a new city had risen along the South Platte at the foot of the mountains. It was easy to reach this new city from the Oregon Trail; one only had to turn south from the main channel of the Platte along the diagonal of the southern tributary to where the river emerged from the mountains onto the plains. Throughout the 1860s, this became an increasingly popular portal of opportunity in the West.

On the trip to Oregon, a funny thing had happened. The trail itself created a way for capitalists and boosters to graft their own dreams for cities and empires onto the emerging corridors of westward travel. And so the means became the ends. Oregon, as a predetermined emigrant destination, was the exception among cities of the West. Most western communities had grown as crossroads, transfer points, or spontaneous speculations along transportation routes: Farson, Rock Springs, Casper, Reno, Cheyenne. Even Salt Lake City, though a preselected location for the Latter-day Saints, only became a modern city because of its advantageous location along major travel and trade routes. Denver, as a base for staging mining prospects and to transport ore, is perhaps the largest example of this pattern.

Within a few years of its founding, Denver thrived as a mining camp, riding the booms and weathering the busts that came with its reliance on mineral extraction. It exploded in the 1860s, receded in the 1870s, and once it secured a railroad spur extending from the main Union Pacific transcontinental line, boomed again in the 1880s before the national silver crash brought it down in the 1890s. By the turn of the century, Denver's population stood at 133,000 residents, the largest city between Kansas City and San Francisco. It was the emergent American West's second-largest metro area.[34]

In these early days, it was entirely possible Denver would end up like Rock Springs or Casper, a way station of resource extraction for companies based far away. But Denver's city fathers had big dreams. Colorado historians Stephen J. Leonard and Thomas J. Noel called Denverites "speculative, mobile, ambitious boosters, proud of their unabashed materialism."[35] Denver would end up as the capital of the Rocky Mountains through determination. The city's boosters willed Denver to become the center of the Rocky Mountain region's network of railroads, both across the plains to the cities of the East and into the mines of the mountains.

Equally as important, mining was Denver's setup, not its destiny. By the end of the nineteenth century, after the booms and busts, city leaders realized that Denver's economy should be more diverse. In the twentieth century they began looking to agriculture, manufacturing, and tourism and also to break free of the economic colonialism that had controlled the city in the mining days. One early twentieth-century Denver capitalist, for example, owned a sugar company, a cement company, a meat packing company, a bank, and a brokerage house.[36] Denver mimicked the diverse urban economies of eastern and midwestern American cities rather than the colonies that had been set up throughout the West.

In addition to being dictated by transport, opportunity in the West had always been in the service of the city. Astor's fur traders had fed New York and the Latter-day Saints needed a dense settlement and capitalism to create their

City of Zion. Abigail Scott Duniway found her calling in the city. As early as Americans settled the West, the city had been its primary development tool.[37]

But the catalyst for twentieth-century cities like Denver was maximizing use of the automobile. Cars transformed Denver's open prairie into thousands of suburban homes. Making outlying areas quickly accessible to downtown and other suburbs kept land costs down for new homeowners and businesses and gave them the room to spread out and enjoy a new kind of city, with open views and rolling lawns. Newer and newer highways moved people from the suburbs to the city. While cities like Salt Lake and San Francisco were geographically constrained, Denver, its center located away from the mountains, was not. As the twentieth century progressed, the Rocky Mountain capital became more and more economically uncon strained as well. Denver's competitive advantage was born from casting out roads and industries into an endless prairie.

Denver eventually spawned a Front Range metropolis of over 4 million people as the dozen counties surrounding it transformed into suburbs that, for Leonard and Noel, perpetuated "the rugged individualism and energetic capitalism of the mining camp days." And Denver's auto-age opportunity increasingly put it at the center of American life. Its population burgeoned, its political power swelled, and its capacity for innovation was as likely to reach toward alternative energy as marijuana legalization. In a nation where the center had shifted west, the Rocky Mountain capital was, as the Brookings Institution observed, America's new heartland.[38]

In this way, the difference between multimillion-resident metros like Denver and their hinterlands is shocking. The West now offers two ver sions of American opportunity. There is the kind I had just come through in Wyoming, with money from resource extraction fueling far-away fortunes. Then there is the kind that was pulling me into Denver: self-determined, diverse, and potentially sustainable, the opportunity of the western wide-open city that doesn't know the constraints of earlier iterations of the American metropolis.

And so, because the West has always been—and will be for the foreseeable future—driven by cities, real economic opportunity in the West is urban opportunity.[39] And the key to finding the new frontier of western opportunity is no longer in the vast distances overcome by routes like the Oregon Trail but in the shorter ones within the cities the trail had created.

Where does Denver begin? Traveling south along the string of urbanized places known as the Front Range, I looked for the outer limits of the metro. I had not been able to sleep on the bus and marked the time by coming in and out of the concentrations of lights along the freeway. Was Cheyenne part of Denver? What about Fort Collins?

There are many ways to define the geographic limits of the urban behemoths that modern metropolitan areas have become. City boundaries, county boundaries, and the limits of urban services like water, power, and sewer are common definitions. There is the way we think of a city—as in, can we see the whole metropolis in one sweeping view? But many demographers measure the extent of a city through the distance people are willing to commute to work. Looking at the patterns of commuting will tell you a lot about a city; you can strip it down to raw economics. Especially in the West, cities are still opportunity writ large on the land. And opportunity, as we have seen, is a slave to transport. The larger the West's auto-oriented cities became, the longer the distances that separated people from the jobs that drew them there. A city in the West can be reduced to pairs of jobs and houses and the commutes that connect them, scattered among the mountains and valleys. These pairs of jobs and houses give a city its shape; changing a city's shape would start with changing the routes between houses and jobs. Today the Front Range is 1.5 million workers spread over ten counties in the Platte Valley, the plains and the foothills. How far are they willing to travel to work?

One answer is Longmont, where the bus dropped me at dawn. The longest Regional Transportation District (RTD) bus ride you could take to downtown Denver from points north was from Longmont, forty miles north of downtown up Interstate 25.

To one set of eyes, Longmont was a small town on the Colorado plains with a quaint, historic downtown. To another, it was a suburb of Denver, with pockets of the same kinds of walled quarter-section subdivisions I'd seen in Las Vegas, alternating with open pasture. As was happening all over the West, the former was fading and the latter was gaining, as Longmont was swallowed into the urban matrix. There were enough Denver commuters here that the transit agency provided Wi-Fi on express buses to the capital's central business district.

It was just becoming light when my Greyhound turned into Longmont's Main Street and let me off on the side of the street, in front of a skateboard shop and a 7-Eleven. I unpacked my hideous bike box, reassembled my bike, and walked it over to the bus stop, a Park-n-Ride where the RTD bus schedule on my phone indicated the 6:27 express bus to downtown would pick me up.

The stop was at a park in the middle of town. Birds chirped and I could see snow-covered mountains to the west through the emerging foliage of the large trees. It was a very pleasant morning on the Front Range. Somewhere in my head I heard the wind raking through Wyoming.

A few people were waiting for the bus when it arrived. The elderly driver helped me put my bike on the rack. With a hop in his step, he opened the bottom compartment for my gear. Coming from Greyhound, I thought he seemed like Santa Claus.

Once the bike was secured, I walked onto the bus—a coach—and found a seat. Then we were off for an hour-long ride to the 16th Street Mall in the middle of downtown. Around me, the passengers—all white professionals of varying ages—settled in to their newspapers, books, earbuds, and sleep. At the next stop was a line fifteen deep, folks in slacks and shirts standing in a parking lot. Two of them had bikes, and because mine was already taking up space, one had to go below.

"Good morning!" said one guy. "Looks like they got new buses."

"Moving up in the world!" the other said.

"Yep! Hear it's going to be a nice day!"

We pulled away from the stop, down the wide road, eastward. The sun rose over the prairie.

We turned south onto I-25 at 6:50, and the freeway was already teeming with traffic. Fifteen minutes later, just north of 104th Avenue, we hit a wall of stopped vehicles. We were still fifteen miles from downtown. About half the people on the bus were asleep, even as the bus lurched and halted with the flow of traffic. There was so much stopping and going, I became concerned about my bike on the front of the bus.

Congestion is the other edge of the sword of opportunity provided by cars in growing cities like Denver. Auto congestion took hold of central Denver as early as the mid-1900s, when motorists in the central business district clogged downtown's narrow streets. A 1931 planning commission report noted a "traffic situation" that was increasingly "annoying."[40] As Denver widened its streets and built freeways out of town, the annoyances of congestion followed and Denver built further out.

And yet traffic is the personification of economic opportunity. Congestion at its essence, wrote commuting expert Alan Pisarski, is "people with the economic means to act on their social and economic interests getting in the way of other people with the means to act on theirs."[41] Millions of aspirations are all competing along the common corridors of opportunity in the West. Put another way, congestion was not a problem in Jeffrey City, though perhaps its boosters wished it was.

Increasingly, congestion is the major constraint that shapes our cities—our roads are built for the largest volumes of daytime traffic. The most congested places in America are, unsurprisingly, the largest cities, which also tend to be old and dense and also walkable, with good public transit systems, such as New York, Chicago, and Washington DC. Denver, though, is part of an echelon of large American cities built mostly for cars, which is worse because there are few other options to get around. A city built for driving better be good for driving. But it was unclear to me whether this was the case in Denver. At one time Denver had been rated America's fourth worst city to drive in the United States, and Denver's average commute time was twenty-seven minutes, two minutes more than the US average.[42] The city had some of the nation's worst freeway bottlenecks.

Denver's ground zero of peak congestion was The Mousetrap, which stood out like a bull's-eye in the center of the region. The Mousetrap was the collision of I-25 with Denver's other major interstate freeway, I-70, a "turbine" interchange where the ramps wrapped around the roadways in circles. The region's first traffic reporter to use a helicopter christened the interchange, which reminded him "of one of those mazes used for mice."[43]

In the bus, however, we avoided the Mousetrap because we had slid into a high-occupancy vehicle/toll lane. We breezed past cars at a standstill. The city's anti-congestion measures were out in force. Metering lights flashed at freeway entrances. We passed a Park-n-Ride lot with a 50-foot line of people waiting for carpools. I had a clear view of the gleaming skyline of Denver, lording over its own western fiefdom. We were motoring toward this glassy Oz of a downtown.

Denver had innovated a lot of transportation techniques, in part to decongest its downtown. In the 1940s, when automobile ownership doubled in

Denver, motorists abused the one-hour limits of its free on-street parking, so the city began using the invention of a bicycle shopkeeper that became known as the Denver boot. The boot, now used nationwide, is a twelve-pound steel device that immobilized an offender's car until fines are paid.

Then there was the reign of Henry Barnes. Barnes, a onetime truck driver and jigsaw puzzle salesman, was hired in the 1940s as the first head of Denver's new traffic engineering department. Barnes took the city by storm. He changed downtown streets to one way, using them to synchronize lights. He put traffic signals in the middle of blocks. While Barnes generally sided with motorists, eliminating sidewalks and trees to create more auto capacity, he did grant one of his inventions to pedestrians: the famous Barnes Dance, which gave walkers their own signal to cross the street corner to corner. Pedestrian-heavy places like downtown San Francisco still use the Barnes Dance, to the great delight of walkers. *Life* magazine called Barnes the "world's greatest traffic engineer."[44]

Since those days, Denver had spun its central business district into a great downtown. The city was a soldier in the army of reawakened downtowns across America. It eliminated cars altogether from 16th Street and built a transit mall. It had light rail and a waterfront along the Platte River where high-rise condos were rising in a way that reminded me of Chicago. At the confluence of Cherry Creek and the Platte, I saw a new grassy circle of a park and a white pedestrian bridge that crossed over the rapids of the river. This was the kernel of Denver, where the first gold miners had settled the city, and now the city had begun to build up around here again.

We went underground into the downtown bus station. The driver announced that we were one minute late. I retrieved my bike from the front rack and my stuff from below. I took the escalator up to street level.

It was nice to be back amid the activity of a city. On the 16th Street Mall, homeless people watched as workers poured out of trains and buses, hustling into offices. A taco cart was already open on the median. I walked over and ordered a carne asada taco, as good a breakfast as I could think of after a sleepless night.

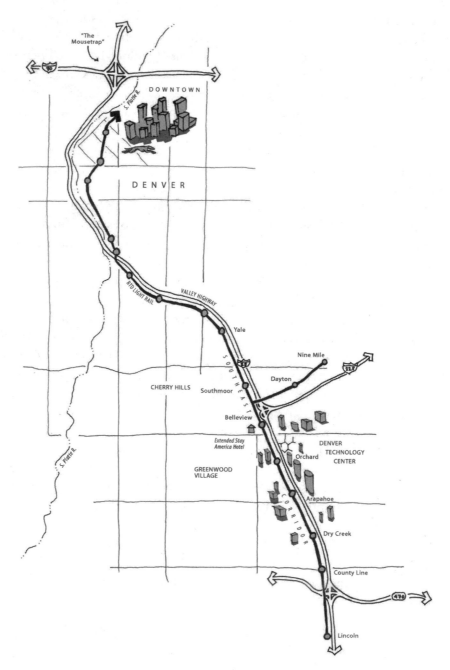

Denver.

Two Economics

Sarah Karjala was the one person in the Denver metro region responsible for understanding how the 1.5 million workers in the region were getting in one another's way on their trips to work. As the congestion management specialist for the Denver Regional Council of Governments—universally referred to as DRCOG, or "Doctor Cog"—Karjala spent her days identifying bottlenecks, assessing delays, talking to cities, coordinating traffic signals, counting turn movements, and retiming streets. She looked at the state highway department's automated traffic counts every day. She broke down traffic volume into fifteen-minute intervals every day of the year. She studied how traffic speed changed and how traffic volume changed. It only took one little hill to screw everything up.

Not that Karjala ever experienced such conditions of congestion in her own commute, a ten-minute bike ride from her apartment in a leafy, old central Denver neighborhood. I planned to meet up with her and join her on her commute to work. I would probably be the only person in the Denver metro area to be commuting twice today.

Karjala came riding around the corner on a 10-speed. She was twenty-eight years old and relatively fresh off her training as a civil engineer at Montana State University in Bozeman. She wanted to stay in the mountains after finishing grad school, but cities called with their plentiful jobs. Denver was a nice combination of the two. Karjala had grown up near Minneapolis and agreed with my observation that Denver seemed like an old midwestern city, but with mountains and eerily healthy people. She competed in triathlons. In Denver, she told me, if you don't do at least three outdoor sports, you're behind.

Her commute was a mostly uneventful downhill ride that didn't even provide enough exercise training for her triathlons. For that she had to tack on extra miles down the bike path that ran along Cherry Creek from downtown to Cherry Creek Reservoir. She pedaled to work along quiet streets while thinking about how to unsnarl that bottleneck at I-25 that was piling up at that very moment.

As big and complex as the region was—and she knew how big and complex the region was—most of Karjala's life took place in the urban neighborhoods of the central city. She liked the city's energy. She estimated that three-fourths of her friends worked downtown, and most lived in downtown neighborhoods. She walked or rode her bike most places and owned a car to get into the mountains and visit her brother in Boulder.

We entered the quiet of Cheesman Park before rolling down the hill to Broadway. Happy to be back on my bike, I was just getting warmed up, but we were already there.

━━━━━━━━━━━━━━━

"It's a new model!" Karjala's boss, Steve Cook, said when he saw us walk into the DRCOG office with bike helmets. "It's psychological, things you can't quantify. It's not just housing units and trips. It's all you young'uns who are finally riding bikes. It took your generation to make biking cool. My generation was 'Cities bad, suburbs good.'"

Cook was in his early fifties but looked ten years younger. He lived in a suburb—a close-in suburb, he emphasized—and, like Karjala, he biked to work.

"Have you heard the *Friends* theory?" he asked. The *Friends* theory, Cook explained, was that throughout the 1970s and 1980s, the most popular TV sitcoms were built around families in the suburbs, *Friends*, which debuted in

1994, was about a group of friends living in New York City. Its popularity, he opined, helped bring cachet back to urban lifestyles.

When the average person tries to solve congestion in her head, which usually happens under duress, she would probably think about the route she takes. Should I have taken the longer road with less traffic? Should I have taken the surface street that parallels the freeway? Should I have left earlier?

To Cook and Karjala, there were more variables. From their point of view, the Front Range was the sum of the 1.5 million pairs of homes and jobs—and the routes between them. When trying to solve congestion, you considered three main variables: the route, the location of the home, and the location of the job. They spent their days adjusting both the routes and the locations of homes and jobs to lessen the impact of one group's economic opportunities on another's throughout the Denver region. The long term solution lay not only with improving the way from point A to point B but changing where point A and point B were in the first place.

In general, they reasoned, houses usually follow jobs. If you wanted to make the biggest difference in the structure of a metropolitan area, you changed where the jobs were located.

Cook, like Karjala, had grown up in the Midwest and loved the Denver region because of its relative lack of segregation and what he called its "interspersed variety." He attributed much of this to the freedom of jobs to locate wherever people wanted them to be.

"There are no factories here," Cook said. "We don't make anything except beer and wind turbines."

So where jobs located was entirely flexible. Employers usually looked for affordable space and one of the region's freeways. Downtown Denver employed about 150,000 workers, but these comprised less than 10 percent of the region's work force. Tens of thousands of jobs lay along the length of I-25, I-70, at Denver International Airport (DIA), in Boulder, and in many other locations.

At the same time, Cook continued, the rates of changing jobs, of two-worker households, and of companies moving offices had all risen across the nation. A lot of things could ruin your commute. Not everyone was as lucky as Sarah Karjala.

If you were somewhat lucky, you were like the folks in the bus I had ridden, with a cushy express coach bound in the direction of your work.

But mostly, you drove your twenty-seven minutes and your spouse or partner traveled in a completely different direction, a rendezvous at home in Arvada or Aurora not expected until long past sunset. People commuted from Longmont to Lone Tree, Brighton to Boulder, downtown to DIA. You could name any combination.

It mostly amounted to long commutes and a high degree of what transportation planners called vehicle miles traveled, or VMT. The number of miles the Denver region drove had increased by over half from 1990 to 2000. Denverites' VMT was on average about 26 miles a day, roughly average for an American metro area and more than in Phoenix or Las Vegas.[45] The Denver road system had about 340 miles of severely congested conditions.[46]

Most expected conditions to worsen. DRCOG predicted that the thirty-eight hours per year of extra travel time each vehicle experienced due to congestion would nearly triple by 2035. The agency predicted that the almost 20 percent of lane miles on freeways and major roads that were congested for three or more hours per day would be 50 percent by 2035. Meanwhile, DRCOG's models had forecasted VMT to continue to rise at this aggressive rate, predicting that by 2010, VMT would rise to 28 miles per person a day, about two and a half more miles than in 2000.[47]

So the city continued to grow and spread out, freeways were expanded and new ones built, and yet travel times increased and people drove farther. After a century of driving cars, one could easily conclude that spreading out did not help congestion—you would always be running away from a problem that would always catch up to you. Yet we still kept building road lanes.

This is one big problem in the American West. The West has long been driven by a conflict between two economics, of concentration and of space. On one hand, the West has always been dependent on the economics of concentration. For much of its history, the dominant transportation modes of shipping and the railroad dictated the processing of resources and the amassing of labor in cities. In such an arid, isolated land, you need to concentrate your resources. The city was and is the most efficient tool for pushing forth the kinds of big dreams capitalists have for the frontier.

But on the other hand, the American West presents a seductive alternative—space. Space sells. Space is appealing. This is the economics of space, of spreading out, the idea that there is plenty of space for everybody to do their thing in the West. As America moved westward, the bad taste of nineteenth-century industrial cities and their overcrowded tenements lingered—and the space of the West was a revelation.

Like an angel and a devil perching on the shoulder of the ur-westerner, the economics of concentration and the economics of space have battled for the soul of the West. Especially as the West moved away from resource extraction and toward the information and service economy, westerners wanted to live on a spacious, spread-out range. But at the same time, higher and higher proportions of westerners lived in cities and commuted to urban jobs, where urban economics still dictated some degree of concentration. The introduction of the automobile into the equation ratcheted the tension even higher. Cars enabled an economics of space yet still needed concentration. Roads are expensive, and cities and states needed bang for their buck in highway projects' capacities, while box stores and fast food franchises required high traffic counts. That left the West in a no-man's land that failed to succeed in either space or concentration. Places would fill up so then people would find more space. Those spaces would fill up and then people would find more space. There was always more space; it just never stayed empty. It was a false summit, disappearing ink. It was exhausting.

The answer is not more space but less of it. The answer is abiding the economics of concentration. Density. Two thousand years of human civilization had proven its benefits.[48] One hundred years of cars had done nothing to change this.

In the language of transportation, space needs mobility, or freedom of movement, and access, the ability to get to the front door of your destinations. But the magic of concentration is that it primarily just needs access. The counterintuitive solution is that once you get enough congestion, you do not need to go as many places because much of what you need is right there. Concentration doesn't reduce congestion, but it reduces the friction of congestion.[49] While cars are essential for the false solution of more space, they just get in the way of the real solution of less space.

But you really have to believe in the solution of less space. It is a phenomenon I have come to call the Leap of Faith. It's like when you need to jump over a wide stream. You have to run as fast as you can and put everything you have into that leap, because if you're too slow and tentative, you'll fall in the stream. You have to be all-in. Usually attempts to solve congestion with half-baked solutions produce worse congestion. This is why a lot of people become angry at city planners.

Steve Cook and his planners were all-in. They believed that fundamentally changing the locations of jobs and the routes that connected them to housing was the key to reducing the friction of congestion and truly nurturing economic opportunity. They looked at the jobs and houses projected to be built all over the Front Range and wanted to focus them into smaller, strategically placed areas. Colorado's largest metro area needed to grow and expand, but the solution wasn't the helter-skelter spreading of roads and the Denver economy, yet neither was trying to concentrate everything in central Denver; not everyone could afford the leafy neighborhoods of the central city and too many restrictions would detrimentally raise the cost of housing for the region's residents.

DRCOG's answer—and one increasingly popular throughout America—was corridors. Corridors are not a city or a neighborhood but a linear unit of development where a transportation route provides the structure of growth. This, in itself, is not new at all. Transportation routes have been providing the structure of growth for thousands of years, from Roman roads to canals to railroads to auto-oriented strip mall highways. The Oregon Trail itself was a corridor.

Yet corridors have usually happened without much regulation, at the whims of technology and the market. The effects of public policy on the resulting pattern of development have usually been unintentional. But in the twenty-first century the corridor is emerging as a flexible but coherent way for a region to provide transportation options and manage growth for American cities. The corridor gives a region a way to say, "this is where growth should occur, there are a wide range of types of places that can be created, and we can offer a range of options to get around." The corridor gives city planners a framework for making walkable, people-oriented places at the scale of the metropolitan region, meaning that it is a way to create a series of connected places that provides a range of options of lifestyle and affordability to the region's diverse individuals, families, and communities. Corridors also work for the network; the corridor connects smaller pieces, such as neighborhoods and districts, to the bigger pieces of cities and metropolitan regions, abiding the important lesson we learned in Utah.

DRCOG planners had designated a series of corridors with light rail lines and streets that spread from downtown Denver outward, thereby providing connections to the small scale of the neighborhood and to the larger scale of the region. They worked with cities to make the areas around the light rail stations walkable and dense while ensuring overall regional mobility. They believed this course of action would create more situations like Karjala's commute and fewer like The Mousetrap.[50]

As the early years of the twenty-first century wore on, the planners were encouraged. They began to notice a few things about changing patterns of transportation and the location of jobs. The first was that people had begun to drive less. Somehow, VMT was flattening, and in some cases, decreasing. Despite the model's prediction that VMT would increase to 28 miles per capita in the Denver region by 2010, the actual 2010 VMT was less than the 2006 peak.

Some of this was due to the Great Recession. But VMT had been climbing since cars were invented; as time wore on, people across America drove farther and farther. Never before had it stopped increasing. As we saw earlier, this was a nationwide trend.

The leveling off of VMT that had occurred was so new that the DRCOG model, which it used to determine a list of priority projects to request money for each plan cycle, had not caught up. Steve Cook thought that the assumptions that the model used—how population growth and specific land uses generate a specific number of trips per day—had been called into question by new preferences for alternate modes of transportation. In its original plan, DRCOG set a goal to reduce the region's 2035 per capita VMT to 23.7, a ten percent reduction from the current VMT.[51]

The second observation was that employers were indeed moving into property along the Denver region's multi-modal corridors, and specifically near light rail stations. DRCOG's effort to focus growth into corridors was built around the region's thirty-five-mile light rail system, with fifty miles under construction in 2013.[52] DRCOG's goal was for at least 75 percent of new jobs to occur in its designated transit-focused centers, but in the last few years, the actual rate had been more like 80 percent. As in the other cities I visited, the new transportation network was overlaying the old one, creating not only new ways of getting around but new economics and a shifting of the framework of opportunity.

Far and away the Front Range's busiest corridor—with the most jobs, the most traffic, the most new development, and, according to its boosters, a quarter of Colorado's gross domestic product—was the stretch of Interstate 25 south of Denver known as the Southeast Corridor.[53] It epitomized the spread-out nature of Front Range development, with office parks and subdivisions dotting the open prairie. And yet the Southeast Corridor was just that—a corridor—inevitably bound to a single strand of roadway and transport. It was a place fighting with itself over the economics of space and the economics of concentration.

The State of Colorado and the regional transit agency had just given the Southeast Corridor a makeover. They widened I-25 and built a new light rail line beside it, and around it developers had begun to build one of the largest concentrations of transit-oriented development in the nation. Had the Southeast Corridor made the Leap of Faith?

I left Sarah Karjala and Steve Cook and rode south.

Corridor of Opportunity

In 1962 an engineer named George Wallace found that his brand-new Lincoln sedan had been dented while parked in its downtown Denver parking spot. Wallace owned a successful engineering firm, and, like many aspiring business owners in Colorado's largest metropolitan area, he located his office downtown.

But Wallace had been noticing that people were moving out to the suburbs south of Denver. As early as 1941, five times as much population growth occurred in the suburbs as in Denver proper. He also noticed that automobiles were fueling Denver's move to its suburbs. A Denver Planning Office report noted that Denver was at the forefront of auto ownership in America. Between 1940 and 1960, automobile registrations in Denver County had more than doubled.[54]

In the years following World War II, engineers came to believe that urban streets were costing the increasing ranks of motorists valuable time. Driving through downtown Denver, for example, took a half hour of time. Cities were often referred to as "obstacles." A "bypass" would provide cost savings for truckers and motorists. Planners agreed with the engineers. The directive of the new Denver Planning Office was "to give the automobile maximum freedom of direction and speed."[55] Wallace eyed the new freeway that led south of town to the increasingly popular suburbs. Originally known as the Valley Highway, the road was Denver's first federally funded highway under the new 1956 interstate highway legislation. It followed the contour at the base of the Front Range, through the Platte River Valley, and was the most basic and intuitive piece of the region's growing auto transportation network.

Construction on the Valley Highway began in 1948, and the first section opened in 1950. In 1956 the highway received the I-25 designation; the federal government reimbursed states for 90 percent of the cost of interstate routes. By the early 1960s, over 60,000 vehicles a day used the Valley Highway.

Wallace saw opportunity in both the shift to suburbia and the new conduit for cars, but at first he reacted on a purely visceral level about his dented car. "I was so goddamned mad," Wallace wrote, "[I decided to] find a little piece of land outside Denver where I'd build my own office, with parking spaces 20 feet wide."[56]

He looked for land along the Valley Highway to build a small development on 4 acres to house his office and perhaps a few others, but the smallest piece of property he could find was 40 acres. So he borrowed $80,000 and hired planners to help him figure out what to do with all the land. The planners were taken by his vision, and they helped him develop a concept for what he called the Denver Technology Center, a new type of office environment for those who, like Wallace, were sick of the crowded conditions of downtown and lived in the growing suburbs.

Apart from new, cutting-edge suburban residential developments like Cherry Hills Village, there was nothing around the Denver Tech Center, just the clean line of Interstate 25 bringing workers to their offices, where they would have open lawns, plenty of parking, and low buildings opening views to the mountains. It was the embodiment of the new opportunity that was luring so many migrants to Colorado and other western states.

Best of all, business opportunities in the Tech Center didn't have to play by the same rules as in downtown—all the space obviated the careful balancing of classes and constituencies, of the management of parking and the timing of lights. It was an endless horizon of green and mobility, the West's latest and greatest economics of space.

After the Tech Center's initial success, Wallace put aside engineering to become a full-time developer, eventually buying a total of 840 acres. The

Tech Center justified the investment. In the 1970s, it began to constitute a second downtown for Denver, as more and more firms moved in. Offshoot freeway corridors such as I-225 lured more suburban development. Denver's freeway corridors exploded the city, spreading and sprawling it all over the plains, a seeming manifestation of the conservative argument that pure mobility leads to opportunity.[57] The result was the All-American suburbs south of Denver along the I-25 corridor. Thousands of people moved to these cities each year, pulled by the opportunities found within the growth of places like the Denver Tech Center and suburbs like Littleton and Aurora and their prestigious Cherry Creek school district.

By 1994, 30,000 employees worked at the Tech Center for 900 firms and Wallace was driving a Rolls Royce and wearing diamond and emerald rings.[58] He even dreamed of building a private mass transit corridor from downtown Denver to the Tech Center.

Meanwhile, other developers channeled George Wallace's innovation, and new office parks took their place alongside the Denver Tech Center. The Southeast Corridor as a whole now had roughly 100,000 employees—putting it in the same league as downtown Denver—and the skyscrapers that housed the workers for eight-plus hours a day dwarfed even Wallace's vision of what the place could become. This was the modern West personified through the new age of white-collar jobs, a land of swashbuckling capitalists in suits. If opportunity in the West in the nineteenth century was Astoria and gold-rush Denver, in the twentieth century it was the Denver Tech Center.

As I rode south, I began to cut through the tree rings of twentieth-century urbanization that had grown outward from central Denver. Four miles from DRCOG's downtown headquarters, I rode through a tight street grid of prewar brick bungalows with huge elm trees. At seven miles, as the grid loosened and streets became wider and occasionally lost their sidewalks, I rode through midcentury ranch houses that looked like my grandma's. By now, the residential streets were serene, but the roads that surrounded them were vicious to a cyclist.

At eight miles, I crossed one such road, Hampden Avenue, and passed into the rarefied air of Cherry Hills Village. I was no longer in Denver. Here was a life in the country—fenced fields of horses, acreage, absolutely no sidewalks.

The loops and curves of the street system made no sense, as if they had been developed piecemeal in a version of the Middle Ages with cars.

As I pedaled along the country lanes, I imagined I was an executive driving from his house in Cherry Hills Village to his office on the I-25 corridor. When I turned onto Happy Valley Road, I began to see the telltale manicured lawns and berms of the office park. Then the road straightened up and the signs of Cherry Hills Village turned to the signs of the Tech Center; they had a kind of no-nonsense blocky font that announced it was time to work.

I wound through another curve, crested a ridge, and there it was: the Denver Tech Center, twelve miles from downtown, a line of towers amid lush rolling greenery. To the west was an awesome view of 14,000-foot Mount Evans and the surrounding peaks; to the north, the distant skyline of Denver.

The area was still growing. Today, the Tech Center and its fellow business parks continue to draw firms. The Southeast Corridor now held six of Colorado's eight Fortune 500 company headquarters and was about to get another.[59] The corridor had an almost mystic appeal to companies looking to relocate or set up a new branch office. A few years ago, for example, the real estate search firm Trulia decided to open another office to add to its San Francisco headquarters and New York City branch. The firm began a nationwide search for the location of its third office, a call center. Trulia developed a short list of cities; Denver wasn't on the list at first. But when some Trulia managers came to a conference in Denver they were approached by the Southeast Business Partnership, a chamber of commerce for the corridor, which convinced them to listen to a pitch. The Partnership showed Trulia about a dozen locations along the corridor. They didn't ask to see any locations downtown.[60]

Trulia located its third office in a low-slung two-story office building on a suburban parkway a mile off Interstate 25 in Englewood, about sixteen miles south of downtown Denver. The suburban location had none of the cachet of Trulia's other, more urban offices on the coasts. But what it did have was one of the most educated workforces in the United States, particularly in regard to telecommunications and call centers. It had a tight-knit network of government contacts. Denver was within convenient travel of both coasts. It had a convenient airport, an easy quality of life, great weather. The cost of doing business was competitive—not as cheap as, say, Omaha, but cheaper than the coasts.

With the opening of the new Trulia office, another one hundred employees were added to the corridor's workforce, another 16,000 square feet occupied.[61] The company held a ribbon cutting with the governor of Colorado in front of their new building with its stone-and-glass façade. On a sunny day in the Front Range, with the mountain views and the new widened I-25 flowing smoothly, life on the corridor seemed limitless, like in the days of George Wallace. In fact, it had changed radically.

"Hell ... It Just Exploded"

George Wallace died in 1995, but many of his associates still called the shots along I-25. I made an appointment to meet with Ray Bullock, the current dean of the Denver Tech Center. He was most well known as the longtime head of its Architectural Control Committee but was also a jack-of-all-trades executive with the company that owned the center. As with many Southeast Corridor luminaries, one of the Tech Center's parks had been named after him.

With the addition of light rail and several new development and street projects, it was clear that the Southeast Corridor was changing in the new century. I wanted to see whether the Tech Center and other office parks were achieving the economics of concentration, and if so, how a place born of the automobile age was becoming a corridor of access rather than just mobility. I started with Bullock, who was semi-retired but kept an office in one of the Tech Center's brand-new skyscrapers that loomed over I-25.

When I arrived, the receptionist led me down a hall decorated with a series of time-lapse aerial images of the Tech Center—first in 1964, then every ten years until the present. In the first image, the buildings and parking lots existed as crisp shapes in the agricultural fields and plains. Then began the slow crowding of urbanization around them, and more buildings, the final shot sifting out into the even density of suburban sprawl.

The receptionist left me in a conference room that had a large window that looked out on the core of the Tech Center. The buildings were so close to the freeway and off-ramps that it seemed to be all one system, the road in the morning delivering the workers to the buildings, which spat them back out at the end of the day. It was about 3:00, and the freeway traffic was just beginning to crowd and slow.

After a few minutes, Ray Bullock walked in, a lanky, sharp presence, wearing a sky blue sweater. His background, unlike many of his colleagues, was not in business but in municipal government. He had helped incorporate the city of Lakewood, Colorado, in the 1970s, and in 1981 he had come across the opportunity to help George Wallace build the infrastructure he needed to keep expanding the Denver Tech Center.

Bullock remembered that at the beginning of his interview with Wallace, Wallace stood up to shake hands and Bullock noticed that Wallace's slacks were tucked into large cowboy boots. Bullock described Wallace as "a colorful character."

"These were men," Bullock said of the original Southeast Corridor developers, "who were so focused, and so determined that when they decided to do something they wouldn't stop."

"Extreme risk takers," said Pete Neukirch, another former Tech Center executive who had joined us in the room. "Wallace wanted complete control."

We looked out the window, which framed the thickening evening commute traffic.

"The growth is not linear," Bullock said, gazing out. "Nothing will happen, and then, boom. Hell, in the '80s, it just exploded."

Bullock agreed to show me around the Tech Center. We took the elevator down to the parking garage and got into his SUV. Despite the carless directive of my trip, it seemed a little much to make him and Neukirch take the train and trudge through the sidewalk-less streets and pedestrian bridges over the freeway. Plus, I had already ridden twenty miles on my bike today. And hadn't gotten any sleep. Besides, the auto was the way you were supposed to experience Tech Center.

It took us three light cycles to get across I-25 into the heart of the original Tech Center. But once we were through, I realized that it was in some ways a museum of the time when people saw no limit to the power of the automobile, especially in regard to space and a lack of western traditions. It reminded me of seeing original Mies van der Rohe modernist buildings in Chicago; they looked like the millions of knockoffs, but the originals had a real quality and integrity to them, and even a richness that was anathema to the whole auto age.

Driving in a car, the Denver Tech Center made sense. The landscapes were lush and green and changed with each turn. The parking was plentiful but hidden to the motorist by strategically placed berms and trees. The original low-slung buildings, which Bullock pointed out amid the skyscrapers, were nestled in mature trees and looked like they belonged to the landscape.

Looking at the aerial photos in the hallway at Bullock's office, I had noticed an interesting hexagonal street pattern in the old part of the Tech Center and had wondered if it had any significance. As we drove on these streets, it became clear: these were three-way T-intersections, with free right-hand turns. No one had to stop. Driving around the Tech Center was like being a pinball in a park. As we drove through T after T, Bullock noted that Wallace had fired an engineer who advised him to build roundabouts instead of the T-intersections. The place was pure automobility. When Bullock first came to the Tech Center, there were not even sidewalks.

I could see how everyone—planners, developers, business owners, employees—could, in the 1960s, see this as America's new landscape of opportunity. It was all, Bullock told me, underlain by a very intentional set of design principles.

The most important principle was the 40–40–30 rule. When a parcel was developed, no more than 40 percent of that parcel could be under a building. No more than 40 percent could be covered by parking. And no less than 30 percent could be open space.

"That way you can have fairly good densities," Bullock said, "but it's not going to look like downtown Philadelphia. You can have seventeen-story office buildings, but they don't go out on the curb. There's a green environment."

The other thing that shaped the Tech Center environment was the Architectural Control Committee that Bullock chaired for decades. The committee evaluated each project proposal for whether the materials and design were of a high enough quality.

The Denver Tech Center was, above all, shaped by developers. Like Charlie Croker in Tom Wolfe's *A Man in Full*, Bullock knew the buildings by their developers, not their architects. He narrated the drive with his friendly, animated drawl, but I wondered what kind of cutthroat skills lurked beneath the surface—skills that anyone associated with Wallace must have possessed to survive on the Southeast Corridor.

Neither Ray Bullock nor the Tech Center was stuck in the past. This place's most important aspect was its flexibility. In the 1970s, as the full possibilities of the Southeast Corridor were becoming apparent, Wallace received a zoning entitlement of 50 million square feet of building space. But unlike the typical twentieth-century zoning practices, in which land uses like residential, commercial, and office were usually segregated, the Tech Center's entitlement allowed them to put any land use wherever they liked. As long as it met the 40 40 30 rule and passed muster with the Architectural Control Committee, it could take any form.

"That flexibility saved our butt over and over," Bullock said.

In the 1980s, for example, office was hot, and developers built office like crazy. But then the Tech Center found itself with an extreme surplus of high-rise office buildings when the market demanded residential, so they built condos. In the last real estate cycle, the office market tanked and the multifamily residential market came back first.

Only 15 million of the 50 million square feet had been built, which reinforced my growing impression of this as an unfinished place. Which was strange for a suburban office park. The whole idea of the suburbs is that it is an ideal, static, unchanging, finished piece. What became clear as I drove around with Bullock and Neukirch was that the Denver Tech Center was constantly evolving.

I had expected an old-timer like Ray Bullock to be clinging to the past of the Tech Center, but he looked straight into the future. I asked him about his favorite Tech Center places, expecting him to name an early example of Wallace's buildings or a verdant view. But he pointed to a glassy skyscraper hugging I-25 known as DTC One, from the Tech Center's era of high-rise offices in the 1980s. He liked a park that had been built in the last few years. His favorite places were always changing.

"I've always had the theory that the Tech Center is like downtown Denver in that you can never say it's finished because it's organic," Bullock said. "I like it better now than I did thirty years ago. I like the vitality."

What *was* the Denver Tech Center? It was not an office park. It was raw opportunity manifested on the plains of the Front Range in transportation, another experiment in the capitalist laboratory of the West. There were no rules here and it was constantly evolving. There were large squares of land between the office campuses and obsolete old buildings. I asked Bullock what he thought we'd see here fifty years from now.

"In fifty years," Bullock said, laughing, "Pete and I wouldn't recognize where the hell we were."

T-REX

But there was one thing to which the Tech Center was beholden and that was its transportation system, its creator in the first place. However the Tech Center, and the rest of the Southeast Corridor, grew and changed, it would have to do so within the constraints of how people got into it, out of it, and around it. The Tech Center was allowed to grow to 50 million square feet, but Ray Bullock thought that if the center ever built out that much, it would look like Manhattan, and there would no way to get in and out of it—at least in a car.

That may have already become the case anyway. When Bullock arrived at the Tech Center, 30,000 cars drove on its segment of I-25 each day; now there were nearly 300,000. Now, fifteen different office parks competed for tenants and access. Likewise, Denver and the suburban jurisdictions created around it also competed for the revenue from the employment centers. Denver and Greenwood Village had fought bitterly over Denver's attempted annexation of the Tech Center.

This fragmentation was the calling card of late twentieth-century suburbia, where nothing was shared, only divided. The infrastructure that had to be jointly or publicly owned—like the transportation system—was far overloaded, and traffic congestion had reached the point where the Valley Highway was obsolete. As the growth crowded around the freeway exits and filled in the spaces between them, the enormous returns of mobility and opportunity seen in the 1950s and 1960s began to diminish rapidly. By 2010, Douglas County, in the southern part of the metro area, had the highest income of any of the Denver region's counties but also the highest commute time. Meanwhile, the working classes who filled many of the jobs along the Southeast Corridor often had to commute from several counties away, creating the metropolitan-scale problems that concerned DRCOG.

A traffic blogger pondered that the intersection of I-25 and I-225, formerly the meeting of two freeways in the open plains—and a respite from the Mousetrap—had become the nation's fourteenth-busiest freeway interchange. He proposed "The Full House" as a nickname. A Douglas County commissioner saw the origin story of the Tech Center being played out over and over, that "with the footprint that has already been laid, there's a very good chance you'll see a strip city from Denver to Colorado Springs."[62]

Congestion not only delayed workers in getting to the Tech Center, it also screwed up the seamless experience of driving through the office park's T-intersections and enjoying its green landscapes, eliminating its two greatest advantages. The corridor began to exhibit many of the same problems it sought to escape. Transportation createth and taketh away. Such is the story of suburban sprawl.

The fathers of the Southeast Corridor had seen it coming. Over the years, it became clear to them that if they didn't stay ahead of the transportation issues, they could not achieve the scale that they envisioned. They could start to see in the late 1970s that the system in place could not handle the commute traffic going downtown as well as the commute traffic going in the other direction.

But they did not decide to re-create the vicious circle. In the West, for hundreds of years, changing circumstances have led the titans of industry to simply pack up and go somewhere else, whether it was a logging camp, a strip mine, or an urban center that had become too crowded. They were abiding the economics of space. It still happened on the windy steppe of Wyoming. The builders of the Southeast Corridor could have done the same thing. In the 1970s and 1980s, lots of plains remained along with a lot of desire on the part of the state highway agency to build more freeways.

Yet the corridor's developers and other leaders instead decided to accept the changing circumstances and adapt to that reality. They first accepted that the very identity of the Southeast Corridor had changed. It was no longer an escape, the employment equivalent of a Hawaiian vacation or a free lunch, but fully woven into the urban fabric of the new West. Commuting had become two-way between the Tech Center and downtown Denver. People lived and worked in both places. The chance of someone denting your Lincoln was the same in the Tech Center as in downtown Denver. As a result, developers accepted that things should be moving closer together rather than farther apart. The economics of concentration came into consideration on the Southeast Corridor.

Then they accepted that while they paid taxes to different entities and had been the focus of aggressive annexation attempts by different jurisdictions, the office parks were not beholden to a city, county, or state. It was something not as small as a neighborhood but not as large as the whole Front Range. Above all else, they were beholden to the line of the Valley Highway, to the corridor not only as a transportation route but as an economic unit.

They also accepted that because they were in for the long term, they must collaborate. In a time when the West's metropolitan areas were fragmenting with suburban jurisdictions and gated communities, the Southeast Corridor's players came together. As Bullock told me, "it would be better than if we put a fence around each one of us."

In the early 1980s, George Wallace gathered together the other major players on the corridor and formed the Joint Southeast Public Improvement Association (JSPIA), a taxing entity focused around one of the natural—yet rarely recognized—units of urban life: the corridor.[63] JSPIA added another tax levy on top of the office parks' separate improvement districts. They set up the Southeast Corridor Transportation Management Authority to mange the money. Turf battles did occur, but JSPIA served as a sort of referee to break down barriers and solve the constant transportation challenges.[64]

At the same time, DRCOG found that the I-25 corridor had exceeded its maximum capacity. Within a few years, with the addition of more jobs to the now-gargantuan Denver Tech Center, the freeway would be gridlocked most of the day.

Those on both sides, public and private, believed that the Southeast Corridor needed a major game-changing redesign of the way transportation flowed along I-25. Both knew that the pure automobility that drove the corridor's original creation was dead. There was no silver bullet in the form of auto lanes; it would have to be a multi-modal solution. Corridor developers took multiple lobbying trips to Washington, DC, and in 1999 voters approved a bond to create light rail in the Southeast Corridor.[65]

In response to the work of JSPIA and DRCOG, the State of Colorado came on board to bond for a $1.67 billion monster called the Colorado Transportation Expansion Project—T-REX for short. Just as the starched developers of the office parks blended conventional business practices with twenty-first century collaboration, T-REX implemented conventional auto-centric congestion mitigation measures at the same time it provided for rail transit. It would widen I-25, as well as add light rail, in an effort to reshape the corridor more around train stations and less around freeway interchanges. T-REX sought to transform the way Denver commuters traveled along the Interstate 25 and 225 corridors. As it turned out, the revolutionary corridor that spawned the revolutionary governmental entity spawned a revolutionary way of rebuilding a highway corridor.

The T-REX project channeled all the revelations of the Southeast Corridor's JSPIA: the project was conceived as a permanent way to move people between two major urban centers, planned a multi-modal corridor as an economic unit, and placed collaboration above just about everything else. In the new millennium, T-REX took on a life of its own as the most important transportation project in all of Colorado and perhaps the West.

In 2000 RTD hired an engineer from Dallas, Rick Clarke, as the project manager for T-REX. He had been a key person in building Dallas's light rail system, known as DART. Clarke frequently brought his family to Colorado on vacation and, because mountains were lacking in east Texas, always thought it would be a nice place to live. I spent the rest of the afternoon riding with Clarke on the light rail. We met at the Belleview station, two light rail stops north of Ray Bullock's office at the Arapahoe station. The Belleview station was in the teeth of the I-25 and I-225 interchange, a node of transport infrastructure majestically rising above the heart of the Denver Tech Center. From an engineering perspective, this was the crux of the project: rebuilding the freeway, adding a train through it, staging traffic, demolishing old structures.

In fact, the tangle of the Full House was a good image of what Rick Clarke thought he was getting into when he came to Colorado. As a pioneering multi-modal project, T-REX was easier said than done. Roads that are built are often the result of the culture of the agencies that build them—from their vision of what constitutes a good network to the standards they follow in their construction details. Traditionally, highways and urban mass transit are built as separate projects by separate agencies, each with its own mandates, funding, culture, and values. In the Denver area, RTD built the light rail and the state agency, the Colorado Department of Transportation, or CDOT, built the highways. They had never jointly built or rebuilt a transportation corridor.

At DART, Clarke had a typical relationship with the state DOT. They didn't work together on a day-to-day basis, each agency wary of the other, doing the dance of stepping around one another's turf. Before Clarke left for his new job, Dallas coworkers said to him, "Do you know what you're going to get yourself into, working with a state DOT? That's not going to work."

But the unorthodox nature of the Tech Center and the Southeast Corridor demanded an unorthodox approach. For the duration of T-REX, Clarke wanted to meld the cultures of the state DOT and RTD into one. They established what became a separate organization, located in its own separate office. Early on, they developed mutually agreeable common goals and committed to adhere to them. Clarke and the state project director, worked out any conflicts amongst themselves, in the T-REX office.

"We had a blank piece of paper," Clarke said. "It became a T-REX culture."

The Full House was a good example. The huge interchange layered a lot of structures. CDOT had to rebuild its interchange and RTD had to put light rail through. Clarke explained that the original idea was to put the trains on bridges 100 feet high. But the contractor made an innovative proposal to keep light rail at grade at the interchange.

We boarded an F train headed south. T-REX had added to I-25 a lane in each direction—two lanes where the road had been most congested—producing a new freeway of up to fourteen lanes. It rebuilt eight interchanges and eighteen bridges and added a fleet of anti-congestion measures like metering lights at on-ramps and EZ Pass electronic toll collection for the high occupancy vehicle (HOV) lanes. Along the west side of the freeway ran the nineteen miles of track through nine stations. RTD added thirty-four vehicles to its fleet and built a new maintenance facility. The state, the transit agency, and DRCOG all now believed that the Southeast Corridor was set for a very long time. They intended never to widen I-25 again.

Being in a train instead of in a car on the freeway took much of the anxiety out of traveling along the corridor. Even driving around as a passenger with Bullock and Neukirch I stressed getting through the interchanges and underpasses. If we had been in a car, neither Clarke nor I could say how long it would take to get from Belleview to County Line, our destination, five miles south on the Southeast Corridor. But trains are usually ruthlessly dependable. Getting from Belleview to County Line was a question of consulting timetables. While you may feel more confident in your car than waiting on a bus at a desolate suburban bus stop, in a high-stakes environment like the Tech Center, you could set your watch to transit. Our train quietly slid through the flyover bridges and performed other freeway gymnastics as we took in the spectacular views of the Rockies.[66]

T-REX finished under budget and two years ahead of schedule in 2006 and became a shining example of intergovernmental agency cooperation. It spent more money on the transit piece of the project than the highway piece and embodied the acceptance that urban corridors are more than mobility out of town but are living, working, diverse pieces of the city. As we have seen, the infrastructure of the twentieth century had given us separation and narrow options. The new century demands collaboration, flexibility, and choices.

Like DRCOG hoped, the corridor started to become more about the possibilities around the train stations than the freeway interchanges. A community could become excited about building up around a train station; it was hard to say the same for freeway ramps. Whether or not a person actually rode the train, the stations provided him with a newer, livelier way of thinking about the line of I-25 running through the Platte Valley. It was a more complex map, but the Southeast Corridor's leaders hoped the people, the goods, and the money would flow as easily as through South Pass.

I needed to crash for a little while, and the hotel where I had made a reservation was next door to the Belleview station. It was an extended stay place across I-25 from the original Denver Tech Center, pushed up against the Full House. It was next to a McDonald's and a gas station on one side, a new housing development on another, the Belleview light rail station on another, and a huge empty piece of land on the other.

It felt good to lie on a hotel bed. It was about 5:00, and I slept until I woke up hungry later that evening.

I decided to ride my bike to a bar in the Tech Center that I had seen on my drive with Bullock. Riding without the weight of my touring gear, I felt light, humming around the streets like a little kid.

At night the Tech Center was empty and shadowy. It didn't matter if I was riding in a street, through a parking lot, or over a berm—they were all empty. The only outposts of life were the occasional bar or restaurant.

Biking and walking the Tech Center was not near as pleasant of an experience as driving in it. On a bike, I felt exposed on the wide streets, and the landscape that was meant to be a moving picture outside motorists' windshields looked like dead space. Many of the streets that spread from the light rail stations did not even have sidewalks, and the bridges that led pedestrians over the freeway dumped them into parking lots.

Likewise, a field of parking surrounded the bar I chose, and it was so quiet I could hear the freeway, but inside it was so full that I could barely find a seat.

The Equation

When you talk to people about transportation problems, you often hear the phrase "You can't build your way out of congestion." They usually mean that the more you widen roads and build more parking, the more they fill up and you have to build even more, per the illusion of the economics of space. But even with a project like T-REX that had arrived on time and under budget, with light rail and pedestrian bridges, it was true in a different sense. In addition to supplying the alternatives, you have to increase the desire for those alternatives. You have to change what people want. Front Range planners had to change the economic calculus of the two-way trip that 1.5 million commuters made every day. They had to change the equation that made getting out of their car a positive factor in their daily pursuit of opportunity.

The Southeast Business Partnership knew this. The organization, which, like T-REX, was the outgrowth of the different corridor stakeholders' solution to corridor transportation problems, extended the project's mission. It would not only change the way people commute along the Southeast Corridor but would convince them to change their habits after the project's completion. The Partnership planned to manipulate all the thousands of individual equations to improve the one larger collective equation—the one that allowed opportunity to continue to flow along the Southeast Corridor.

Another day dawned over I-25. Unlike my days in Las Vegas or Wyoming, the temperature was perfect. It was a cloudless morning. I left my bike in my motel room and walked over to the Belleview station. Trains were speeding down the tracks, passing the cars on the freeway.

Once the light rail opened, the Southeast Business Partnership began asking why a Southeast Corridor worker would want to take transit and why she would not. First of all, who were these workers? The companies in the Tech Center and other office parks specialized in financial and telecommunications industries like cable TV. Most were white-collar jobs. But many did not pay more than, say, $15 an hour. So workers likely would not be able to afford housing nearby, and therefore their ability to access the jobs along the corridor was an issue. Yet now they had another potentially less expensive transportation option: mass transit.

The Partnership sold transit passes to workers and tracked the usage of those passes. It found that light rail made jobs available to people from other areas. A surprising number of people from far-flung suburbs like Arvada, Westminster, North Glen, even Greeley, were taking a bus to light rail. And 30 percent of the people participating in the transit pass program came from north of I-70. The Partnership began to see that light rail opened up opportunities for households with only one car, enabling, in many cases, a carless spouse to get a job.

The major problem the Partnership faced in increasing train ridership was that, in most cases, workplaces were not very close to a light rail station; after all, most of the corridor had been built for cars, not trains. This dilemma had become known as "the last mile." For an uber-suburban environment like the Tech Center, even a standard walking distance such as a half mile was a concern, as that half mile was fraught with dangerous, boring, and unpleasant walking.

I caught an RTD shuttle designed to take care of these last miles and extend the reach of light rail to office campuses. The shuttle left at nine minutes and thirty-nine minutes past the hour and the driver dropped you off wherever you wanted, as long as it was close to the route. The ride was free with your RTD ticket.

When I got on, the shuttle was half-full of women dressed in suits. Everyone knew each other, including the driver.

"We just got a dress code, no sneakers in the office," announced one of the women in the shuttle, carrying a pair of dress shoes. She wore running shoes for her commute because it involved a large amount of walking. She worked at a medical services company in One DTC, Ray Bullock's favorite Tech Center building.

It was easy to ask people about their commutes. In the Tech Center world, people put a lot of thought into commuting and would spill forth information, as if they had been waiting for someone to ask them to lay out the logic of their strategy. Each had different factors that made riding the train the best choice. The woman with the new dress code, for example, said she lived in central Denver and walked fifteen minutes to a station. She paid $100 a month for her transit pass. She usually took the train to Belleview, then walked across I-25, then along the streets to One DTC, but if she arrived at :39 she took the shuttle. Taking the train made sense in terms of money and time.

I asked another woman why she didn't drive. "Traffic is terrible," she said. "This is so much faster." She had a three-leg commute that involved a five-minute bus ride to light rail, the train ride, and then the shuttle, to her job at a debt holdings company. Her employer gave her a free transit pass.

A woman from Aurora told me that her forty-five-minute commute beat the I-225 traffic. "The shuttle is brilliant," she said. "I call it my limo."

These Call-n-Ride shuttles, in conjunction with light rail, were making a substantial difference. A 2008 customer satisfaction survey completed by RTD suggested that these shuttles had changed the predominant commute patterns when compared to services operated prior to the opening of light rail. Many of the agency's suburban Call-n-Rides operated at over 95 percent capacity.[67]

I asked to be let off at the Starbucks that appeared to be the eye of the Denver Tech Center's morning commute hurricane. A line of customers snaked out the front door and a few al fresco business meetings were occurring at the tables out front.

Once inside, I asked the barista who made my mocha about her commute. She lived two-and-a-half miles down the I-225 corridor and rode her bike to work. She couldn't take the train because she had to be at work at 4:15 a.m.

And even if the train ran, she was wary of her personal safety while commuting at nighttime.

You applied for a job at Starbucks online, and they tried to keep you in a five-mile radius. But people who worked at the Tech Center Starbucks lived all over the metro area. "We had one girl who came from Broomfield," the barista said. Broomfield was clear on the other side of the metro area. "She didn't last too long."

The Southeast Business Partnership had big ambitions to capture these commutes. It was trying to reduce commuting by car on the Southeast Corridor over a seven-month period by 1 million miles, a project it called the Million Mile Challenge. It was going well; they had been at it for two months and convinced commuters to pledge to reduce their driving by 600,000 miles.

The Partnership had myriad tools to accomplish this goal, including a carpool service, which helped companies match up commuters for riding together. To encourage commuters to double their use of transit, it subsidized transit passes for people to try light rail for three months for free. It gave away free stuff; a pledge would yield a $25 gift card. It raffled off an i-Pad.

Ultimately, though, changing the equation would happen with the companies themselves. It was how and where companies located, how they designated parking and incented different types of commuting that shaped the use of the Southeast Corridor's transportation system. And indeed, light rail had fundamentally changed how companies made these decisions: many of them increasingly wanted to be near light rail.

The company with the most participants in the Partnership's Million Mile Challenge was the telecommunications media company Dex One. Occupying the intersection of telecommunications and advertising, Dex One was the bread and butter of the Southeast Corridor. It was a firm that, like Steve Cook's description, didn't make anything (except phone books), so it could locate anywhere. Dex advertised local businesses through both the book and digitally, so it valued being close to its workforce and its customers. The company stressed the mobility of its work, encouraging its employees to telecommute; being on the road provided an opportunity to connect with customers. In fact, parts of the Denver region had some of the highest telecommuting rates in the United States.[68]

After a bankruptcy and an acquisition a few years before, Dex needed a new office for its 600 employees. It wanted to remain on the Southeast

Corridor, near much of its workforce and customers and potential customers as well as the mobility of the freeway. It had no reason to locate downtown. Dex chose two brand-new Class A office buildings right next to I-25 and the Lincoln Avenue light rail station. Visible and easily accessible from the freeway, the site met all the traditional suburban criteria that the Denver Tech Center had pioneered.

But the light rail was also a major factor for Dex. One reason was that it afforded it the potential for a respite on its parking requirements. Even more than the last mile, parking was the factor that, for those with a choice, drove the decision to take transit or drive. In downtown Denver, and most major cities, land is too expensive to allow free parking. Paying for parking tips an employee's equation toward transit. But in a suburban place like the Southeast Corridor whose very genesis was based on a non-downtown parking situation, free parking was as much a part of its identity as the rolling green lawns.

Yet even along the Southeast Corridor, parking constrained how much a business could grow. The free and available parking was also part of the package of how firms competed with one another. Before light rail, an employee had no other way to get to work that competed with an automobile. If a developer or a company wanted to grow in the increasingly crowded corridor, it had to densify, and that meant more parking, which either takes up a lot of valuable land in parking lots or a lot of money in parking structures. Parking was, from just about any perspective, an inefficient use of land.

Dex had negotiated a lease giving it overflow parking in the adjacent seven-level parking garage, which had been jointly built by RTD and the property owner. Without more parking, Dex could not add any more employees, unless they didn't drive to work. With light rail now running, workers could get to work without driving. Dex could monitor how many employees took the train, prove to the landlord that a certain percentage of its employees took transit to work, and receive permission to add more employees. Employees riding light rail would lessen the burden of parking, the company got more capacity, and the landlord got more rent. Everybody won, and so the company was economically incented for its employees to ride transit.

These real estate economics still depended on the individual commute decision. Each of Dex's six hundred employees was faced with the choice of whether to take the train to work or drive on I-25. For example, the person the Southeast Business Partnership worked with at Dex, Bruce Holter, had explained to me on the phone that he commuted thirty-five miles to the Lincoln station office from the suburb of Arvada, in the northwestern part of the metro area. He drove I-70 to C–470, which looped him around the whole southwest chunk of the metro area. He avoided I-25 like the plague. As per DRCOG's recommendation, he adapted to the congestion, leaving the house by 6:00 a.m. He usually arrived at the office at 6:45.

When the company moved to its Lincoln station buildings, the Southeast Business Partnership offered its employees a 50 percent discount on the $160 monthly light rail pass. Holter took advantage of it and for four months rode the train every day from Arvada. It added about a half hour each way to his commute, but he didn't care; the time on the train was of a much higher quality than in the car.[69]

After a few months, though, the discount reduced to 30 percent, and then it went away. Holter stopped taking the train and went back to driving, purely because of the price. If he had, say, an older Chevy truck and gas cost more, he might still have ridden the train.

Dex continued to wrestle with the equation of its employees' commute. Before the discount went into effect, when the company was still at its previous building near another light rail station, it conducted a survey and found that 85 of its employees commuted by transit at least one day a week. Since it had moved, more and more people were beginning to ride. Holter was considering buying a FlexPass for all Dex employees, which would give them a yearlong transit pass for $150, a 92 percent discount. Was the $82,000 worth it? Would people use the train enough to justify the firm's real estate economics? Perhaps more importantly, would the increased demand for transit raise light rail station area land values enough that the sacrosanct free parking was no longer possible or palatable to the companies, further incenting alternative transportation—creating more momentum for the Southeast Corridor's new path?

This is what opportunity had become in the West: fragile equations that negotiated their way though a sprawling metro area. These equations are what shape our regions in the new West. With each shift to transit, the map of the corridor changes, and demand increases on the side of the train rather than the car.

The Evolution

Or maybe you *could* build your way out of congestion. As we recall from my conversation with Steve Cook and Sarah Karjala at DRCOG, truly adjusting opportunity through transportation means changing not only the route but the origin and the destination. Building traffic lanes to free the flow of traffic all over the Front Range was one way to move people between places, but decades had shown that more lanes are not the best way to achieve better traffic flow. And new, expensive light rail lines are not a silver bullet. You also need to build places for jobs and housing that are closer together in the first place.

With light rail built and the Southeast Business Partnership working to promote it, the actual built environment around these transportation improvements became the critical factor in determining whether the Southeast Corridor would continue to prosper. Everyone seemed to agree that this change needed to happen. But it was like turning around an oil tanker.

Yet this, too, was beginning to happen along the Southeast Corridor. The City of Greenwood Village, perhaps the corridor's key municipality (it was home to just 14,000 residents but 50,000 employees commuted to its jobs every day), was leveraging light rail to create the downtown it never had. The city had built a three-level plaza connecting the Arapahoe light rail station to new office towers and lured a few restaurants to occupy plaza-fronting spaces. It had redesigned the surrounding streets for pedestrians and collaborated with RTD and CDOT to build a shared parking garage and maintenance facility next to the Arapahoe station that preserved a large piece of land for future development.[70]

The train was reorganizing how developers thought about the corridor. Despite the myth of the single-use office park, other uses had been mixed into the Southeast Corridor for a long time. Forty percent of Greenwood Village's housing units, for example, were condos and apartments, mostly clustered along I 25. The mixing had accelerated with T REX. Greenwood Village had seen a stunning amount of development built in the last decade, much of it spurred by light rail.

The Center for Transit-Oriented Development undertook a study of development along three new light rail lines in the United States that included the Southeast Corridor. The study found that development along the corridor increased dramatically after the 2006 opening of light rail and that the stations became magnets for new projects, which often included several different land uses.[71] Notably, more intense projects such as the Landmark, which included a twelve story condo tower and a Main Street of restaurants, theaters, and shops, filled in the huge pieces of land left in the patchwork of office parks.

Yet taking the Southeast Corridor to the next level of quality urbanism depended on the details. Even with mixed-use projects, the corridor still exhibited the same suburban symptoms of disconnection and auto dependency. The Landmark, for example, though a half mile from the Orchard station, did not even have sidewalks connecting it to the station platform. Its Main Street restaurants faced out onto a sea of surface parking across the street.

Much of the transit-oriented development around the Tech Center still lived on the bare utilitarian bones of the commute equations of its workers. The previous evening, when I had been walking from the Belleview light rail station back to my motel, I ran into a man named Mohammed, who lived in the apartments next to the station. He and his wife both worked downtown but couldn't find very much for their money there and thought it was not very safe. They had chosen this location because it was right next to the light rail station. His work subsidized his pass. People in his complex were there because of either the light rail station or the Tech Center. He walked exactly four-and-a-half minutes from the station to home. His equation led to riding transit.

But even being a four-and-a-half-minute walk from the Belleview station didn't mean it was part of their lifestyle. "We drive to restaurants around here," he said. "Transit lifestyle—that's Tokyo."

This, too, was changing though, with some pioneering projects. The best new transit-oriented development built along the Southeast Corridor was called Vallagio at Inverness, after its location next to the Inverness business park. Vallagio was a mixed-use development, with units that ranged from 700-square-foot lofts to million-dollar 4,000-square-foot golf villas. It had a Main Street of ground-floor retail and extended the pedestrian bridge from the Dry Creek light rail station so that your walk home from the station dropped you onto a carefully curated row of locally owned restaurants, dry cleaners, and salons.[72]

Other developers had an even bigger transit-oriented vision. Along the Southeast Corridor, it wasn't just newfangled interlopers who were building token transit-oriented, mixed-use projects. The very families who built the corridor in the first place were changing its foundations.

Walter Koelbel was, along with George Wallace, one of the pioneer developers of the Southeast Corridor. Koelbel started his development business, Koelbel and Company, in 1957. At roughly the same time that Wallace found his dented Lincoln, Koelbel was watching the development of the Valley Highway and acquiring a gut sense that being close to the growing freeway system would be advantageous. Property adjacent to that kind of thoroughfare, Koelbel believed, would see a more dramatic acceleration of value and activity than those that weren't. Besides, he already lived along the corridor, near the Wilshire Golf Course, in Cherry Hills. There would be a lot of people like himself who wanted to work closer to home.

Koelbel began to buy property along I-25. Unlike Wallace, he bought several pieces of property interspersed along the corridor. Eventually he owned six different sites, including the 900 acres that became Inverness Business

Park. He moved his own office from downtown Denver to the I-25 and Yale interchange in 1963. His son, Walter Jr., nicknamed "Buz," joined the family business and grew up in the new suburbs of the Southeast Corridor.

"It was awesome," Buz told me later that afternoon in his office, still at Yale and I-25 but that now sat next to a light rail station. "We rode our bikes to school. It was a classic neighborhood lifestyle. County Line was a dirt road in 1974 when I graduated from high school. We used to go out there and party."

I sat in the Koelbel conference room with Buz and his son, Carl, the third generation of Koelbel developers. Both men wore the sharp attire of real estate developers—Buz in a white shirt and yellow and brown diagonal striped tie, Carl in a red pinstriped shirt and pointy brown shoes.

Walter Sr. had just died a few months earlier. Carl had joined the company after earning an MBA at the University of Colorado Boulder. He graduated from Cherry Creek High and went to college in L.A. as an econ-government major. He wanted to work for the State Department until, as he said, he "realized that it's in my blood," meaning both real estate and the Front Range. "I love Colorado. It's a special place, skiing, biking, rafting," he said.

"Everything in life's an evolution," Buz said when he sat down. "In 1962 even the thought of suburban office was revolutionary. It was all in the central business district. Nobody understood what that meant."

As growth occurred in cities throughout America, Buz continued, people called it suburban sprawl, but it was accommodating what people wanted. Why not put offices close to where people lived?

"We always listen to what the market is telling us," Carl added.

Walter Koelbel Sr. had been a naval officer and a University of Colorado Buffaloes tight end before be began to work in real estate. After a few years, he struck out on his own and looked southward. He was a land developer, meaning he bought large pieces of land and put in the infrastructure and zoning entitlements so that builders could put offices or shopping malls or subdivisions on them. Some considered his biggest achievement to be the Pinehurst Country Club, the first master planned golf course community in Denver.

When Buz began to work alongside his father in the 1980s, the Southeast Corridor was hitting on all cylinders, and he ventured into vertical development. He built The Breakers Resort, which contained 1,500 luxury apartments around a 60-acre lake in Denver, and Centennial Village, an office complex near Boulder.

Now they had entered a new era of Koelbel development, embodied by a 16-acre parcel of rare vacant land right next to the Arapahoe light rail station in Greenwood Village. Walter had acquired the property in 1978 as part of a 76-acre assembly. The company had developed the first 60 acres as an extension of the Denver Tech Center, with strip malls and office buildings. Highway visibility was the key selling point for the first tenants, like Sheplers, a western wear store that Walter had made a deal with before he even bought the property. In the 1980s, Buz and Walter developed conventional three-story office buildings on one piece. On another segment, they built 142 apartments in the mid-1990s.

That left the extreme southern portion of the land. In the late 1980s, at the height of the Tech Center's first office park bonanza, Koelbel had come close to building a group of office buildings there. Buz fished out a presentation board with an image of the kind of brick and black glass buildings popular in the 1980s titled "Orchard Valley Centre I."

"The design wasn't rocket science," Buz said, when I asked about how that particular plan came about. "It was standard office product."

But then the market crashed in the late 1980s, and developers were stuck with a massive oversupply of office. Walter estimated that the corridor had a decades-deep supply. Orchard Valley Centre I stayed on the boards and the land sat fallow for decades. By the time they returned to thinking about developing the remaining 16 acres, in the mid-2000s, things had changed along the Southeast Corridor. As Buz said, it had evolved.

Some of the evolution had been a matter of public agencies and office park leaders responding to congestion and growth, producing infrastructure such as the T-REX project. But another piece was that what the market wanted had changed. They had learned that if you simply have a single-use office park, you'd have a ten-hour community with no energy or place created. And the asset classes—the real estate industry's term for different types of properties—that retained their value were those closer to energetic, round-the-clock urban centers.

Koelbel did a planning exercise in 2004 to see what it could do with the Arapahoe parcel with this latest evolution in mind. Their planners drew up concepts with vertical mixed-use buildings, the variety intended to activate the places twenty-four hours a day. The new name of City Green emphasized everything that was different from Orchard Valley Centre I.[73]

"The mixing of uses was an appropriate way to extend the evolution of office parks," Buz said. "There's more energy and amenities. We're in the early stages of understanding what that means. We're taking advantage and utilizing the dynamics of this evolution."

"It's a psychographic shift," Carl said. "People want the ability to walk more. Boomers who are retiring want an easier lifestyle to maintain. The issue is can you get a critical mass?"

"And when you add the transit component, adding high density, mix of uses," Buz added, "it allows the transit to be more viable."

"Light rail is saying, 'Here is a place where density should exist,'" Carl said. "It's a direct market result of what happens when the proper transportation is put in place."

"We were working our way out," Buz said. "Now we're working our way back in."

Buz had to leave to catch a flight to the East Coast, and Carl agreed to walk me over to the Yale light rail station, where the company had just developed a project. As we walked, he explained that Koelbel's new building came about because the old one was condemned for the light rail. It was part of the evolution.

The company built the mixed-use residential project on the land between its office and the light rail station. Its five-story building contained fifty apartments and a dentist's office on the ground floor. The apartments were reserved for people, as the building's website said, "55 and better." They were also subsidized.[74]

Koelbel had controlled the land for over forty years. Affordable housing was outside its comfort zone but financeable, and so the company partnered with a non-profit developer experienced in affordable housing. On its fourth application, it received tax credits. The company had to provide less than one parking space per unit because it was a senior project and next to a light rail station. The building leased up in two months. Koelbel found that 25 percent of residents commuted to jobs on the light rail.

The project was something Koelbel never would have done before Carl joined the firm. Buz found it interesting to listen to what Carl and his friends were saying. Carl's input, as Buz said, allowed the company to fortify its directional change, that "unless you're twenty-nine years old, you don't know how a twenty-nine-year-old thinks."

I asked Carl, who lived downtown, if he planned to move out here eventually, back to where he grew up.

"No way," he said. "I hate it out here. You can't walk anywhere. Every time I eat lunch here, I have to get in the car or else bring a peanut butter and jelly sandwich."

I was surprised. The family had such a legacy in these southern suburbs. I imagined Carl slipping into a life in Cherry Hills at the country clubs his family had developed. But he liked living downtown and being able to go everywhere he needed to go. He told me that he had walked to the Nuggets game the night before. And, in fact, he could walk to the Broncos' and the Rockies' stadiums too. He planned to buy a townhouse in a project the company was developing just across the Platte River from downtown Denver.

"What about when you have kids?" I asked.

"My kids can like the city," he said.

Carl even wanted to move the office downtown. He projected in his mind to when he might run the company and worried that Koelbel still owned several acres out on the eastern plains. "I mean," he said, "what's the exit strategy there?"

—————————————

It was Friday and happy hour, so I rode the train back to the Arapahoe station and walked into the bar that faced onto Greenwood Village's hope of a downtown. There was a bar stool open amid a line of professionals looking at their smartphones. The plaza may have been empty, but the bar sure wasn't.

The guy next to me, who was drinking light beer out of a tall thin cylinder of a glass, said he used to work downtown. His firm split parking with him.

"It was $100 a month," he said. "That's like paying to go to work."

Then he got a job at the Tech Center. He still lived in Denver, two blocks from the Louisiana light rail station. He took the train downtown all the time to eat and drink, but he split his commute between his car and the train.

"If I leave at 7:20, it takes me seven minutes, but if I leave at 7:21, it takes me forty minutes," he said. The train was somewhere in between. It wasn't the fastest, but it was at least reliable.

"When I found out I had to work at the Tech Center, I was pissed," he said. "But this area has changed a lot in the last five years. The Tech Center's not downtown, but it's better."

Indeed, I saw how the new economics of opportunity in the West were beginning to manifest in metros like the Front Range, where the daily work and household trips that were the tiny building blocks of the massive metro region were transforming. Transportation corridors were evolving and equations were changing. What kept the corridor moving wasn't the freedom of the auto but the multiplicity of different strategies and careful planning: an eye on the shorter distances rather than the longer ones. Again, not division but connection. In the cities of the West there would always be people doggedly pursuing opportunity—as there should be—but it would require humane concentration rather than space and speed for them to not get in each other's way. While we had been working our way out, as Buz Koelbel had said, now we were figuring out how to work our way back in.

Next, I would be slowing down, dropping out, and relaxing in a trip through the Southwest. I'd take a breath and consider the meaning of two quintessential totems of the American West—freedom and trains—and how westerners are reinventing both of them.

Greyhound IV: Denver to La Junta

On my bike ride back to the light rail station I got hit by a car. I was winding along what I thought was a low-traffic street that meandered through an office park. A woman turning her SUV right out of a parking lot was in a hurry, didn't look hard enough left, and nicked my pannier. This was one of the most common car-bike collisions—the right turn sideswipe; a driver not used to bikes on the road isn't inclined to crank his head far enough left. Even as a parallel world of transit and walking was emerging in the Southeast Corridor, the autoscape of the Southeast Corridor remained, each roadway and intersection flooded with huge vehicles trying to get somewhere quickly. In this sea full of big fish, it was hard to notice the small ones.

In crashing to the ground, my first thought wasn't whether I was hurt, but what would happen to my bike. The driver burst out of her vehicle, panicked, but my bike and I were both fine. I kept riding, got on the train, and took it all the way downtown. I was headed to a far less appealing kind of station: the one where Greyhounds went.

And the Denver Greyhound station was the worst one yet. Where the Vegas station had been too small, this one was too big, with hidden corners all over the place. A security guard walked through it asking to see people's tickets.

The bus to Pueblo came at midnight. It wound up in Dallas eventually, and many of the passengers who lined up with me were heading to the South. At last we pushed off, south on I-25, finally traveling the freeway in a vehicle. We drove through the Tech Center, its office windows lit by late-night workers grinding away.

Notes

1. Ray Ring, "When a Boom is a Bust," *High Country News*, September 13, 2004 and Jennifer Steinhauer, "In a Red State Rolling in Green, a Relaxed Attitude," *New York Times*, October 4, 2008.

2. Although signs seemed to indicate the boom was coming to an end, as the 2010s wore on, companies were abandoning natural gas wells throughout Wyoming. See Dan Frosch, "Wyoming May Act to Plug Abandoned Wells as Natural Gas Boom Ends," *New York Times*, December 24, 2013.

3. William G. Robbins and James C. Foster, eds., *Land in the American West: Private Claims and the Common Good* (Seattle: University of Washington Press, 2000).

4. Robert Stuart, *The Discovery of the Oregon Trail: Robert Stuart's Narratives of His Overland Trip Eastward from Astoria in 1812–13*, ed. Phillip Ashton Rollins (1935; Lincoln: University of Nebraska Press, 1995), lxxiv.

5. Julie Fanselow, *Traveling the Oregon Trail* (Guilford, CT: Falcon, 2001), "Chapter Four: Halfway to Heaven: Wyoming."

6. Stuart, *The Discovery of the Oregon Trail*, lxxiv.

7. Ibid., 157.

8. Ibid., 133.

9. Ibid., 162.

10. Ibid., 163.

11. Ibid., 256.

12. Ibid., 162.

13. Ibid., lxvii.

14. Fanselow, *Traveling the Oregon Trail*, "Chapter Four: Halfway to Heaven: Wyoming." This quote is attributed to Lorenzo Sawyer, the California judge who emigrated across the country in 1850.

15. Ibid, "Chapter Four: Halfway to Heaven: Wyoming."

16. "Oregon State Library: Oregon Trail Emigrant Resources," oregon.gov, accessed July 17, 2014, http://www.oregon.gov/osl/gres/docs/oregontrailbibliog raphy.pdf.

17. The story of the Scott party is adapted from the journal of Abigail Scott. *Covered Wagon Women: Diaries & Letters from the Western Trails, 1852*, ed. and comp. Kenneth L. Holmes and David C. Duniway, vol. 5, *The Oregon Trail* (Lincoln: University of Nebraska Press, 1995).

18. Ibid.

19. Ibid., "Journal of a Trip to Oregon: Abigail Jane Scott."

20. Ibid.

21. Ibid.

22. P. L. Platt and Nelson Slater, *The Travelers' Guide Across the Plains, upon the overland route to California Showing Distances from Point to Point, Accurately Measured by Roadometer* (Chicago: Daily Journal, 1852).

23. Ibid., "Journal of a Trip to Oregon: Abigail Jane Scott."

24. Ibid.

25. Ibid.

26. Ibid.

27. Ibid.

28. David Dary, *The Oregon Trail: An American Saga* (New York: Knopf, 2005), 60.

29. Holmes and Duniway, *Covered Wagon Women.*

30. Ibid., "Journal of a Trip to Oregon: Abigail Jane Scott."

31. Ibid.

32. Ibid.

33. Jeremy Fugleberg, "County OKs 1,000-Turbine Wind Farm in Wyoming," *Casper Star-Tribune*, October 4, 2012.

34. "Population of the 100 Largest Urban Places: 1900," *US Bureau of the Census*, last modified June 15, 1998, http://www.census.gov/population/www/documentation/twps0027/tab13.txt.

35. Stephen J. Leonard and Thomas J. Noel, *Denver: Mining Camp to Metropolis* (Boulder: University Press of Colorado, 1990), 1.

36. Ibid., 126–27.

37. As historian John W. Reps writes, the typical community of the American West was the "instant city," a settlement built in one orchestrated act and fastened into the grid established by the township and range. Historian Bradford Luckingham observed that early western cities were not the results of decades of agglomeration of organic growth but spearheads for future hoped-for settlement. John W. Reps, *Cities of the American West: A History of Frontier Urban Planning,* (Princeton, NJ: Princeton University Press, 1979), ix–xi. Bradford Luckingham, "The American Southwest: An Urban View," in *The American West: The Urban West,* ed. Gordon Morris Bakken and Brenda Farrington (New York: Garland, 2000), 261–62.

38. Leonard and Noel, *Denver,* 253; Robert E. Lang and Mark Muro, "Western Perspective: Mountain Megas," Brookings Institution, October 14, 2008. http://www.brookings.edu/research/opinions/2008/10/14-intermountain-west-muro-lang.

39. One could draw a parallel between this discussion of economic determinism in the West and the West's public lands dispute, wherein a narrative is spun that the federal government, as the distant owner of a majority of western lands, is the wrongful controller of the region, and the longtime ranchers and the county and, in some cases, state governments that support them, deserve the determinism

of control of the lands on which they have worked for generations. However, the argument I am making here is that the West is fundamentally an urban civilization, and so its true path to sustainable self-determinism is through good cities and diverse urban economies rather than an illusion of hardscrabble rural or mountain communities whose economic destiny is really just controlled by people in other cities, just like the frontier days.

40. Leonard and Noel, *Denver*, 265.

41. Pisarski quoted in Tom Vanderbilt, *Traffic: Why We Drive the Way We Do (and What It Says About Us)* (New York: Vintage, 2008), 134.

42. Bert Sperling and Peter Sander, *Cities Ranked & Rated: More than 400 Metropolitan Areas Evaluated in the US* (Hoboken, NJ: Wiley, 2004), 101.

43. Leonard and Noel, *Denver*, 273.

44. Ibid., 271.

45. "Vehicle Miles Traveled (VMT)," Blueprint for American Prosperity, accessed July 17, 2014, http://www.brookings.edu/~/media/Research/Files/Reports/2008 /6/metropolicy/vehicle_miles_traveld.PDF. High VMT can have serious economic consequences for a household. A Center for Housing Policy study found that for every dollar saved on housing, people spent $.77 on additional transportation. Barbara J. Lipman, "A Heavy Load: The Combined Housing and Transportation Burdens of Working Families," Center for Housing Policy, last modified October 2006, http://www.cnt.org/repository/heavy_load_10_06.pdf.

46. "2035 Metro Vision Regional Transportation Plan: Updated and Adopted February 16, 2011," Denver Regional Council of Governments, accessed July 17, 2014, http://www.drcog.org/documents/FINAL-2035%20MVRTP-2010%20Update%20 with%20App%202-9.pdf.

47. "2010 Annual Report on Traffic Congestion in the Denver Region," Denver Regional Council of Governments, last modified May 2011, https://drcog.org/sites /drcog/files/resources/2010%20Annual%20Report%20on%20Traffic%20 Congestion.pdf.

48. "A certain size of settlement and density of population is an essential feature of civilization," noted archaeologist V. Gordon Childe, "The Urban Revolution," *Town Planning Review* 21 (April 1950): 3–17. This applies to both human productivity and ecological footprint, and especially how the interconnections of dense cities are able to affect both at the same time. As William Rees and Mathis Wackernagel noted, "While urban regions certainly disrupt the ecosystems of which they are a part, the sheer concentration of population and consumption also gives cities enormous leverage in the quest for global sustainability . . . Most importantly, the shift in incentives and modal split [to non-auto alternatives] would not only be ecologically more sustainable but also both economically more efficient and socially more

equitable. (It should therefore appeal to both the political right and left.) Over time, it would contribute to better air quality, improved public health, greater access to the city, more affordable housing, more efficient land use, the hardening of the urban fringe, the conservation of food lands, and levels of urban density at which at least direct subsidies to transit become unnecessary. In short, because of complex systems linkages, seriously addressing even a single issue in the city can stimulate change in many related factors contributing to sustainability." William Rees and Mathis Wackernagel, "Urban Ecological Footprints: Why Cities Cannot Be Sustainable—and Why They Are a Key to Sustainability," *Environmental Impact Assessment Review* 16, nos. 4–6 (July–Nov. 1996): 242–43.

49. As the Victoria Transport Policy Institute writes, "Smart Growth tends to increase traffic congestion *intensity* (the delay that motorists experience when driving during peak periods) but tends to reduce per-capita Congestion delays because residents drive less and take shorter trips." "Congestion Reduction Strategies: Identifying and Evaluating Strategies to Reduce Traffic Congestion," Victoria Transport Policy Institute, last modified May 22, 2014, http://www.vtpi.org/tdm/tdm96.htm (italics in original). A study by the Arizona Department of Transportation on the relationship between land use patterns and congestion in Phoenix found that compact, mixed, and multimodal communities are normally less congested due to fewer vehicle trips, more use of public transit and/or walking, and more connected street networks, which offer plentiful options to reduce congestion on major urban arterials. Residents in these more compact areas drive about 33 percent fewer daily miles than those in suburban areas, the study found. "Arizona DOT Releases Study on Correlation between Land Use and Congestion," *AASHTO Journal*, last modified November 2, 2012, http://www.aashtojournal.org/Pages/110212Arizona.aspx.

50. DRCOG hoped to decrease VMT by 10 percent by 2035.

51. Denver Regional Council of Governments, "2011 Annual Report on Traffic Congestion in the Denver Region," July 30, 2012, 3.

52. "RTD West Rail Line to Open Early: First FasTracks Line to Open 8 Months Ahead of Schedule," RTD FasTracks, last modified May 23, 2012, http://www.rtd-fastracks.com/media/uploads/main/RTD_West_Rail_Line_Opening_Early_5-23-12.pdf.

53. "Two New Transit Programs Introduced in the Southeast Corridor," *SOUTHEASTconnections*, last modified May 2009, http://www.southeastconnections.com/newsletters/2009/May-Newsletter-LR.pdf.

54. Leonard and Noel, *Denver*, 269.

55. Owen D. Gutfreund, *20th Century Sprawl: Highways and the Reshaping of the American Landscape* (Oxford: Oxford University Press, 2004), 89 and 95.

56. Wallace quoted in ibid., 97.

57. This theory has been most visibly championed by the Cato Institute's Randal O'Toole: "The benefits of mobility are huge and undeniable . . . Increased travel speeds allow people to reach more potential jobs in a given commute time." *Gridlock: Why We're Stuck in Traffic and What to Do About It* (Washington, DC: Cato Institute, 2009), 5.

58. Paul G. Lewis, *Shaping Suburbia: How Political Institutions Organize Urban Development* (Pittsburgh: University of Pittsburgh Press, 1996), 148–49.

59. Greg Griffin, "Denver Area's Corporate Power Base is Shifting South from Downtown," *Denver Post*, June 12, 2011.

60. This story of Trulia's office search is adapted from an interview with Steve Klausing of the Southeast Business Partnership.

61. "Trulia to Open Customer Service Office in Denver," Inman Select, last modified January 19, 2011, http://www.inman.com/news/2011/01/19/trulia-open -customer-service-office-in-denver.

62. Kevin Flynn, "Name that Interchange," *Inside Lane* (blog), November 24, 2009, http://www.inside-lane.com/2009/11/24/commentary-name-that-interchange-i -25225-full-house/ (blog discontinued).

63. Even early in its life in the 1980s, JSPIA was being recognized for its innovation. A US Department of Transportation report on alternative financing methods recognized its pioneering use of the metro district to finance a freeway interchange project. See "Alternative Financing for Urban Transportation: The State of the Practice," July 1986, Federal Highway Administration and Urban Mass Transportation Administration, http://ntl.bts.gov/DOCS/afut.html. As Paul G. Lewis notes in *Shaping Suburbia*, the JSPIA was a quasi-government for the corridor. Lewis argues that JSPIA and the office parks other districts essentially privatized land use in the corridor, a darker aspect of the developers' innovation.

64. It was crucial that the private landowners initiated the process. The biggest stories of urban success in the West involve collaborations between the public and private sectors.

65. "Southeast Corridor Light Rail Line: Facts & Figures," RTD Denver, last modified January 2013, http://www.rtd-denver.com/FF-SoutheastCorridor.shtml.

66. In addition to reformulating the relationship between transit and highway builders, T-REX also broke down the wall that usually divides designers from contractors. The T-REX team collaborated with the construction company contracted to build the project, a process known as design-build. Design-build is often employed in houses and sometimes in commercial buildings. But applying this approach to such a massive piece of transportation infrastructure was a pioneering practice. Design-build meant that the project could change with evolving demands, saving millions of dollars. With the widening of I-25, for example, RTD's

old pedestrian bridges weren't long enough; they would have paid 100 percent of the cost to redesign and lengthen the bridges, but having it rolled into one process saved $200 million, the cost distributed between the different agencies. It could accommodate things that different communities wanted in places along the corridor. Around each light rail station, community processes had played themselves out and the builders were able to respond. One vocal group that lived near the Dayton Station, out along I-225, didn't want anything to do with light rail; they wanted a wall. But one citizen spoke up and argued for sidewalks to that station, and the contractor changed the design on the fly. Now the Dayton station had widespread support.

67. "Final West Corridor Service Plan, 2013," RTD Denver, last modified October 2012, http://www.rtd-denver.com/PDF_Files/ServiceD/ServPPP_Final_West_Corridor_Service%20Plan_October_2011.pdf, 6.

68. A US Census Bureau report found that the Boulder, Colorado, region had the highest rate of telecommuting in the nation, with nearly 11 percent of its workers working from home. Peter J. Mateyka, Melanie A. Rapino, and Liana Christin Landivar, "Home-Based Workers in the United States: 2010," US Census Bureau, October 2012, http://www.census.gov/prod/2012pubs/p70-132.pdf, 18. The study also found that two of the most likely sectors to telecommute included management/business/financial and sales, the bread and butter of the Southeast Corridor.

69. Once at work, being so close to the train opened up a new map of potential daily destinations for lunch or other trips. It was much easier to get on light rail and go to Park Meadows Mall rather than driving there. You certainly didn't want to leave your parking spot, or you'd end up in the sticks when you came back. "The last thing people want to do," Holter told me, "is look for a damn parking spot."

70. On the other side of I-25, next to the Arapahoe station, RTD and CDOT had planned a parking garage and a maintenance facility. Greenwood Village, eyeing the prime land around the station, asked if the two facilities could be combined. The city joined together with CDOT and RTD and figured out how the magnesium chloride trucks and snowplows would get in and out and paid $7 million to stack the facilities into one building, using less land. In return, they got a prime piece of land. Now they owned another 3 acres right next to the Arapahoe station that they could leverage to get the kind of development they wanted. Someone once told me that good planning was simply leaving future generations with options.

71. "Rails to Real Estate: Development Patterns along Three New Transit Lines," Center for Transit-Oriented Development, March 2011, http://ctod.org/pdfs/2011R2R.pdf, 36.

72. Vallagio took seriously the connectivity missing from most other Southeast Corridor development. The developer, Peter Kudla, envisioned that there would

be connections between the residents and merchants—for example, that a family would get to know the staff of its favorite restaurant. Perhaps most impressively, Kudla held out for locally owned businesses, which was a difficult thing to do, because often, only chains can afford the rents of new buildings. Ground-floor retail spaces of mixed-use buildings are notoriously difficult to lease, especially in the suburbs, and many of the spaces had taken a long time to rent; but Vallagio had made it work. They had filled the back of the Main Street block with easy surface parking. When they opened the restaurants, Vallagio's sales office undertook a massive marketing campaign, trying to attract the denizens of the world headquarters scattered around them in Inverness Business Park. They gave out 20,000 lunches.

73. At the same time, the Koelbels were wary of vertical mixed use—or putting retail on the bottom floor with offices or residences above. In what Buz called the "frothier times" of the boom of the mid-2000s, the plan they had proposed for Center Green was full of vertical mixed-use buildings. But the plan they were about to move forward mixed uses horizontally, or next to one another, which was easier to finance.

74. Through my conversations with people on the Front Range, the piece that still didn't sit well was the cost of housing in places like the Southeast Corridor, where jobs and other amenities continued to concentrate along improving transportation options. Many of the corridor's jobs were, as the Southeast Business Partnership explained, on the lower end of white collar, and the incomes they afforded could not buy very much in the corridor's communities. Cities like Greenwood Village had a tax base of 40,000 jobs but had to provide services for only 15,000 mostly well-off households. Greenwood Village acknowledged the problem but tried to address it by improving transportation access to its jobs from elsewhere, sidestepping the thorny issues associated with more affordable housing. Front Range housing affordability advocates treated the Southeast Corridor like it was a lost battle. Groups like FRESC see the Southeast Corridor as privileged at the expense of lower income corridors like the West and East Corridors. But as we have seen, housing follows jobs—and the jobs continued to flow to the Southeast Corridor. It would be easier to allow people to live near their jobs than try to bring jobs to where people live. The Southeast Business Partnership told me that affordable housing was less of a concern to them than it was ten years ago.

PART IV

Freedom

1ST STREET HARVEY HOUSE & RAIL YARD   LA JUNTA, CO

1930

CENTRAL AVENUE, PHOENIX, AZ

2012

DOI: 10.7330/9780874219937.c004

The Junction

My Greyhound itinerary gave me a thin margin for sleep. I was scheduled to change buses at Pueblo, two-and-a-half hours down I-25, at 2:30 in the morning. Then it was only a few hours along US 50 to La Junta, my destination on the plains of eastern Colorado.

I didn't sleep at all on the bus. At every stop the driver pitched the break as a chance to "have a smoke," and nearly every single person on the bus took him up on it, clumsily shuffling past me and having smirking inside conversations. It always seemed like half of the passengers on Greyhound buses already knew each other.

But my second bus was almost empty. Drifting in and out of sleep, I heard the voice of the driver announcing the motley names of the towns we passed rolling east: Avondale, Fowler, Manzanola, Rocky Ford. The further destinations—Cimarron, Dodge City—were right out of a Western.

Through my half-conscious haze I gauged our progress, noticing around 4:00 when we finally passed though the dark railroad yard of La Junta. I recognized the names of the motels I had searched on my phone the day before. Empty Burlington Northern Santa Fe freight cars sat on the tracks. The town was motionless.

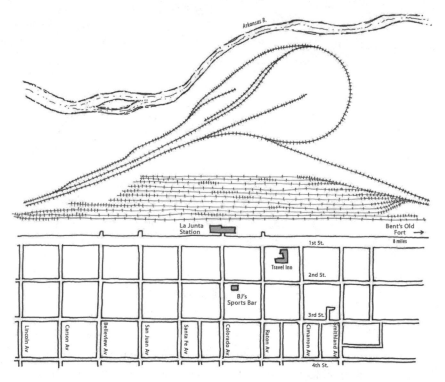

La Junta.

   But the driver zoomed straight through town and came to a halt at a dark motel a few miles outside it. This, apparently, was my stop. I unloaded my bike box and bag from the bottom compartments. The bus took off into the darkness.

   I started reassembling my bike in the carport of the motel. My plan had been to find somewhere to hang out for the hours until the day began and then check into my motel, right across the street from the train station, in downtown La Junta.

   I also wanted to make sure to reuse my bike box. I didn't know what Amtrak was going to charge me for a box, or whether they even had any for sale, so once my bike was assembled and loaded with my touring gear, I walked it around with one hand and carried my box with the other.

   Despite the hour, it felt good to be walking in the countryside. It was the kind of warm spring morning where the sound of birds transcends the darkness. Cottonwood trees arched over the sidewalk-less streets. I passed several auto repair shops and a few churches. No traffic passed me and everything was quiet.

It soon became apparent that I needed a motel room. I was exhausted and couldn't see whiling away the morning in public spaces when all I wanted to do was sleep.

The Travel Inn sounded like it should be a national chain, but it wasn't. It was a two-story L-shaped building across the highway from the rail yard. At 4:45, I rang the bell at the front desk, and an Indian man with rumpled hair walked out wearing an undershirt. He was kind enough to check me in early and didn't even charge me for the extra night.

La Junta means "The Junction," or "The Meeting." At one point in time, it had been one of the most important junctions in the West: the point at which the Santa Fe railroad, heading west from Chicago, split north to Denver and Salt Lake and south to Los Angeles. It was another of the lost transportation nodes of the West. Now La Junta was just a middle-of-the-night stop on the Route 50 Greyhound line, a dot far off the more important trajectory of the interstates.

La Junta had branded itself "The Smile Hi City," perhaps to distinguish itself from the hurried cosmopolitanism of the distant "Mile High" state capital. It seemed to me a small plains town with a certain completeness, upstandingness, and civic quality. La Junta seemed to have all the key institutions intact: banks, churches, schools. Like Rock Springs, the town was oriented to the train line but had less of a transient feel.

I didn't intend to stop here. I was on my way to Phoenix; the trip there was my only opportunity to take a long-distance train—the Amtrak Southwest Chief—which I'd ride to Flagstaff and then take another Greyhound to Phoenix. I'd planned to board the train in Raton, New Mexico, but learned that I wouldn't be able to check in my bike there, so I boarded one stop earlier, in La Junta.

It was a fortunate turn of events. As I read more about La Junta, I realized its significant place in the West's transportation history, and so I decided to spend a whole day here, recuperating from the go-go schedules of my bike tours and trips through Salt Lake and Denver. There would be no traveling today, just a lazy Saturday in the Arkansas Valley.

I slept until 10:00 and felt good when I woke up. And as my predawn walk had indicated, it was a beautiful day. I walked over to what appeared to be one of the town's only coffee places, a café called Barista in one of the stately red brick buildings along Santa Fe Avenue.

"I came back to get out of the rat race," the owner, a young woman, said to me as I ordered breakfast. She had grown up in La Junta and left to attend the University of Colorado Boulder, but she couldn't stand the city.

"You can't even have a conversation with people," she said.

La Junta was shrinking. The town had lost about 15 percent of its residents since 1980 and now sat at about 7,000 people. The Bay Valley Foods pickle factory had closed, the bus plant in Lamar had shut down, and the prisons throughout the Arkansas Valley were under the ongoing threat of closure.[1]

But that wasn't the point of La Junta anymore. More and more, people moved here not for opportunity but for liberation. The median home price was less than $100,000 and a Barista couldn't have been more different than the Starbucks in the Denver Tech Center. The Tech Center Starbucks defined the rat race. This was its opposite. You could definitely have conversations here. As fascinating as the Denver Tech Center had been, I felt a little like washing out the taste of the office park with some time in the Smile Hi City.

The laid-back atmosphere of La Junta pointed to the aspect of the American West that we most need to reclaim from the automobile: freedom. Like with opportunity, the engine for freedom in the West had been the automobile; like with my truck, liberation had been defined by where your vehicle could take you.

A Corridor of Ideas (Phase One)

I decided to spend the day riding to Bent's Old Fort, an outpost on the Santa Fe Trail six miles east of La Junta along the Arkansas River. I crossed the Arkansas on the other side of town and then I was riding on the historic trail.

The intuitive route along the river through the plains now took the shape of the cross-country Route 50 and the BNSF Railway (formerly the Burlington Northern Santa Fe Railway), but its original blazing by Anglos had come with the Santa Fe Trail. The nineteenth-century trade route linked St. Louis to Santa Fe—the Americans to their Mexican trade partners. Unlike the Oregon Trail, the Santa Fe Trail had been largely lost under tilled fields. I could see the thick cottonwoods surrounding the river; unlike the ones along the road, they already had their bright green leaves. Cicadas and frogs chirped loudly. The road had no shoulder and no traffic, save for the occasional combine rolling along. It was nice to be riding six miles on a beautiful day instead of eighty on a frigid, windy one.

A little ways down the road I came upon an auction. I turned off the road. A man who looked like Steven Spielberg stood on a red metal stepladder selling off old pictures, sewing machines, and doors. A crowd of about fifty people—half Latino, half Caucasian—sat in camp chairs in the shade created by parked vehicles. Cans of soda were for sale. I passed a man with a red mesh hat that said "YUUUUP." I parked my bike and watched.

"Five-n-a-five-n-a-five-n-a-five-n-a-five-n-a," Spielberg called, "Four-n-a-four-n-a-four-n-a-four-n-a . . . Goin' once, goin' twice, goin' three times, SOLD! To Buyer 87."

Buyer 87 had himself a box of Cabbage Patch Kids dolls for $4.

Bent's Old Fort lay between the road and the river. The original fort was long gone, but the National Park Service had rebuilt it in the 1970s. A few families were parking in the lot when I arrived.

The Bent brothers, Charles and William, built the fort in 1833 with their business partner, Ceran St. Vrain, to trade with the bands of Southern Cheyenne and Arapaho Indians who lived in the area. Like the Oregon Trail, the means of the Santa Fe Trail had become ends, as Santa Fe Trail traders like the Bents saw as much opportunity to trade with Indians as they did with the Mexicans in Santa Fe.

The Bents built their fort with walls 14 feet thick made almost entirely of mud. They hired 150 Mexican laborers to make the adobe bricks out of sand and silt and water from the Arkansas, mixed and trampled by oxen. The fort was a classic Spanish design, with a ring of rooms arranged around a central *placita*. Stairs led to the roof, where the fort's men could look out onto the river, its unending line of cottonwoods, and the expanses of the plains.

St. Vrain and Company was in the business of buffalo. The company bought tanned buffalo hides from the Indians to make robes and sell down the road in its stores in Taos and Santa Fe. In exchange for the hides, they gave the Native Americans more horses so they could hunt more buffalo. They also hunted the bison themselves. St. Vrain's hunters covered an area that encompassed most of modern-day Colorado and reached as far north as Wyoming and as far south and east as Texas and Oklahoma.

In this way, the Santa Fe Trail was like the Oregon Trail—a corridor created by pure capitalistic opportunity, with just enough specks of civilization to support the commerce. Bent's Fort was really just another boomtown that mined the resources of the West, the demand for a fashion trend recklessly running its course and dooming a generations-old Native American livelihood.

But the trail and Bent's Fort also created something less tangible, and probably more important. Today the fort appeared to occupy a random location along the Arkansas River, a mundane part of a state that had more spectacular parts. But its geography was remarkable. In the 1830s, the Arkansas River was the border between the United States and Mexico, as well as several Indian nations—the Cheyenne and Arapaho to the north and the Kiowa and Comanche to the south. As the only permanent American settlement between Missouri and the then-Mexican border, Bent's Fort thrived off the commerce across these borders. But because of the distances around it, it served perhaps even more as a multinational respite from the rigors of the Santa Fe Trail. The fort was a who's-who of American frontiersmen in the 1830s and 1840s. Kit Carson was employed as a St. Vrain buffalo hunter in 1841. John C. Frémont and Stephen Watts Kearny both staged their respective expeditions and attacks from the fort in the 1840s.

Within two years after its completion, wrote David Lavender in the colorful *Bent's Fort*, "the mud fortress west of Purgatory Creek was the center of a primitive empire that spread across the entire watershed of the upper Arkansas." A visiting reporter observed that Bent's Fort was "as though an air-built castle had dropped to earth . . . in the midst of the vast desert."[2]

At the fort, weary travelers found silverware, tablecloths, and chandeliers as well as billiards, musical instruments, and liquor. They ate buffalo, buffalo, and more buffalo. Buffalo innards staved off dehydration. Out on a hunt with a fresh kill, William Bent liked to eat a piece of bison liver sopped in bile.

This was in the more optimistic frontier times before the Indian Wars and the dark days of the 1850s and 1860s (the notorious Sand Creek Massacre would take place about one hundred miles to the northeast in 1864). American travel through the West was light enough that Anglo-Americans and Indians saw mutual advantage to occupying the same area.

The difficult but very important thing we as modern Americans should grasp is that before more modern modes of transportation, the openness of this landscape mainly meant aridity, ruggedness, and isolation—as Escalante and Dominguez, Robert Stuart, and many others knew too well. Routes like the Santa Fe Trail and places like Bent's Fort provided the foundation for the connection and modernity we now take for granted. We associate the openness of the West with freedom, but freedom needs structure in the form of routes, roads, and places to rest and meet.

These meeting places along the frontier were like small versions of port cities, with many of the attributes of a diverse, urban place. Seven languages

were spoken at the fort, and its placita was a theater for the various ritu-
als of the different cultures crossing through it. The white frontiersmen
enjoyed seeing a band of Cheyennes, faces painted black with the ash of
burned grass mixed with bison blood, come "howling up to the gate with
fresh scalps stretched on hoops that were carried at the ends of long willow wands," as Lavender wrote. "The trappers liked the spectacle as much
as the Indians did . . . in the center of the [placita], fire glow brightened.
Women formed a square, gaudy in blankets, some brandishing arms, some
waving the scalps . . . The glistening bodies of the men moved among them
or squatted amid the thumping drums."[3] The Santa Fe Trail was a corridor
for people and goods, but it also carried culture and ideas. And at Bent's Fort,
these cultures and ideas were exposed to one another to begin to create the
modern West.

Sadly, the Park Service had planned no reenactments of Cheyenne war
dances on the day I arrived at Bent's Old Fort. The rebuilt fort was the same
kind of simple pueblo ring of rooms around the central courtyard. It had
replicas of the machinery for drying and tanning buffalo hides. A troop of
Cub Scouts was poking around the rooms.

I locked my bike to a restored antique cannon and walked out to the
Arkansas. The river was slow and shallow, moving around sandbars through
the corridor of newly green cottonwood trees. I took off my shoes and sat on
the bank, my feet in the clear water.

Americans didn't find freedom in the open spaces of the West. They found
freedom in the ability to traverse and understand them, to make them part
of the modern world. Places like Bent's Fort were the first step in this process. The next step would be the biggest breakthrough, nothing less than the
annihilation of time and space in the West: the railroad.

Órale

When I returned to La Junta, I found a sports bar named JT's around the corner from the Travel Inn. It was across the street from a variety of closed down businesses, including a tavern called the Kit Carson, which advertised its "Fine Foods and Steaks" from what had once been a gorgeous neon sign. I found myself wishing it had still been open.

Inside JT's, the Negra Modelos cost $3 and the bartender's name, I surmised from the banter of the customers, was Carlos. Carlos wore a handlebar mustache, a ponytail, and a black "Mexican Energy" T-shirt tucked into Levis. The customers were mostly Latino, and I guessed they could have been part of the Chicano culture that had lived in southern Colorado for hundreds of years. Carlos, though, was from Chihuahua, a Mexican city I had visited twice and enjoyed. It was the only place where I had ever seen real swinging waist-high doors in a bar like you see in Western movies.

I ordered a beer, and Carlos slid the Negra Modelo over to me. I laid a tip down on the bar.

Carlos gave me a fist bump. "Órale," he said.

The regulars began to round up money for the jukebox. One of the only Anglos in the bar, an older guy, told me he'd buy me a drink if I ponied up some jukebox money. I gave him a few dollars. He gestured to Carlos and another cold Negra Modelo was passed my way.

They selected a list of *ranchera* and Whitney Houston songs and began to pair up and dance on the large dance floor in the dark bar. On the wall, I noticed a framed photo of a Latino man with John Elway. I asked Carlos if that was the owner. He said it was—the picture had been taken at Elway's restaurant in the Front Range.

"Cherry Hills," Carlos said, raising an eyebrow and making the universal sign for "money" by rubbing together his thumb and index finger.

After the basketball game on the bar TV was over, I walked over to Lucy's Tacos for a burrito. It had gotten to be evening, and the sun shone down the empty streets. Outside a bar around the corner named La Bamba, a guy strummed three chords on a guitar and blew a harmonica, singing, "On the rooow, woooo, wooad . . . " in the dying of the day. It was the only sound around, except for the occasional noise of the train.

The next day loomed, my longest travel day yet: 650 miles on the train. By this time tomorrow, I'd be almost to Phoenix.

The Santa Fe

William Bent abandoned his fort in 1849 and burned it down a few years later, and for a few years, its place along the Arkansas remained fallow. But such a natural transportation corridor would die hard.

In 1859 a railroad tycoon named Cyrus K. Holliday chartered a railroad in Topeka, Kansas. Holliday had helped found Topeka, and like many frontier boosters at the time, he desired a connection to the continent's growing rail network. He also saw opportunity in making Topeka a conduit of settlement along the Santa Fe Trail.[4]

Holliday first named the railroad the Atchison and Topeka, after the eastern terminus of the road on the bank of the Missouri River. But searching for something a little more inspired, he branded the new road with the addition of the name of the legendary Native, Spanish, Mexican, and now American place of the Southwest he aspired to reach with the new train.

With the advent of the railroad, the Santa Fe Trail had become obsolete. Yet Holliday's railroad followed the same route through the plains, along the Arkansas River Valley of eastern Colorado, and over the Continental Divide through a low point of the Rockies to within a few miles of its namesake (it never actually served Santa Fe due to the rugged terrain surrounding it).

The Atchison, Topeka and Santa Fe Railroad, which became known as the Santa Fe, came right through the site of Bent's Fort. In 1876 the railroad's construction crews were racing west toward Raton Pass in a bid to beat out the Denver and Río Grande Western Railroad for the easiest access point into New Mexico. Six miles west of the site of Bent's Fort, a third railroad—the Kansas Pacific—had established a camp at the end of its line on the bank of the Arkansas. The Santa Fe crews arrived there, and the camp became a town named La Junta, and with its fork in the road, an important one. At the height of passenger service on the Santa Fe, La Junta had a roundhouse and a yard for assembling trains to climb over Raton Pass.[5]

The next morning, I woke up early, packed up my bike in the box I had lugged through town, and dropped off my key. I walked through La Junta's museum of ruins, boarded-up storefronts amid the survivors of the early railroad days. I hefted my bike box across Highway 50 to the station. The town was still in the way that only a small town on Sunday can be.

The train station, too, had experienced better days. It looked not of the vintage of the American rail's turn-of-the-century glory days but of its mid-century last gasps and decline. The station was an unremarkable rectangular building that looked like what it more or less was: a freight office for Burlington Northern that happened to have a ticket window and a bench.

I presented my paper ticket and checked in my bike and walked outside to put my bike box on the baggage cart. In the rail yard was a gleaming orange engine with a line of black freight cars that ran to the horizon. The BNSF was mostly a freight line now. Passenger service had been kept on life support by the government subsidization of Amtrak.

Amtrak had renamed the lone remaining passenger route on the old Santa Fe line the Southwest Chief. I'd ride this route across the Colorado plains, over Raton Pass, through the New Mexico mountains, south through the Río Grande Valley to Albuquerque, take a right westward through the southern edge of the Navajo Reservation into Arizona, and alight at Flagstaff, where I'd catch a late-night bus to Phoenix.

Inside the train office, there were no down-on-their luck travelers, runaway kids, or security personnel aggressively keeping order. I saw only one person, a small elderly woman sitting on the bench. I didn't pay much attention to her until she commented on my bike.

"The train's so bad these days that you need a bike, I guess," she said.

Her name was Beverly. She was a nearly lifelong La Juntan who was bound for Santa Fe to celebrate her daughter's sixtieth birthday. Her daughter would pick her up in Lamy; the train still did not reach Santa Fe.

"I usually drive my Prius there, which is maybe an hour quicker, but it's not as fun," Beverly said. "You go through better country on the train."

The Southwest Chief arrived right on time, at 8:15. The train agents stepped off the cars onto the cement of the La Junta platform, stretched and looked over the sad scene of what was left of the once-mighty junction. I waited on the platform until I saw one of them load my bike onto the train.

Beverly instructed me that no matter what seat I had been assigned, I needed to sit in the lounge. I envisioned a dark, smoky, perhaps seedy car But she led me through two or three passenger cars until we came into a space awash in sunlight, with windows on all sides and above and reclining seats looking outward to the freight cars full of coal on one side, 1st Avenue and its empty storefronts on the other.

"We're going to go through some beautiful country," Beverly said, selecting a table to sit at.

I sat down in one of the window seats. In front of me were four electrical outlets and side tables for my stuff. Beer and wine and spirits were available after noon. It was a traveler's heaven. Today was going to be like watching a movie of scenery.

We pushed off, rolling past the town graveyard, the ball fields, then the open plains along the Arkansas. Soon the blue and white of the Sangre de Cristo Mountains came in sight. With the first sight of the Rockies over the plains, I experienced the best part of traveling across the country without having to travel across the country. I knew this from several cross-country trips, many of them through Colorado. At first, you think that it's just a bank of puffy clouds floating in the horizon, then you speculate whether they might be mountains but decide they're clouds, and then you know you've arrived in the West.

I remembered from those drives how the plains started to slope subtly upward until suddenly you're a mile above sea level in Denver. I turned on my GPS and saw that, sure enough, we were climbing quickly. Having started at 4,000 feet in La Junta, we hit 5,000 feet quickly, but with no real sense of climbing. Accordingly, the land began to speckle with piñon and juniper and stark, dry buttes. We were climbing toward Raton Pass and New Mexico.

A professor-type in a khaki-colored shirt, pants, and hat sat across the aisle from me pointing out old railroad infrastructure and the ruins of a stone fort that we were passing. Several other passengers had crowded around him to listen, and he had begun to hold court like a tour guide. That was the thing that I always liked about riding trains in the Bay Area—transport became a collective experience, like a moving public space. Any great or terrible thing you experienced together, like a baseball game victory, the end of a work-week, or a fight. There was satisfaction and weariness on the last train on a weekend night. This was my first long-distance train trip in the United States, and it was the same feeling, perhaps even magnified by the adventure of going several hundred miles.

I also realized how much nicer an experience this was compared to the Greyhound. It wasn't that anything was fancy; it was just more civil. It wasn't even that much more expensive.

We were entering the mountains through shallow ravines. This was one of the segments of the route that had split from the highway. So the view from my seat through the wall of windows made it feel as if we were hovering in the landscape, magically detached from any piece of transport infrastructure.

I walked over and sat across from Beverly at her table. She looked up from her book.

"There's going to be a herd of elk coming up on the right," she said, and there was.

Death Valley Scotty, the Super Chief, and the Annihilation of Space (Phase Two)

I was aboard the remnant of a legendary train. Other railroads indulged the fantasies of Americans by pioneering connections across the continent, but the Santa Fe tapped a different imagination: speed. The Santa Fe gave America an almost unthinkably fast link between the West and the rest of the United States, shooting through the plains, mountains, and deserts that would eventually become known as "flyover country."

Cyrus Holliday had predicted that his railroad would one day connect the great cities of the West. He died in 1900, and by then he had an idea that his prophesy would be fulfilled. By the beginning of the twentieth century, the Santa Fe extended to and through the urban hubs of the day: Chicago, St. Louis, Kansas City, Denver, Salt Lake, San Francisco, Los Angeles. It had won the battle for Raton Pass with the Denver and Río Grande Western by an inch. In February 1878, engineers from both railroads rode the same Río Grande train to El Moro, right below the pass. But while the Río Grande engineers checked into their hotel, the Santa Fe engineers had gone straight to the owner of a toll road over the pass to secure the rights to the route, laying claim to the pass before their competitor.

The Santa Fe had also established a reputation for extreme speed. In 1889, when Pulitzer reporter Nellie Bly circumnavigated the Earth, beating the fictional time of the character Phileas Fogg in Jules Verne's *Around the World in 80 Days*, she rode a Santa Fe train for the leg from Los Angeles to Chicago. In subsequent years, this 2,265-mile L.A.-to-Chicago route became a measuring stick for speed, as the Santa Fe continually bested its record times on the route, achieving a standard of fifty-two hours in 1903.

In 1905 a man named Walter Scott walked into the Santa Fe depot in Los Angeles and demanded that a train take him to Chicago in forty-six hours. "Death Valley Scotty" was a former cowboy in Buffalo Bill's Wild West show who had made a fortune in a mine near Death Valley, California. Scotty had taken to riding the trains of the West; he had already ridden the Santa Fe across the West thirty-two times. The Santa Fe management agreed to bring him to Chicago for the sum of $5,500. The train would leave the next day.[6]

The Scott Special was comprised of only three cars—a baggage car, a dining car, and a Pullman sleeping car—pulled by a series of Santa Fe locomotives. The train left L.A.'s Union Station at 1:00 p.m. on July 9, 1905, reaching 84 miles per hour just outside the city. A little after 2:00 the train was climbing toward the 4,000-foot elevation of Cajon Pass with the aid of a "helper" engine, uncoupling from the helper at the pass's summit without stopping. On the way down to Barstow, the train reached a speed of 96 miles per hour. The train whipped around curves, spilling Scott's fine meals, which included caviar, consommé, and Porterhouse steak.

The Scott Special arrived at Chicago's Dearborn Station just before noon on July 11, which meant a travel time of under forty-five hours. Its average speed was 50 miles per hour, with a top speed of 106. The train had risen over 7,000 feet above sea level four separate times, climbing over 18,000 feet total. Scotty sent a telegram to President Theodore Roosevelt.

While it is true that the Scott Special was a one-off, the Santa Fe had pulled off the feat with twenty-four hours notice with its regular locomotives, cars, and crews. And by then, the Santa Fe's standard passenger service, the one on which Scott rode back to L.A., was plenty fast. The California Limited, its all-Pullman once-a-day passenger service from Chicago to Los Angeles, had debuted in 1892 and defined the direction that cutting-edge passenger service through the West would take over the next half century.

Like Walter Scott, California Limited passengers ate gourmet meals and slept in luxury accommodations. They had access to a two-car diner, a club-lounge, a soda fountain, and a barbershop. Sleeping cars had inlaid wood and polished brass lamps. Uniformed boys came onto the train at Cajon Pass with free boutonnieres for the men and roses for the ladies. In 1911 the Santa Fe began to offer an even more luxurious experience in the de-Luxe. It was hugely popular, with up to twenty-three trains leaving each day. As happens with technology, once only available to the rich, long-distance rail travel became affordable to the middle class. The speed of the Santa Fe and the access it brought to the West became a central piece of the nation.

In the 1920s and 1930s, the Santa Fe continued to outdo itself. In 1936 the new Super Chief did the trip in thirty-nine hours and forty-five minutes, regularly reaching speeds of over 100 miles per hour. Sadly, the Southwest Chief I was riding was not traveling nearly as fast.

Just a few decades earlier, Americans had toiled for months to cross the West in such uncomfortable conditions as Abigail Scott (no relation to Walter) had endured. Now, not only could we cross the entire West in a day and a half, we could experience it in luxury, with our feet up.

What speed really meant was the compression of the space that defined the West. Until the railroad era, the West's space had been something to overcome, not enjoy, except for the hardiest and most masochistic of mountain men and women. Americans could now enjoy and consume the West's space. Our sense of having the West at our fingertips originated on trains like the Super Chief. While automobiles and the roads they traveled provided more options, the trains collapsed the West to something the average American felt that he could picture in his mind and access if he wanted to.

The hallmarks of modern life began to appear in the suddenly open West: speed, connection, mass production, commercialization. The Santa Fe trains that ruled the early twentieth century created perhaps the height of civilized modernity in the West: eating a Porterhouse steak while zooming through the canyon country, alighting to explore spectacular places, meeting the conquered Indians, and then buying their goods. Yet on the now-accessible open range, America searched for more freedom.

Beverly had traveled by train since she was six, and for her whole life, it felt like magic. She loved how it animated La Junta when she was a little girl. Passengers traveling from L.A. to Chicago came to her small town and walked its streets and shopped in its businesses. La Junta even had a Little Italy of immigrant laborers, which the city had scrapped in its own era of urban renewal.

Riding the train was an experience Beverly cherished, one that had been much more civil and classy than it was now. She remembered the mahogany and plush of the Pullman sleeper cars and the tuxedoed waiters. She said she and other La Juntans were trying to get Amtrak to reinstate the train to Denver.

She knew the route of the Santa Fe by heart: the racing across the plains to the mountains, the gentle curves of the foothills, the climbing to Raton Pass, the desert at the foot of the Sangre de Cristo peaks, and the final grade up into the red clay and piñon majesty of northern New Mexico.

Beverly got off in Lamy, which was little more than a train station that served Santa Fe.

"Tim, have a great trip," she said, grasping my shoulder strongly before walking down the stairs of the car. I watched her move down the platform to a middle-aged woman who must have been her daughter.

I had another four hundred miles to go. We wound through Ansel Adams country: voluptuous clouds, old Hispano churches, spots of juniper on the rolling hills and carved mesas. We stopped for forty-five minutes in Albuquerque and then turned west. Past the Arizona line, the sun began to set over the low mesas of the Navajo Reservation. The lounge car became a lightbox, its windows turning the colors of the sky, patches of blue and white and the charcoal gray of storm clouds. I was back on the Colorado Plateau with its long cliffs of red Wingate sandstone, the same stratum that Jonny Wilde and I had ridden past on the trail of the padres.

Next to me sat a young Latino from Albuquerque headed for Los Angeles, in a large white T-shirt and baggy black jeans. He was reclining, listening to music with headphones, watching the same scenery out the lounge car's wraparound windows. I asked him if he had ridden the train before.

"Nah," he said. "You?"

"No, this is my first time."

"Pretty nice," he said. "Better than the bus."

Amen. We leaned back and watched the poor suckers on the freeway. Now we were more or less following the route of I-40. We occupied the same space and had the same views, but as had happened throughout my trip, taking a different mode of transportation put me in a different world. I liked watching the arc of a gorgeous day from a rolling train, the sun making its way across different points of the lounge car's skylights. The evening light casting through storm clouds over the mesas awed my fellow passengers, many of whom held cocktails. The train was a glowing public space, the lounge car a lively happy hour rolling through the desert.

We were traveling through a corridor where all the chronological threads of western transportation wove together in a parallel braided strand: the Santa Fe Trail, the stagecoach, the Santa Fe railroad, Route 66, and Interstate 40. Not to mention the trails of the various Native American nations: The sacred peak of Mount Taylor was visible, marking one corner of Dinetah, the Navajo homeland. We crossed the trade routes leading to Chaco Canyon and its thousand-year-old Anasazi city.

In the chronology, we should have been pressing the gas on the interstate, but we were on the train, taken out of time, just a bunch of people looking out the window with no other goal than heading west.

Greyhound V: Flagstaff to Phoenix

We arrived in Flagstaff early, at about 9:00. It was dark, and the neon Hotel Monte Vista sign was my signal that we were in Flag. I had attended college here for a semester in the late 1990s, and I remembered the red brick train station in the middle of town. Back then, to my teenage mind, it seemed like a relic; I didn't think of it as an actual living part of the town or its transportation network, just one of the keepsakes that gave Flagstaff the transient train town aura that I liked. That it was still a working train station seemed too hard to believe.

But the Southwest Chief rolled right into the station; it was, in fact, still the town depot. Lots of people were getting off here, and the Grand Canyon–bound tourists, baggage handlers, and cabbies enlivened the deadness of a Sunday night.

At the exact moment that I realized I needed my luggage, I also realized that I had no idea how to get it. Soon the train would shove off silently without warning. Suddenly in full panic mode, I sprinted to the nearest train attendant, who was vacantly looking at her smartphone, and asked where the luggage was going. She said it would be in the depot building. I raced over. The window was closed, no sign of life. I raced back to the agent. She shrugged. Finally I saw a train worker in the act of leaving a cart of baggage in a seemingly random location next to the building. My duffel and bike box were on it.

I would have loved to stay the night in Flagstaff, but unfortunately, my journey continued on the Greyhound to Phoenix, scheduled to leave in less than an hour. The Greyhound terminal was not located next to or even any-where near the train station. The walk was too far, and I would not be able to catch a bus in time. Greyhound called this a "self transfer," which I found funny because there was no way you could actually do it by yourself. I tried to imagine if an airline attempted to do this. You fly into Kennedy and look at your ticket and see you have a self transfer to La Guardia for a flight leav-ing in an hour.

"They had to downsize and find a cheaper place to rent, further away from the center of town," explained the cab driver as he drove me the mile to the Greyhound station.

The station turned out to be a squat hovel in an industrial, dark part of town where I had never been. The place was sterile, empty, and lit by loud fluorescent panels. One man stood at the counter.

"You're not gonna like this," he said, looking at my ticket. "That bus is four hours late. It broke down."

I had been scheduled to arrive in Phoenix at 1:00 a.m., an arrival time tee-tering on the edge of reason. I'd ride my bike from the Greyhound station—interestingly located at the airport—to downtown, where I would finally crash at my motel. Now my journey had fallen to the floor of the absurd, another sleepless night courtesy of Greyhound.

I brought in my bike and put it on the scale.

"Dude, you're really not gonna like this," the man said, chuckling like a jubilant elf. "That bike's gonna cost you an extra 50 bucks. We gotta ship it."

Fortunately, or unfortunately, I was a road-hardened Greyhound traveler and ready for this kind of BS. I calmly responded that everywhere else on my trip I had been allowed to check the bike as an extra bag for a $10 charge.

He shook his head. I shook mine. Finally, I got the man to call some sort of superior in another city.

"This guy says that we're supposed to let him check his bike as an extra bag," he said into the phone.

Silence. "Uh huh," he said. Another silence. "Oh. When did that change?" He hung up and looked at me. "Ten dollars," he said.

I had four hours to kill. Against my better judgment, I left my baggage under the man's watch and gave him my cell number in case the bus's timetable changed. I still hadn't eaten dinner, so I walked to one of Flagstaff's many brewpubs and devoured a burger and a few pints of beer.

I returned to the station at midnight. The bus was still two hours away. More people were waiting in the station and the typical Greyhound scene was building. When the bus finally arrived at around 2:30, I expected to be hustled aboard in an effort to make up time. But the passengers stumbled out as if on just another smoke break. I instinctively gathered my pieces of luggage and walked outside toward the bus. The driver, a skinny man with a thick white mustache, had gotten out of the bus and I approached him, expecting him to offer an apology for being four hours late.

"Get back inside!" the driver barked in my direction without directly looking at me. He took out a cigarette and began smoking. I went indoors until we were ordered onto the bus. We left at 3:00. The bus was the same circus I had come to expect on other Greyhounds, although a boy and girl who were conversing passionately through the night on either side of me thoughtfully offered to switch seats so I wouldn't be in the middle of their conversation. The drive to Phoenix was two hours down Interstate 17. I knew from traveling it that it was one of the more beautiful interstate drives in the West: a plunge down a vertical mile over the edge of the Colorado Plateau, through the Verde Valley, and into the magic of the Sonoran Desert. But as with my other Greyhound trips, it was dark, and so I was not traveling through scenic Arizona, just as I had not traveled through Nevada, Utah, Wyoming, or Colorado. I was in the dark parallel reality of the Greyhound.

I arrived in Phoenix fully awake. The Phoenix Greyhound station did not even pretend to be a civic fixture in the center of town; it was part of the sprawl of Sky Harbor airport. Back in the Sunbelt, I walked out into the hot morning and got on my bike.

The Anti-City (Phase Three)

"If you've got a burning ambition to do something," the longtime Arizona politician Bruce Babbitt once said about his native state, "there's absolutely no limits." As another Arizona booster put it, "this country pumps new life and energy and thinking into a man! . . . release from the staid ordinary ways of thinking."[7]

As I rode out of the tangle of Sky Harbor toward downtown Phoenix, it was light enough to see the city's skyscrapers glistening. They were glassy and shimmering but short for such a big metro area. The jagged, prehistoric-looking brown peaks beyond made them look like part of a fake city built for a giant waterslide park. The surreal upward thrusts of saguaro cacti were everywhere, along with the incongruous palm trees. The sandy riverbeds sat empty and so were the wide roads.

Even with its 4 million residents, Phoenix and the metropolitan area that occupied the Salt River Valley—often called the Valley of the Sun—was in another category than New York or Philadelphia, or even Salt Lake or Denver. It was not a harbor city of dense assemblages of workers and their ghettos around a waterfront. It was not a factory city, with tenements crowded around railroads and the engines of capitalism. It was not a city of the nineteenth-century West that reached out to a hinterland of mineral and resource wealth. It was a city custom-built by people of the twentieth-century West to suit their new technological abilities and the values that came with them. And so, as was evident to anyone visiting Phoenix, the place strangely lacked the things that Phoenix's builders specifically avoided: density, complexity, walking, and anything smacking of oldness.

That these were the qualities most valued by the reawakening of urban culture taking place across the country made Phoenix a little off-putting in the twenty-first century. But Phoenix was a vital part of the evolution of America. Everything about the direction of transportation in the twentieth-century West—the rapidly developing technology, the emerging ability to define space, the increasingly fast movement of not only people and goods but ideas, the West at one's fingertips—had headed toward Phoenix. Transportation had brought freedom through the release and exchange of ideas at the melting pot of Bent's Old Fort, and then freedom through overcoming geographic barriers and collapsing space along the 90-mile-an-hour California Limited. And up until then, the freedom and modern life that the West offered had been about people coming together, modern civilization lifting Americans to experience its frontier with one another. But the automobile accelerated Americans' concept of freedom by individualizing it. Literally and figuratively, the West began to run off the tracks, and no more so than in Phoenix.

As America looked out over the West in the middle of the twentieth century, the cities that we built in the industrial era had little to do with our new concepts of modernity and freedom. Automobility had provided the final ability to spread out and segregate our lives how we wanted—home from work, left from right, rich from poor. With this new modern life and freedom, America needed a new place to live. Phoenix, wrote historian Bradford Luckingham, "represented the modern urban center in America." Modern Americans, Luckingham quoted an observer as saying, "desired not a unified metropolis but a fragmented one." So we "opted for the dissolution of the city" and created the "dispersed and fragmented" metropolitan world that we had come to know in America.[8]

Phoenix was conceived as an anti-city in an environment that just decades earlier would not have been habitable for 50,000 people, much less 4 million.

The twentieth-century innovations of massive dams and air conditioning were the very kernel of Phoenix's existence and success. But the main enabler was the car, and because of this codependency, Phoenix was arguably the most auto-oriented city in America. In 1900, when the first cars arrived in Phoenix, the town had a little more than 5,500 residents, and over the ensuing century, autos catalyzed the city's population to almost 1.5 million and its area to an unruly 516 square miles.

Which is not to say Phoenix did not have a pre-auto iteration. The city was originally conceived as a quaint farming community, which can now be viewed almost as a mulligan. In 1867 a Civil War veteran named Jack Swilling led a group of unemployed miners into the valley of the Salt River, which back then had water in it. Swilling's men revived a network of ancient Hohokam Indian canals. They founded a permanent townsite in 1870 and convinced Maricopa County to make it its county seat a year later. They platted a small network of streets, naming the east-west streets for presidents and the north-south streets for Native American tribes (that were replaced by numbers in 1893).[9] Phoenix's relentless boosters attracted the railroad, which served as a sort of life support for the desert settlement until cars arrived.

When they did, America embraced the anti-city. Phoenix's geographic area dovetailed with the number of autos people owned. The city was half a square mile in 1870, before the auto was available. In 1910 Phoenix contained 352 licensed autos. By 1913 ten auto dealers had opened, the number of autos in the city had almost doubled, and the city limits had grown to encompass over 3 square miles.[10] Phoenix had 11,539 cars in 1920 and 53,064 in 1929.

After World War II, these trends took on epic proportions, as Phoenix grew by over 300 percent in the 1950s alone.[11] The city reflected the dominant values of its citizens: businesslike, flexible, pragmatic, and growth-oriented.[12] The "clean city" attracted non-polluting industries associated with increased federal defense contracting like electronics.

These companies had no trouble convincing new hires to relocate to Phoenix. As a Motorola manager stated in 1957, "We can run an ad in the trade magazines mentioning three places to work—Phoenix, Chicago and Riverside, in California. We'll draw 25 to 1 replies for Phoenix compared to the other cities." As the manager said, the premium for relocating was free—sunshine.[13]

Phoenix innovated the American life of leisure with year-round warm temperatures and roomy, open ranch houses. People worked and played together at the Arizona Country Club and the Phoenix Country Club. As one former New York City executive explained in 1957, "I used to commute . . . an hour and a half each way. Now I live in the desert just beyond town and it takes me only 20 minutes to get to work. I can go home at lunchtime and take a dip in my pool. After work or on weekends, I play tennis or golf . . . I just enjoy life about 10 times as much."[14]

Cars and air conditioners had obviated America's only concerns about living in the Valley of the Sun. Now we were free to enjoy the life of leisure in a booming economy of sun, growth, and clean industry. Phoenix became the swimming pool capital of America and landlocked Arizona had more boats per capita than any other state except California or Florida. Employees worked from 7:00 'til 3:00 and drove home in ten or twenty minutes to relax with their families and friends.

But something had been lost, something basic and human. As early as 1920, one prescient observer commented, "The people in this town have forgotten how to walk. If they have to go 2 blocks, they have to get in a machine and drive."

————————————

Now, in twenty-first-century America, Phoenix was far from what Americans seemed to desire. Especially since the Great Recession pummeled its real estate market, Phoenix had been exposed as an anti-city in the worst sense. Like much of the West, it had all of the bad parts of urbanization and none of the good parts. Phoenix was the American symbol of sprawl and a cautionary tale of auto dependence.

It was now clear that Phoenix, in its rush to build the modern anti-city, had shed basic human necessities—namely, the city. People need connection. We need density. We need things that last.

Meanwhile, the city's image of tough western independence had been exposed as a thin veneer hiding a web of sad dependencies. Phoenix was a slave to the ephemera of the real estate market, its booms largely the result of construction activity, requiring more and more exponential growth to sustain the economic health of the region. The creation and maintenance of an image drove the real estate market, and so it drove the city.[15] And as the capital and cultural hub of one of the reddest states in the United States, Phoenix had always been dependent on the federal government, whether it was water from the dams of the New Deal or federal funds to pad municipal budgets running on low taxes.[16]

The automobility of the twentieth century was as much a ball and chain as freedom, and Phoenix seemed imprisoned by its choices. Urban planners and the media universally disparaged the city. In a documentary on auto dependence in the recession, PBS interviewed members of a household in a Phoenix suburb that drove 120 miles a day; when the price of a gallon of gas reached $4 in 2008, their sizeable transportation costs doubled. "We don't think about it," they said, "we do it."[17] Phoenix had seemingly turned into an anti-city of anti-thinkers, rolling around on belt routes to nowhere.

Which is why it was strange that Phoenix had one of the most successful new mass transit lines in the United States.

Why Are People Riding the Light Rail?

The ride to downtown Phoenix was, like my walk into La Junta, a quiet journey that served as a nice exhale after my latest Greyhound ride. Luckily, Sky Harbor was strangely close to downtown Phoenix. The route to my motel was straightforward. I had only to ride to Washington Street and turn left, then ride two quick miles into downtown.

At Washington, I saw the light rail tracks. What may have been the first train of the day glided into the center of the city.

I checked into my motel, the Budget Lodge, at 4th Avenue and Washington, and slept for a few hours. When I woke up, Phoenix was in the throes of Monday morning. The motel was three blocks from the central station of the Valley Metro light rail, so I left my bike in my room, which was protected by a steel security gate, and set out on foot into the already-warm morning for a day of riding the train.

The Valley Metro Rail opened in December 2008. The system could transport 12,000 passengers per hour, roughly the same as a six-lane freeway. On its opening day, some 150,000 passengers crowded into the new trains for a free ride. They gave various reasons for their excitement over the train:

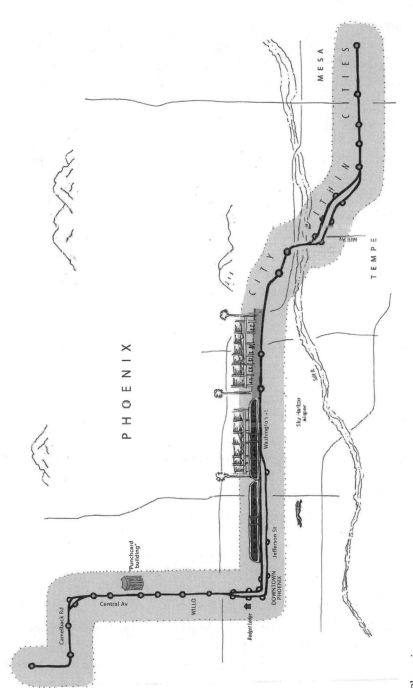

Phoenix.

skipping traffic, getting to destinations faster, environmental sustainability, and a more relaxing way to get around. The enthusiasm did not wane in the following weeks, months, and years. Like in other western cities, ridership on light rail exceeded expectations (by over 30 percent), and the presence of light rail had influenced new development and revitalization of neighborhoods along the line.[18]

Skeptics questioned whether light rail was the most cost-effective way of offering residents a more environmentally sustainable option for getting around. One blogger bet that the agency could buy each daily rider of the system a new Toyota Prius and gas for 10,000 miles per year for its $1.4 billion cost.[19] It still reached a very small percentage of the Greater Phoenix metro area.[20]

Others viewed Phoenix's light rail as a canary in a coal mine. Even exceeding ridership expectations, the system carried only a fraction of the riders of the world's busier transit systems. One hour on one of Tokyo's typical subway lines dwarfed Valley Metro Rail's best day.

Before my trip, I spoke to Emily Talen, an urban planning professor at Arizona State University (ASU) who was, like many in the valley, from the Midwest and couldn't get away from comparing her adopted city to her home of Chicago.

"I came here kicking and screaming. I hated Phoenix," Talen told me. "It's the non-city that is here, I really don't like it."

Talen was also lukewarm about the light rail. She acknowledged the higher-than-expected use of the train, but she was disappointed in the lack of what she called "community building" around the train. Despite the enormous investment in rail transit, the city hadn't done enough to encourage the real estate industry to complement the train with the appropriate development around the stations.

"Some days," Talen said, "you wonder, why bother?"

Others who lived in larger coastal cities like the one where I lived, seemed perfectly happy to let Phoenix decline and empty, its ruins covered in blowing sand while America thrived elsewhere.

But I always had a soft spot for the Sonoran Desert. I thought it was a compelling place to pass time as a human. I identified with the reasons people wanted to live here. And it wasn't like the Northeast or California did not have their environmental and economic challenges and liabilities.[21]

In conversations in Bay Area cafés or bars, I often found myself being a Phoenix apologist.

The Valley of the Sun had to restart somewhere. To me, Phoenix just needed to approach being Phoenix differently. And to do that, it needed a fundamental move to reverse the spreading out, to balance the private desert retreats with a public realm, to curb the disposable sprawl. The fallout from the Great Recession suggested that maybe what was modern and liberating in the West was something that pulled people together, not dispersed them. Perhaps we needed to go back to Bent's Fort and the California Limited—and away from the anti-city—for our concept of freedom.

Was light rail that thing? Or was light rail the urban lipstick on a suburban pig destined for slaughter?

In America, the train is no longer the king of speed. It does not provide the competitive advantages of convenience and saving time, as the omnibus and streetcar had over walking a century ago. In a vacuum, the car is faster. Now we take the train for other reasons. In Phoenix, the auto capital of the world, I wanted to know what those reasons could be.

Waiting for the Train

Jack Tevlin, dressed in white shorts, a denim shirt, and boat shoes, a sweater wrapped around his shoulders, embodied Phoenix's lifestyle of leisure. But Tevlin was a veteran of battle, and he had won. Jack Tevlin was known as the godfather of light rail in Phoenix.

Tevlin walked into the grand lobby of the downtown Phoenix Sheraton, where we had arranged to meet, and then led me out of the hotel through the promenade of the ASU campus. The campus was the new jewel of downtown Phoenix. We walked to where the buildings opened onto a pedestrian promenade with desert palo verde trees, the orange and red panels of the buildings rising above us. Many Phoenicians had testified that the new ASU campus would not have materialized without light rail.

We stopped at Central Avenue, busy with trains running up and down. Civic Space Park lay across the street, fronted by a block of palo verde trees and a few of downtown's rare pre-auto buildings that had been renovated. Down the street was one of the light rail stations, sleek and modern, its shade structures pointing up like sails on a desert ship.

"There's something about going down the street and seeing people waiting for the train," Tevlin said, a satisfied smile on his tanned face. Then he told me the story of how this train had come into being in the most car-happy city in America.

The crusade for light rail had actually begun with the battle over freeways. By the early 1980s, other Sunbelt metros, like Los Angeles and Houston, had built new networks of expressways to take their residents nearly anywhere they wished to go. But Phoenix was behind. New freeways had been on the boards since the 1960s but were never built. Interstate 10 through downtown had not been completed, the last missing piece of the coast-to-coast freeway. Some in town liked it that way. Phoenix had a grid of wide arterials, and building more freeways would turn the city into another Los Angeles. But not building them might turn the city into something even worse. Congestion was thickening, and the Maricopa Association of Governments (MAG) didn't think the surface roads could handle all the traffic.

In 1985 Maricopa County voters approved a half-cent sales tax to build a set of new freeways throughout the region. Tucked into this measure was funding to study an increase in transit funding by another half cent.

Tevlin was a young planner for the City of Phoenix, and it had been clear to him that the city needed to improve its transit service. The city ran buses, but up to an hour apart, even on a well-used line. Most routes ended at 8:00 p.m. Famously, there was no Sunday service. Tevlin remembered people telling him they couldn't get to church. Phoenix was the ninth-largest city in the United States, but it had the thirty-seventh largest transit system.

"It kind of fell into my lap to start a conversation about transit," he said.

It was a chicken-and-egg problem. Few rode the system because the system was poor, and it was poor because few rode it. It suffered for a few specific reasons. For example, the city's funding stream for transit was arcane; it paid for its buses using general fund monies and surrounding cities bought into the bus routes with their state lottery money. So no city in the valley had a dedicated funding stream. Another problem was that the people who rode the bus had no power to make changes, and the people who had that power did not ride the bus. And then there was the reality that the valley was full of residents who used to live in older, denser, less car-centric eastern or midwestern cities. In many cases, they came to Arizona to escape the hardships of the city, including long commutes in rattling old train cars.

Tevlin had grown up in New York City. He went to high school in Queens and took the Long Island Railroad. But he had fond memories of the train. He remembered it as a nice lifestyle. He used to do all his homework on the train.

"I thought it would provide another lifestyle transportation mode," Tevlin said. "We're Phoenix. We're a car community, but I had no doubt that we weren't any different than other cities."

At first Tevlin tried to expand the bus system. Each year he invested more and more general fund money in buses, but it was only enough to garnish what, at its core, was a rotten asset. He knew the city needed a rail system for transit to be successful, so he and other officials hatched ValTrans in 1989, envisioning elevated rail arcing over the valley's wide streets, not taking up space and not bound to street routes.

ValTrans lost, badly. Voters rejected it by a two-to-one margin. Tevlin believed that they became confused as to what the rail system really was and that the city had no clear transit vision.

By the mid-1990s, though, the problems of congestion were worsening, even with the new freeways. New voices such as the Chamber of Commerce agreed with Tevlin about the valley's need for mass transit. Phoenix had always been a city of boosters, and those boosters began to back transit. Workers were having a difficult time traveling to work. In 1997 the city decided to approach voters again, this time for a sales tax increase to support light rail. The measure lost by 122 votes.[22]

"A killer blow," Tevlin said.

Yet a few years later, in 2000, a committee of citizens decided to create another measure. By now, Tevlin had become passionate about light rail. He saw the appeal of light rail to a new type of mass transit rider, a person who owned or could afford a car but who chose to ride. Light rail provided a classy urban rail experience for this new rider but was less expensive to build, operate, and maintain than the heavy-rail urban metros of the East Coast, so it could be accomplished with less population density. This was the equation driving the success of new rail systems in cities that, like Phoenix, had been built around the automobile. Tevlin and his growing group of transit supporters used these other cities—Denver, Dallas, Sacramento, Portland, and Salt Lake City—to sell the rest of the metro area on light rail. The committee took a dozen people at a time to these cities to talk to business owners and citizens.

Dallas, in particular, helped change Phoenicians' perceptions because Dallas was like Phoenix in its size, newness, and spread-out geography.

Tevlin and his growing ranks of supporters showed community leaders what the system could be, how well it could be used, and its potential effect on economic development. As a fixed investment, for example, light rail acted the same as a freeway interchange, providing certainty to developers and others managing risk.

To communicate to voters and community leaders exactly what they were buying, the city and the system, renamed Valley Metro, drew a clear map of the alignment of the first and subsequent phases, with projected completion dates. Three factors drove the initial alignment. Existing transit riders and their "desire lines" came first; by far, the highest demand for transit was the bus system's Red Line running up Central Avenue. Destinations that needed to be connected came second, such as downtown Phoenix, uptown Phoenix, and ASU. Last came development potential. Phoenix had a lot of vacant land, even within its core. Light rail boosters thought that more and more people would want to live in the central city because they were tired of the congestion.

These directives produced a consensus starter line that ran between Mesa on one end and uptown Phoenix on the other, with downtown Phoenix, Arizona State University, and Sky Harbor in between.

Yet even with a large coalition of public officials, business owners, and citizens, the City of Phoenix was thick with skeptics. Jack Tevlin became the spokesman for the massive campaign. He spoke to a hundred citizen groups, merchant groups, and other organizations. A public meeting led by Tevlin at Christown Spectrum Mall in 2000 became a NIMBY mob to which the police were summoned. After that, police attended all meetings.[23]

The Transit 2000 vote was a landslide. Voters approved it by a two-to-one margin. This key piece of funding ensured the ability to construct the twenty-mile starter Valley Metro Rail line. Federal funding and contributions from Mesa and Tempe paid the rest of the $1.4 billion, and the train opened in December 2008. Valley Metro estimated that it would cost $184 million per year to operate, with 25 percent recovered from fares.[24] For the first few days, the train was free. After that, an all-day pass cost just $2.50.

What would justify such an enormous public investment? The train's ten-year projection was 28,000 riders per day. Six months into service, the novelty having worn off, weekday ridership was over 33,000 per day. Then, in the steep slide of the recession, Valley Metro began instituting a series of service cuts and fare increases.[25] According to transit history, that should have snuffed out the popularity of the train, especially in such a fragile transit environment as Phoenix.

But people kept riding, more of them every month. A month after the first service cuts in 2009, the transit system added a half million boardings. By August 2011, it added almost a million new riders. Now the daily ridership averaged around 45,000, nearly reaching the 2020 projection. On a September Friday in 2011, with weekday commuters, students, people going out to dinner, and both Arizona Diamondbacks and Arizona State Sun Devils home games, the system carried 60,437 people, a record for ridership. For Phoenix, 60,000 people packing urban rail cars was unthinkable.[26]

I boarded a train running north on Central Avenue. Jack Tevlin was right. There is a timeless quality to riding the train: the line of people waiting on the platform checking their watches, the smooth glide coming into the station, the rise of activity that comes with the quick exchange of passengers.

But the appearance of Valley Metro's light rail was carefully designed to exude modern. Mass transit seemed incompatible with Phoenix in part because of the public image of transit as something like a trolley or rickety New York subway cars screeching through dank tunnels. Phoenix had no history with transit and, fortunately, light rail advocates did not pretend the short-lived streetcar era held any weight. Opponents had dubbed the project the "trolley folly," so a regurgitation of East Coast train memes was the last thing Tevlin and rail supporters wanted. They wanted to communicate to the valley that transit was about moving forward, not backward.

The resulting stations in the middle of the street were a strange sight, a mirage of what a more urban Phoenix could be. The most notable feature of the stations was their distinctive shelters. Valley Metro had studied where shade fell at certain times of the day and emerged with a sail design that used pieces from the wall and roof to cast shade from all angles. They chose white surfaces that wouldn't absorb heat.

Where I stood on the platform at just about noon, as the temperature approached 90 degrees, the sun shone from overhead, so the sails rendered a spiky shadow over the benches below. Later, during rush hour, when the sun dipped into the horizon, shade duty would shift to the walls of white louvers.

Then there were the smaller touches. Drinking fountains gave the train platforms a Parisian or Roman quality. Vines grew through screens. Bars for leaning against ran along the screens. Lighting was plentiful.

I was standing on an island of comfort in the desert, and being a desert rat, I took no greater pleasure than being in the cool shade looking out into the hot midday landscape. It was rare to have this feeling in an American desert city, in a public space designed just for this purpose.

When the train arrived, it was a rolling relief from the Arizona heat. Each car carried two 5-ton HVAC units. If one city knew how to use air conditioning, and valued spending money to do it, it was Phoenix. When you spread out 4 million people, diverted Colorado River water over three hundred miles, and spent millions of dollars cooling it just so each house can be a refrigerator, that is a questionable investment of the Earth's resources. But it's less objectionable when you're directing those resources into a public space, especially one that collectively transports people in an efficient way.

The Valley Metro Rail system was what urbanism has to be in the desert Southwest: comfortable and concentrated, the exact opposite of what had been there. It seemed to be the one thing in the valley that fearlessly looked forward to Phoenix's urban future rather than the ruins of the twentieth century. It's hard to envision what you have never seen, and when people in most of the West think of cities in their region, they think of the wretched urban fabric that occupies most of the Valley of the Sun.

Valley Metro's light rail provided a concrete alternative vision. Its finery reminded me of what I'd heard of the mahogany and brass of the California Limited, a moving bastion of modern civilization before modern had gone awry. It had planted itself in the middle of the most important street in Phoenix as a permanent fixture in a city that had been built on disposability.

As one Valley Metro staffer told me, "People take better care of nicer things." Fewer, nicer, better things, placed closer together—that was the light rail's message for liberating Phoenix from its anti-city.

A City within Cities

Shortly after Phoenix's light rail opened, a new blog appeared called *RailLife*. *RailLife* had become the chronicler and clearinghouse for Phoenix's new mass transit system. At a basic level, the blog alerted its readers to events happening along the rail line. For example, on the previous Fourth of July, approximately 5,000 people had visited the site to find out about two giant fireworks displays along the light rail, over Tempe Town Lake and on Central Avenue. It promoted events, such as when a church organized eighty women taking light rail to Mill Avenue. One *RailLife* page called "Light Rail Drinks" received hundreds of thousands of hits a year. Like many blogs, it was ostensibly utilitarian but became a touchstone for the burgeoning lifestyle of riding the train to access the region. While some of the blog's committed followers were preexisting transit wonks, it mostly attracted people who just wanted to try out the train and explore the valley in a new way.

That included its author, a valley native named Nick Bastian. Bastian was a real estate agent who, earlier in the decade, had been part of the region's sprawl machine. He specialized in something called contingency management—when homebuyers approached a builder to build their new home, but they had to sell their old house first. Contingency management was a common concern in the valley's real estate market, and Bastian made a living selling yesterday's houses. Buyers traded Tempe for Chandler and Chandler for Apache Junction as they moved farther and farther out.

In the middle of the 2000s, when homebuyers were paying over $250,000 for houses in the outer areas of Queen Creek, a formerly rural city nearly forty miles from downtown Phoenix, Bastian said to himself, "That ain't right." The driving-'til-you-qualify was driving him nuts. He became aware of the hours in the car and the gas expense his clients incurred. Even Bastian, who made a living on the growth, began to question why residents would want to compromise their lifestyles so much for square footage, homeownership, and newness.

Around the same time, Bastian heard about the Valley Metro light rail. Like others in the valley, he enjoyed using transit in cities like New York and San Francisco but never thought about it at home. He vaguely remembered the failure of ValTrans. He did walk and ride his bike to the grocery store and was aware that Arizonans drove too much. In 2004, even as both tax measures were in place, the vision of a train running through Tempe and the rest of the valley struck him as too good to be true. He went online to find out where light rail would go and how much it would cost. He started attending public meetings.

Meanwhile, as blogs spread on the Internet, Bastian was trying to figure out something to write about as a hobby. He didn't necessarily want to write about real estate. Perhaps he could write about light rail. He didn't know much about public transportation. But that, apparently, was what the Valley of the Sun wanted.

I spent much of the afternoon riding the light rail around Phoenix, eventually taking the train to Tempe to meet up with Bastian. The train car was already full of commuters, many of them with bikes hanging on the train's racks. We arced over Tempe Town Lake, a blue clot of dammed water in the otherwise bone-dry Salt River, and I got off at the Mill Avenue station.

I identified Bastian immediately from the picture on his Twitter feed. He was wearing a blue "Tempe Towers" golf shirt, and he was grinning broadly. Bastian's smile was infectious. I had asked him to take me on a light rail pub crawl, even though it was Monday. I didn't have to ask twice. Although he was a virtual guide for thousands of people, he seemed excited to show me around.

We walked south from the station onto Mill Avenue, the heart of ASU's student business district that was in the middle of a boom of new businesses.

"It's a whole different mindset," Bastian said. "As people use it recreationally, they think, 'This isn't so bad, it's not just losers on this train.' People look at the map and plan to go to Hooters, but then they see this other dot, and they say let's check this out. I just think it's cool as hell."

He continued, "For the first few years of the blog, it was people curious about what the light rail was all about. There were some transit geeks, but my audience became more diverse. A lot of people don't want to fight traffic or pay to park. There are rail-gating parties. Some people are like, 'It's cool to be there, but I'm not selling my car.' There's the whole spectrum."

When light rail opened, Bastian found that it led him to parts of the valley he had never been to. He used to visit Phoenix infrequently, maybe for a game every once and a while, and he always drove. He went there and back, that was it; garage to garage to garage. Stopping at other places was inconvenient and defied the inertia of driving. Now he launched full-scale adventures with his three kids, six-year-old twins and a seven-year-old. They went to games, but they'd also go to the Phoenix Public Market or hiking on "A" Mountain, then out to lunch. They'd make unscheduled stops at places they thought looked interesting. Even being on the train was part of the adventure.

Large swaths of the valley had forsaken these places in the heart of the metro area. Phoenix was well known for its nonexistent downtown. But even worse, the downtown that existed was intimidating for suburban residents to drive to. There were one-way streets and tall buildings. There were homeless people. Parking was plentiful but, somehow, it was just easier to go to the chain restaurants at the nearest shopping center than the ones downtown.

Nothing is inherently wrong with staying local. Many New Yorkers are "hood rats," staying within a close distance of their apartment to do everything from laundry to nightlife. But New Yorkers still share common, iconic experiences of the city that bind them together: Central Park, the subway, Times Square, the long shore of Manhattan along the East River. Phoenix had nothing. No shared public experience existed for the region except for freeways and traffic. Many people told me that Phoenicians wanted a downtown, but eventually I came to believe that what they really wanted was a common humane touchstone.

By many accounts, that had begun to happen since the opening of the light rail. People who would normally stay within a few miles of their house in the suburbs were now coming into Phoenix to try restaurants, attend sporting events, or visit a museum or library. Nearly everyone I spoke to in Phoenix had mentioned this. They called it "the exploration"—group after group emerged from the trains with backpacks and water bottles to poke around vintage clothing shops and lunch spots. Arizona Public Interest Research Group interviewed owners of businesses along the light rail line about the impact of the Valley Metro light rail on their businesses and found that not only had light rail created additional foot traffic and visibility, it had prompted curiosity and sales from bases of customers who had never shown an interest before. An owner of a business targeted to Indian customers, for example, reported a spike in non-Indian customers curious about his business specifically because of light rail trips. A jewelry store owner spoke of patrons taking light rail "just to see what's out there." These new urban explorers were not just college students and barflies but families and senior citizens.[27]

Light rail planners did not expect such explorations. MAG undertook the modeling to forecast light rail ridership and, like many regional agencies, it assumed that most of the system's ridership would occur on the commute. MAG believed a modest number of valley residents, both existing transit riders and new riders, would commute on light rail, and this would drive the ridership.

The models did not emphasize other trips, such as a resident of a rail-adjacent neighborhood riding to a restaurant in Tempe or a resident parking at Christown Mall and riding to a Suns game. Yet many of these trips occurred every day in the valley. Valley Metro had seen people come into what it called "the transit fold." They were starting, as Nick Bastian described, to think about transit in a new way. It was fitting that in a city built on leisure, those riding for fun would drive the transit system. Slowly, light rail had become a venue for collective experiences in a region that had grown used to fragmented ones.

Bastian was telling me that Mill Avenue was undergoing a change parallel to the rise of light rail, whereby local businesses were beginning to displace the chains that had taken hold. People were coming from all over the valley on the train to try new local businesses.

Bastian wanted to check out a new pizza restaurant on our walk. He looked at his smartphone and located the spot.

"Like this pizza place, guys taking a chance," he said, walking in.

Inside the restaurant, Bastian's large smile drew the owner's attention.

"We just opened," the owner said. "We're trying to orient the place to all the increasing foot traffic. Kitchen's open to the sidewalk."

"Nice," Bastian said.

We each got a slice and kept walking. Bastian checked in on Foursquare and Twitter. He had 5,000 followers on Twitter. People were already asking him about the new pizza place.

"Nick how is that new pizza place on Mill?" one tweet said.

"It doesn't suck!" Bastian wrote.

We got back on the train, rode east toward Mesa, and got off at the McClintock stop, out on Apache Boulevard. While Mill Avenue had always been a walking street geared to the university, Apache was a suburban wasteland. But in the last five years, six-story apartment buildings had risen around the rail stops to house ASU students. These were classic Arizona fun-and-sun party shacks, with twenty-four-hour concierges, free tanning, and rooftop terraces with drains for spilled keg beer. But they were transit-oriented development just the same, giving the valley a better version of itself.

We visited two more bars, a renovated dive at McClintock that had a buy-one-Pabst-get-one-free special and a brewpub off the "A" Mountain stop. As our pub crawl wrapped up, Bastian told me he liked to call the light rail a "city within cities"—a parallel universe stretching across the boundaries of Phoenix, Tempe, and Mesa, and eventually other municipalities, that offered a fundamentally different way of living in the Valley of the Sun. If you're in the city within cities, he pointed out, you can do everything via train. Like I had discovered in Salt Lake, getting out of the car and into a train, onto a bike, and on your feet changed your perception of the world around you; the city within cities showed us that it opened up more possibilities, too.

I headed to the Mill Avenue station, rode back to downtown Phoenix, and walked to Chase Field. I bought a ticket for a Diamondbacks game against the Phillies and spent the next few hours relaxing in the climate-controlled wonder of the ballpark.

After the game, people flowed out of the stadium to the train. I sat next to a sixties-ish couple from Cave Creek, north of Scottsdale. The man carried a baseball mitt and told me the train was faster than driving to the stadium.

"It hasn't let us down yet," he said.

Next to them was a rough-looking, wild-eyed man bouncing around the car ranting about NASA. The Cave Creek couple remained stone-faced. A collective experience indeed.

The Ball Boy

Nick Bastian didn't live on the light rail line, as people were surprised to find out, but many others chose to live in the city within cities. They wanted to use the light rail to invent a completely different place than the disposable, fragmented, over-leveraged, and just all-around cheap one that had been built.

In 1996 a thirteen-year old named Aaron Kimberlin found himself wandering through the empty streets of downtown Phoenix among the warehouses around the railroad tracks. The Phoenix Suns basketball team had just built its new arena there, but little else drew people to the growing city's withering core.

Even then, Phoenix and the surrounding region realized that it had lost its downtown and desperately wanted it back. Developers who wanted to build there were scarce because they were all spreading the same subdivisions over suburbs like Chandler, where Kimberlin's family had lived since the 1970s.

He enjoyed growing up in Chandler. It felt protected, and he could be carefree. There was nothing challenging about it, even if it felt a little vanilla. His life was hanging out at home and going to the nearest strip malls with friends.

They drove everywhere. There was nowhere to bike and nowhere to walk because everything was so spread out. Taking public transportation was unheard of among Kimberlin and his friends. Glimpsing one of the mostly empty buses felt strange, that poor people got around that way. If you didn't have a car in Chandler, you were nobody.

He had been an enormous Suns fan since he was six. His dad had season tickets through his job. They would drive to games at Veterans Memorial Coliseum in the inner suburbia of McDowell and 15th Avenue, but the team had moved downtown into the brand-new America West Arena in 1992. It was a good time to be a Suns fan: they had Charles Barkley and Kevin Johnson and during the 1993 NBA Finals had taken Michael Jordan and the Chicago Bulls to six games. In 1996 they drafted an unknown point guard named Steve Nash, who would capture back-to-back league MVPs in the 2000s.

It happened that Kimberlin's brother-in-law knew the Suns trainer and was able to get him a job as a ball boy. He worked for free for two-and-a-half years. Until he learned to drive, his parents drove him back and forth between Chandler and downtown Phoenix.

One of Kimberlin's jobs involved fetching meals for players and their families. The restaurants he frequented lay within two or three blocks, but he often found himself wandering beyond this radius to the empty streets and old buildings. He recognized that sports teams played perhaps the most important role in the public's enjoyment of downtown, that the empty central business district didn't serve much purpose. He had visited the bustling downtowns of San Francisco and Chicago, so he knew what was possible in a city core. He kept wondering how Phoenix could create a place where people wanted to go.

When Kimberlin started college at Arizona State, he majored in urban planning because of all his evenings wandering around deserted downtown Phoenix. Downtown had begun to change; ASU had built its downtown campus on Central Avenue, where he took some of his courses.

During one of Kimberlin's classes, the mayor of Tempe had given a presentation about the effort to build light rail in the valley. Kimberlin was still of a mind that mass transit didn't belong in Phoenix or Tempe or any other valley city. He wondered why cities would build the system if it would benefit 1 percent of the valley's population and go just 30 miles per hour. He posed this question to the mayor.

The mayor told him that the train was about much more than just moving people. It was economic development. It was public space. It was the revitalization Kimberlin had craved as a kid. Light rail began to become part of the downtown Phoenix of his mind's eye.

Kimberlin moved to Chicago to get a masters degree in urban planning and to live in a real city. He rode the "L" and explored the city on the train and on foot. He noticed how Chicago was different than Phoenix. Chicago got things done, and its strong mayor system and aldermen truly represented their districts. It had neighborhoods with identities and frequent block parties. In Phoenix, Kimberlin realized, people never even went outside.

At this point, the strange connection between Phoenix and Chicago must be noted. All over Phoenix I ran into people from Chicago or who had family from Chicago.[28] It was one of the major corridors on another of America's great migrations: the white flight out of the Midwest's frigid cities to the Sunbelt. The two cities had as little in common as is imaginable within the United States, yet they were strangely linked. But instead of bringing great traditions with them, as America's other swaths of migrants had done, new residents put their cars in the garage and turned up the AC.

Kimberlin put a twist on the tiresome pattern. Despite how much he appreciated and enjoyed Chicago, he always intended to return to Arizona. He came from Phoenix to Chicago, and then brought the inspiration of that great city back with him. He moved back in 2009, as the Great Recession settled in, his home state one of its most devastated victims. He had trouble finding work. He lived in a suburb while working three part-time jobs and networking. He temped as a housing development specialist, then as support staff for multifamily affordable housing. He worked briefly for a developer.

Meanwhile, the light rail that Kimberlin had scorned in 2003 had become reality. He compared it positively to the "L": it was clean and there were not a lot of weird people on it. He thought that the light rail would someday be a key component of the revitalization of downtown Phoenix.

At about the same time, Valley Metro undertook a survey of some 15,000 transit riders and found that, by-and-large, they were much like Aaron Kimberlin. They were much younger than four years earlier, pre-train. University students made up the largest group of riders. Light rail riders were, like Kimberlin, overwhelmingly riding by choice and to save money in the heart of the recession.

When I talked to Metro's CEO, Steve Banta, over the phone before my trip, he mentioned that his twenty-four-year-old son, who lived in Portland, refused to get his driver's license. "The younger generation, they work to live. His mind works different than mine," Banta said. "It's the freedom. He doesn't have to get a license, he doesn't have to get insurance. I always say to him, 'You should get your license, just in case.' When gas prices went up, he said, 'I'm pretty smart, huh?' And I run a transit agency."

———————————

One of Kimberlin's part-time jobs was as a barista at the Phoenix Public Market. The market had just opened next to the downtown ASU campus because of an activist from Chicago named Cindy Gentry. She often joked about the impermanence of Phoenix, that after thirty-five years in the valley, she was thinking about staying. She remarked that Chicagoans carried such strong identities with their city and their neighborhoods. In Phoenix she noticed that these connections were much weaker. You got in and out of your car in your driveway and went right into your house. It was that way where Gentry lived, in northeast Phoenix, just like in most parts of the valley. Changing this situation was at the front of Gentry's mind when she started the market.

The market began as an extension of Gentry's organization, a nonprofit called Community Food Connections that sought to keep farmers on the land, increase access to food for the poor, and help small businesses. The owner of the property on Central Avenue let the group use the parking lot for a market if it paid his property taxes. She renovated a small storefront next to it.

As soon as it opened, the market became a hub for the increasing number of valley natives who, like Aaron Kimberlin, hated the suburbs and were moving to central Phoenix. Like in many American downtowns, Phoenix had no downtown grocery store for almost twenty years. It would be a stretch to call the Phoenix Public Market a grocery store, but it was a destination just the same, a kernel of a neighborhood anchor.[29]

The market's spot on Central lay between two light rail stops. Gentry liked light rail because it became the connector of the smatterings of small local businesses and art venues opening downtown. Like the train, the market was a major enabler of the lifestyle that many of Phoenix's young natives wanted, and the two became simpatico. In the two years the store was open before the light rail, it struggled, employing one full-time and one part-time person.

Once the train got rolling, so did the market. Two to three thousand people came to the outdoor market on Saturdays, each year bigger than the one before. By 2011 the market employed fifteen people. It was just one example of how light rail shaped a business's location decision; up and down the corridor were restaurants, ethnic malls, stores, and galleries that invested in their property specifically in anticipation of the train.[30]

To Aaron Kimberlin and others moving downtown, these businesses and the light rail that connected them were everything the valley where they grew up was not. They were locally owned, interesting, connected, and not financially overleveraged. They were authentic. And at the center was ditching the car. Many of Gentry's customers walked to the market. Most of her staff biked. On Saturdays, she saw sixty bikes locked to any piece of metal while people poured in from the Valley Metro Rail stops. Certainly, this was still a stark minority of the valley's residents, but now they had an option to live this way, and their ranks were growing.

For Kimberlin, working at the market allowed him to create a new community in his old home. Through good networking, he landed a job at the Phoenix Urban Research Laboratory at ASU. He didn't waste any time moving to central Phoenix, right next to the light rail.

When I met up with Kimberlin the next morning to ride to work with him, he had just moved into 800 square feet of living space in a red brick 1920s bungalow in the historic Willo neighborhood, a few miles north of downtown, just off Central Avenue. He had just walked out the front door onto the shady street and his tall thin frame was unmistakable, especially because he was dressed impressively in a white dress shirt with a red collar and bow tie, tight brown pants that displayed his long legs, and pointy shoes.

The 800 square feet, the size of most Phoenicians' garages, was double what he had in his last place, in the same neighborhood. He wanted to convert his garage into more living space. He planned to fix up the kitchen, trading his labor for credit against his rent. He had learned how to fix up houses from his dad, who had a shop in their house in Chandler.

"It's living within my means," he said.

He told me the story behind the bow tie as we walked to the train station. He had started his own cottage industry finding old ties and turning them into bow ties. He called his business Dapper and Dash. He told me how architects in the old days had preferred bow ties because regular ties would smear their drawings as they hunched over them. So he packaged the ties in the kind of tubes that held architectural drawings. The blue and brown diagonal-striped tie he was wearing happened to have been made by Goldwaters department store in the 1950s, the paragon of midcentury Phoenix. Dapper and Dash was emblematic of Kimberlin's entire economic philosophy. He hated the cheapness of his city and exuded a real anger about the economic values of his forebears. He was close to his parents, but he did not necessarily want to live the same way their generation did.

"Phoenix was giving away land," he said. "The Phoenix economy was all land sales. You sold high. You're not getting that anymore, so what's left?"

What was left was a lot of bank-owned property in the suburbs and unemployed people, but many people like Kimberlin were trying to do the exact opposite of everything that had put the valley in its sad predicament. The urban lifestyle he experienced in Chicago—living in proximity, not overextending, living simply—resonated deeply with him, and he didn't see a reason he couldn't continue to live like this in Phoenix. Kimberlin thought that, having been molded in the Great Recession, people his age had received a formative lesson in the value of things. So he salvaged the value of old ties and made them new again.

To him, the light rail, which took us two minutes to reach, fit perfectly with this worldview and, perhaps in Phoenix, had begun to provide a hefty frame for it. It was for the freedom of the automobile that many of the grisly compromises that had sunk Phoenix had been made.

The way Kimberlin saw it, life was difficult and the light rail was simple, a clean line to creating a new city. He had even convinced his parents to move downtown because his dad would have a ten-minute walk to work.

To change cities away from car dependence, the first step is to enable the people who want to live a different lifestyle to live it. That's what the Valley Metro light rail had done.

━━━━━━━━━━━━━━━━━━

The ex-Chicagoans that pervaded Phoenix couldn't help but compare their city of broad shoulders to the Valley of the Sun. Aaron Kimberlin made these comparisons, but he took a different perspective than most. He pointed out a basic difference between Chicago and Phoenix: in Chicago everything finds you and in Phoenix you have to find things. But that gave Phoenix its charm. It was like going in a restaurant though the back door.

After we got off the train at the Van Buren stop, where I had stood with Jack Tevlin the day before, we passed an example of what he was talking about, an old building advertising "AE England & Motors Inc—1926." It was Arizona's first car dealership and had been converted into an event space.

The office where Kimberlin worked was also in a rare prewar building, a Deco-era skyscraper. The top floor was bathed in sunlight because in the horizontal world of Phoenix, there weren't many buildings taller than it.

Kimberlin was investigating whether it would be possible for 30 percent of the valley's new growth to be accommodated within walking distance of light rail stations. He now saw the light rail as bettering the community in multiple ways: as mobility for thousands of people, as an investment in urban vibrancy, as the pride of a city, and as a shaper of the future growth of the valley.

To someone like Aaron Kimberlin, I'd ask, why not stay in Chicago? Why not move to Portland? Why stay in Phoenix, viewed by many prominent urbanists as doomed to fail and wither in the sands of time and climate change?

"The vacant lots," Kimberlin answered. "Here it's fight or flight, and I choose to fight. People are either really committed or they leave. I see the potential of something that could be huge. You go to San Francisco, New York City, those places have already been established. They already have their people. Here it's about youth. There are a lot of smart young people here, people my age, working on making Phoenix more vibrant. The city can reinvent itself if it wants. I feel connected to Phoenix because of the potential."

Evaluations of American cities are often made with the assumption that US metros are like a menu of places that one can choose to live in. And for many rootless Americans, this is true. But there's another perspective, for those tied to their hometowns but not entirely satisfied with them. Phoenix was home for Kimberlin and millions of others, and to them it was fixable.

We walked out onto a marvelous terrace outside Kimberlin's office that faced north over downtown. "It's the 1950s all over again," he said. "I want to build."

The Changing of the Guard

One of the "smart young people" Kimberlin was referring to was the City of Phoenix's light rail station area planner, a thirty-two-year-old named Curt Upton. Like Kimberlin, Upton was a valley native and had a similarly interesting urban awakening. One day in college, he approached an intersection with a green light on Camelback Road in Scottsdale. At the same time, another driver was approaching the intersection from a perpendicular direction, into a red light. The driver, another teenager, drove into the intersection at the same time as Upton. Upton's head went through the windshield, but the windshield was ejected from the car, so he only received a few lacerations. Upton spent his settlement check on a trip to Europe. While he was there, the overriding thoughts going though his mind were "These are real cities" and "Why isn't my city like this?"

There were several deeply entrenched and depressing reasons, as Upton found out when he became a city planner. The biggest one had almost killed him: the car. Yet light rail had been built. It was popular. It had drawn suburbanites out of their walled subdivisions and into the city within cities of the light rail line. It had fortified an alternative way of living in Phoenix.

But even with people shifting away from driving to riding transit and walking, several obstacles stood in the way of changing the landscape of the city. If Phoenix wanted to get the most out of light rail, it needed to completely rethink how it approached regulating the environment around the train stations.

This was Upton's job. As we walked up Central Avenue later that morning, he explained that Phoenix had one of the most over-parked downtowns in the nation.[31] Parking had been free and plentiful since the city realized it needed to compete with the suburbs to have a chance of survival. Phoenix had required developers to build one space per 300 square feet of floor area for most commercial uses, a ratio closer to what would be required for a suburban shopping center. A 2006 study found that downtown Phoenix possessed nearly 10,000 more parking spaces than it needed.[32] We passed the downtown Arizona State campus, where a football-field-sized surface parking lot on Central Avenue symbolized the prevalence of parking.

A vast supply of free parking at popular destinations is a good way to discourage people from riding your transit system. The city had tried to remedy the parking problem by reducing parking minimum requirements by over three times. It allowed flexibility. It allowed, as Upton said, the market to take care of it. It instituted maximums. It allowed shared parking.

Other hidden maladies also festered. Along Central Avenue, we saw huge vacant lots along the street where it seemed like buildings should be, as this was some of the most visible high-value property in the valley. But these lots were an obstacle, not an opportunity. In the 1970s, as the city's central business district was creeping northward, city leaders envisioned a high-rise corridor along Central so they zoned it for 300-foot heights. As Upton explained, "We wanted to be the biggest and best of everything."

So property owners engaged in a winless game of holding out for higher land prices. In Maricopa County, property tax rates were set entirely by the value of the improvement rather than the land itself, so taxes remained low for property owners holding onto their vacant lots. These rules were practically written for land speculation. Upton estimated that central Phoenix had a one-hundred-year supply of vacant land zoned for high-rises.

The fallout was distrust and fear from the neighbors living on either side of the corridor. The city had not only allowed high-rises to come in against their single-story neighborhoods, they had created a situation where huge vacant lots could remain for decades. Upton remembered hearing the urbanist Andrés

Duany telling Phoenicians that they sold two things: lots and views. There was no in-between.

We arrived at a development named Roosevelt Square, which had successfully combated both problems and had become a symbol of a different urban path for Phoenix. Roosevelt Square was in-between: a four-story U-shaped building wrapped around a hidden parking garage consisting of mostly apartments, with a few commercial spaces on the ground floor. It was tall, but not too tall, and its friendly frontage complemented the light rail station across the street. It was similar to the Vallagio I saw in suburban Denver. Phoenix urbanists agreed that this was what was missing from the city; perhaps it would create the community that slipped through the cracks between the lots and the views.

Roosevelt Square was the type of project that made an outsider like myself ask, why aren't there more of these? But I already knew the answer. These projects were very difficult in most places in the United States, which made them extra tough in Phoenix, with its onerous parking expectations and zoning and tax structures geared toward land speculation.

Upton thought that perhaps the biggest challenge was that Phoenix didn't have any urban neighborhoods. Like with light rail itself, it was difficult to sell investors on a vision of something that didn't exist. Upton explained the gymnastics Roosevelt Square performed to clear these obstacles.

But Curt Upton was much more interested in something more unique to Phoenix than replicas of the same mixed-use developments that were rising in central cities across America—modern architecture. Midcentury modern was Phoenix's golden era, especially along Central Avenue, which had been the showcase of the latest automobile models cruising down its wide lanes.

"People automatically write Phoenix off because it doesn't have much prewar building stock," Upton said. "But there is enormous potential to reuse modern buildings. You don't look at those buildings and think urbanism, but in Phoenix you have to."

We were across from a building that was far out. It was officially named the Phoenix Financial Center but was better known as the "Punchcard Building," for the pattern of tiny windows staggering up its facade. It also inspired allusions to the Jetsons.

"Those round buildings, they look like wedding cakes," he said, pointing to another building with a For Lease sign in its window. "Wouldn't they be great as nightclubs?"

The irony that Upton wanted to take buildings designed for the auto age and rebuild them for walkers and transit was not lost on him. "They're not pedestrian-friendly but they can overcome that," he said. He pointed to a glass curtain wall across the street and hypothesized that taking the glass out of the first floor would yield a nice shady arcade.

Upton's interest in adaptive reuse was driven by his wariness with Phoenix's culture of disposability. The process of real estate development had burned Phoenix too many times. The natives looked to cut bait and reuse what they had to solve the problems of creating a city around its new transit system. They were tired of disposing their buildings to build new ones, even if they were being told again that *No, really! These ones are better than the ones before.*

Part of the appeal of transit to Upton was a reason to build a better version of Phoenix's unique self, not a copy of every other American city rediscovering its downtown and building condos around its new light rail system. That, he worried, would just result in the same placelessness and chain dominance that he and everyone else his age hated about their hometown.

Plus, there was just something optimistic and forward-looking about Phoenix's midcentury buildings. They had attitude and verve. That those doing the looking forward fifty years ago were plumb wrong was beside the point. It was the idea of looking forward to a modern life free of the constraints of the past. That was why Jack Tevlin wanted the system to look modern too. Modern was not only Phoenix's future, it was also its past.

Upton's favorite example of the pedestrianization of modern Phoenix was a restaurant called the St. Francis, which took its name from the neighborhood around it. The restaurant owners had taken most of the building's parking spaces in front and turned them into a patio and opened up the facades for that Arizonan Ranch–style blend of inside and outside.

To the city planner in Upton, it was the perfect blend of private initiative with a little help from the public sector; the city had reduced the parking requirement by 50 percent. That was a benefit of being a property rights town, where the government usually let people do what they want.

"If you multiply this, you get an authentic place," Curt said. "It's pent-up demand for something authentic and not a chain."

As Aaron Kimberlin had said, you have to go looking for things in Phoenix. As we walked along Camelback Avenue, Upton pointed to buildings I would have dismissed as strip malls but were actually interesting independent businesses, slowly converting car space to people space.

We'd been walking for miles. I checked my phone. The temperature was 103 degrees. The air conditioning of the light rail really sounded enticing, and I suggested we catch a train. Upton had to get back anyway. We walked to the nearest stop, at an old streetcar turn at Central and Camelback.

I went straight for the drinking fountain. I quaffed at the fountain at every train station. Upton drank no water, like a camel.

"I'm a native," he said. "But I underestimate the heat. Every year in September I question why I live here because of the heat."

I told him it was 103.

"That's nothing," he said and kept walking.

<hr/>

The guard was changing in the neighborhoods along the light rail too. Long wary of the lots-and-views dynamic, neighborhoods felt lorded over by Phoenix's real estate mess and guarded themselves against any high density. Curt Upton had just worked with four neighborhoods around Central and Camelback that feared the worst with the coming of light rail but had agreed that the mid-rise type of development would be OK.

In Aaron Kimberlin's Willo neighborhood, neighbors were making a similar transformation. I got off the train at the same stop where Kimberlin and I had boarded and walked a few blocks to the center of the neighborhood to meet with Brad Brauer, Willo's neighborhood association president.

Brauer had come to Phoenix to attend ASU and then had stayed because "You don't have to shovel sunshine." We walked along the pleasant sidewalks. Willo looked like a classic L.A. bungalow neighborhood. It always stunned me how, unlike Tucson and other Sonoran cities, Phoenix yards had grass, like they were pretending not to be in a desert. Brauer was a realtor, so he knew a lot about what was going on with the houses. He deemed most of Phoenix a "garagescape" whose biggest implication was that you never got to know your neighbors. Willo was different. He had lived in Willo for eight years and described his neighbors as "so amazing, so not Phoenix." When he moved in, neighbors had brought over cookies and exchanged phone numbers.

Still, like many Phoenix neighborhoods, Willo feared mass transit. In the 1980s, when the ValTrans plan had floated around the valley, Willo residents only saw the incursion of traffic and made the city agree to build gates at the entries to their neighborhood.

On the night of the 2004 election, Brauer was on a cruise in the Atlantic Ocean, checking the voting on the Internet. It blew him away that Arizonans— whose cars you had to pry from their cold, dead hands—voted for light rail.

Now, Willo and Valley Metro Rail were good with one another. Brauer saw his neighbors on the Central Avenue light rail platform where he never saw them on Central before. That past week, friends had come in from Mesa, and they had all walked to the station and rode it to Roosevelt and had dinner. It wasn't a novelty. They were all used to it. Brauer considered it a paradigm shift.

"Once you ride it, you realize you're not just riding with homeless people, which is what people on the outside think," he said.

We walked out to Central Avenue, where restaurants were beginning to fill in the anonymous facades between the skyscrapers and empty lots.

Sometimes, Brauer said, "you don't want all these people here. But that's what you're supposed to do, concentrate everything. Central Avenue is supposed to be a high-density area."

━━━━━━━━━━━━━━━

I rode back up Central to Camelback to look for some lunch and ended up emerging at a Rolberto's Taco Shop. Cars flowed by on both sides of the A-frame building, but the place had a window in front where people could order food.

"Man! That looks good," said a fiftyish white guy who was the only other pedestrian within sight. He was pointing to one of the meal photographs on the counter window. He was wearing a New Jersey Devils hat and bright neon green shoelaces on his sneakers. "These 'Berto's are all over the place now. I think it started with Filiberto's. Then it was Alberto's. Now it's Rolberto's!"

We were competing with the heavy stream of drive-through traffic for attention. Three Latino guys were eating at a picnic table under an awning.

I ordered two shredded beef tacos and took them to go, eating as I walked. On Camelback, I took a right, back toward the light rail station at Central. I passed a taco place in an old drive-through with shaded tables in the old parking lot, an architectural office with a decorative concrete paver parking lot and a midcentury modern furniture store. Amid the Rolberto's and other drive-throughs on Central, Camelback, and every other big Phoenix street, I never would have noticed the shops if I hadn't been walking slowly through the Sonoran heat. You had to find things in Phoenix.

A Nice Ride

As reluctant as I was to leave the city within cities, I needed to go somewhere that was not on the light rail line—at least not yet. Glendale City Hall was eight-and-a-half miles from where I was at Camelback and Central. Glendale, an inner suburb adjacent to the City of Phoenix, was scheduled to receive one of the next light rail extensions, but as the valley's fiscal situation worsened, the extension kept extending into the future.

For now, to get to Glendale on transit, I would need to take two buses—one along each of the township and range grid's x and y coordinates—up 19th to Glendale Avenue and west to downtown Glendale. At 19th and Montebello, I stepped out of the Metro's desert oasis and into the hellish Sunbelt urban inferno of most of the rest of the valley.

I waited for awhile at a shelter in the Christown Mall parking lot, but after talking with some youths, I learned I should wait at the shelter on 19th Avenue. I walked across the lot to the other shelter, and the 19 actually came quickly and was quite full.

At the next shelter I encountered a group of people waiting for the same bus as me. It was the 70, the trunk line for Glendale Avenue, one of the city's most popular routes. After waiting for fifteen minutes I told a white-haired woman with two enormous bags of KFC that the bus was ten minutes late.

"Par for the course," she harrumphed.

Her name was Alice, and she lived near 35th Avenue. She used to work for the Arizona Department of Transportation. She was originally from Philadelphia, where "the buses ran all the time, and you didn't even need to think about it. They even ran in the snow." She was bringing the chicken home to her roommate.

"I just want to get home while my coleslaw's still cold," Alice said. In Phoenix, you didn't worry about your food getting cold, you worried about it getting hot.

I asked Alice if she ever took the light rail.

"I have, but it doesn't take me where I want to go," she said. "It goes through the nice part of town. It hits the highlights."

Another man at the stop overheard our conversation and added pointedly, "It doesn't benefit everybody."

"But it's a nice ride," Alice said.

The bus showed up, and we got on. This bus was completely packed. It was 2:30 in the afternoon. It reminded me that we were in the fourteenth-largest metro area in the nation, and even if it was the most car-centric, tens of thousands of people lived here who couldn't afford cars and needed transit. They took it regardless of the slick appeal of the light rail or the bump and grind of this bus I was on.

It was standing room only for Alice and me. We were smooshed against a row of seats. I asked her if she had a car.

"I used to," Alice said. "I was in an accident three years ago and totaled it. I didn't want to go through buying a new one. I take the bus, and if it doesn't take me where I need to go, then I have four kids that can take me." She smiled ruefully. "If they can't, then I have a problem."

Alice got off at the 35th Avenue stop. I continued to marvel at how crowded and unpleasant this bus was.

It was on rides like this where the 1 percent argument of light rail opponents began to seep into my thoughts. Despite the attraction of suburbanites driving to the park-and-rides and the exceeded ridership expectations, when you got out of the train's range, you realized how much of the valley saw the smooth air-conditioned light rail as a glimmer of Oz in the distance.

The vision of Valley Metro recognized the sprawl of the valley. The 2004 measure was projected to pay for several extensions, making more of a complete regional network, like the Wasatch Front's rail network in Utah. By 2032 the train was supposed to run fifty-nine miles into all corners of the city, reaching the western and northern ends of Phoenix, Glendale in the northwest, Paradise Valley in the northeast, and further into Mesa on the far east. Then came the Great Recession and the decline in public revenue. Cities like Glendale never had a decline in sales tax until this recession. Annual sales tax in the city fell from $391 million in 2007 to $290 million in 2011.[33]

Meanwhile, many might argue the real transit need in the valley isn't taking suburbanites to baseball games or satisfying the lifestyle desires of middle-class millennials who choose to ride but instead comfortably transporting people who are dependent on transit. South Phoenix, for example, the city's poorest area, had barely received a whiff of light rail attention; Valley Metro was just beginning an analysis of alternatives for mass transit on the Central Avenue corridor through south Phoenix. Riding on the 70 bus through mile after mile of dense suburbia told me that transit still had a long, long way to go in the Valley of the Sun.

Glendale agreed. It was one of the original four cities to join Valley Metro Rail, and the other three had light rail trains running though their towns. Glendale had been paying for the system, and yet it came nowhere near the city's limits.

I arrived at city hall a half-hour late for my appointment with Jamsheed Mehta, the city's transportation director. I wasted no time blaming it on the bus. Mehta, was floored that I would even think of taking the bus to Glendale from central Phoenix. I told him about my road trip.

He could relate. "Light rail now is like an expedition," Mehta said. Like Alice, he recognized it as a nice ride, but it served little utility for most of Glendale's residents, who didn't go to baseball games or happy hours.

Mehta called Glendale a "transition city," located between Phoenix and its suburbs. This meant that it wasn't the exciting new center city downtown and it wasn't the brand-new suburbs. It was yesterday's news. It was exactly what you didn't want to be in a Sunbelt metro like Phoenix. It also meant that every day it bore a disproportionate level of traffic traveling on its freeways and arterials between jobs in Phoenix and Tempe and the exurbs of the West Valley.

Glendale's struggle to realize its planned light rail extension illuminated another lurking problem facing Valley Metro Rail. The starter line worked largely because it leveraged almost all of the valley's major urban activity centers. The planned extensions had far fewer of these. The extensions would be less glamorous workhorses that transported commuters.

Yet corridors like Glendale Avenue clearly demonstrated the need for better transit. The city had just finished a study that cemented its decision to route its light rail extension along Glendale Avenue, mostly to serve the need of the transit-dependent people riding with me on the 70 bus, a more blue-collar modus operandi than the starter line's, but one that would likely result in major ridership. But such a vision was far away for Glendale.

"It was 2017, then 2019, 2021, now we're shooting for 2025 or '26," Mehta said. I asked him if the city was frustrated.

"It took a lot of political courage to do this," Mehta said, "and we don't even get the benefit?"

I worked my way back to Phoenix as the workday ended. Traffic was a mess. Congestion still hadn't changed how valley governments thought about roadway improvements. But the poor economy had also led the Arizona Department of Transportation and MAG to put one I-10 widening project on hold. It was just not worth it to add the lane, and MAG held out hope that a future light rail project could accommodate the demand. Grand Avenue, a diagonal road built along an old Santa Fe rail line running from downtown Phoenix northwest to old downtown Glendale and beyond was slated to be a new freeway, which would cost over $1 billion, with large community impacts. MAG urged others to consider building transit instead. At least now, with a living example of a train breezing through the valley, it was a conversation. It had proven worth it to consider transit.

Aaron Kimberlin and I had made a plan to meet for a drink at the end of the day. He texted me where we'd be meeting, a place on 3rd Street called the Roosevelt. The bar was in a converted brick bungalow, the kind of old building Kimberlin loved. When I got there, he was sitting at the bar talking to the owner, who he knew. His bow tie still looked immaculate.

"I had my twenty-sixth birthday here," Kimberlin said. "A lot of friends saw it for the first time and then they became regulars."

Some of them were friends from his college days who had landed jobs with construction companies in 2006 when they graduated from ASU. They bought houses and cars. Now practically all of it was gone: laid-off, fore-closed, repossessed.

As it happened, my Utah Jazz were playing the Suns in Salt Lake that night. I had wanted to watch the game with Kimberlin, but it was on late and he had somewhere to be. He suggested I go to a sports bar downtown called Majerle's, owned by legendary Sun "Thunder" Dan Majerle, who I remembered as a vicious Jazz killer. Before we parted ways, I asked him who was his favorite Sun.

"Nash," he said, "then Charles Barkley."

<hr/>

Phoenix showed me how freedom in the modern West wasn't built on the disconnection, monoculture, and disposability of the anti-city—and defi-nitely not on the automobiles that created it—but on the quality, richness, and connections of the city. I saw how these things had liberated the West before, in frontier communities and the crafted experience of passenger trains. And I saw how trains, once again, are liberating the West.

The road beckoned. In the next segment of the trip I would explore the sole reason many came to the West: adventure. It, too, had come under the cloud of auto dependence, and I'd see how getting out of our cars was reclaiming personal drama in the western landscape.

The next morning I took the Metro back to Sky Harbor. I wasn't getting on Greyhound and I wasn't getting on a plane. I was renting a car.

I had come to redraw my mental map of Phoenix through the city within cities of the Metro, and even the bus lines. I was used to getting around the city on trains and buses, so its freeways were a new game for me. They seemed like a maze.

I drove back to my motel, picked up my bike and gear, and selected Grand Avenue as my route out of town, a diagonal arrow pointing toward the Sonoran Desert. Grand provided a transect of Phoenix's tree rings: its small downtown, inner-ring suburbs, midcentury suburbs, Sun City, and brand-new exurb of Surprise with its Trader Joe's and new mall.

I hit a brief traffic jam right at the final edge of the Valley of the Sun's urbanization, where cars mysteriously stacked up on a Wednesday morning, and then I was free.

Notes

1. Kristi Arellano, "SE Colo. Reeling As More Jobs Cut," *Denver Post*, November 17, 2005 and Joe Zemba, "BCCF Will Remain Open," *La Junta Tribune-Democrat*, July 1, 2013.

2. David Lavender, *Bent's Fort* (Lincoln: University of Nebraska Press, 1954), 196.

3. Ibid., 182.

4. Steve Glischinski, *Santa Fe Railway* (Osceola, WI: MBI Publishing, 1997), 11–12.

5. Ibid., 16.

6. The story of Walter Scott is adapted from ibid., 32–33.

7. Bradford Luckingham, *Phoenix: The History of a Southwestern Metropolis* (Tucson: University of Arizona Press, 1989), 210, 161.

8. Ibid., 9.

9. Ibid., 19–20.

10. Ibid., 52, 49.

11. From just over 100,000 to over 439,000. Ibid., 153.

12. Ibid., 151.

13. Ibid., 156.

14. Ibid., 168.

15. Ibid., 90.

16. Phoenix was receiving \$10 million annually from the federal government by 1937. Ibid., 104.

17. "Stretched To the Limits: Still Driving to Qualify After the Housing Crisis," October 22, 2010, transcript, Blueprint America, produced by Fac Moore, http://www.pbs.org/wnet/blueprintamerica/reports/profiles-from-the-recession/video-stretched-to-the-limits-still-driving-to-qualify-after-the-housing-crisis/?p=1138.

18. "Phoenix: Light Rail Opens, Ridership Soars," Light Rail Now Project, last modified February 2009, http://www.lightrailnow.org/news/n_phx_2009 02a.htm.

19. Yes, \$1,400,000,000/45,000 = \$31,111.11. The sticker price of a new Prius starts at \$24,200. But in thirty years, the Priuses would be in a scrap heap while the light rail will still be moving 45,000 or more people a day and will likely have helped to reshape the central piece of the Phoenix metro area for the better.

20. Warren Meyer, "Urban Light Rail Fail," *Forbes*, last modified September 22, 2010, http://blogs.forbes.com/warrenmeyer/2010/09/22/urban-light-rail-fail/.

21. How sustainable is heating New York City all winter or piping drinking water to 7 million holier-than-thou Bay Area denizens through the earthquake-prone Sacramento River Delta?

22. Against Tevlin's wishes, the city presented the benefits of transit to Phoenix as relieving congestion and cleaning up the air. These were good objectives, but

Tevlin had studied transit long enough to know that transit does not singlehandedly solve congestion and air quality. His preferred message would have been "creating more options for people for transportation." The day before the vote, the governor asked the heads of ADOT and the Air Quality Division of the state Department of Environmental Quality to hold a joint press conference urging Phoenicians to vote "no" on transit. The credibility of the congestion and air quality messages was put in question. The day after the election there was an inversion. The LED message signs along the freeways read, "Air Quality Alert—Use Carpool or Bus."

23. The opposition's primary argument was that only 1 percent of valley residents would use transit. They had derived this number by dividing Maricopa County's current transit ridership by the county's population. Tevlin couldn't argue with that number, but he thought that to evaluate potential light rail ridership, one had to focus on the corridors that already had good transit service and provided a real option. He told his staff to go out to Central Avenue, where the train would run, and figure out what percentage of people traveling along Central were traveling by transit. Central's transit service was as good as any in the metro area; it had three bus lines with six-minute headways during rush hour. His staff returned and told him that they found that 25 percent of people rode transit on the Central corridor. Light rail advocates thought that number portended a similar situation if you made the quality better for other routes.

24. Glen Greno, "Coping with Light-Rail Costs: Tab for Operating Trains Puts Burden on Cities Already Tightening Budgets," *Arizona Republic*, last modified December 9, 2008, http://www.azcentral.com/news/articles/2008/12/09/20081209lrail-money1209.html#ixzz2M1GbErrA.

25. The cuts totaled 10 percent of service and the costs increased the base fare by 40 percent. Sean Holstege, "Transit Ridership Up," *Arizona Republic*, January 27, 2012.

26. Thanks to Valley Metro's John Farry and Steve Banta, as well as Hillary Foose, for helping me piece together Valley Metro light rail's origin story.

27. "The Businesses of Light Rail: A Compilation of Local Business Interviews," Arizona PIRG Education Fund, April 2010, http://www.arizonapirg.org/sites/pirg/files/reports/The-Businesses-of-Light-Rail.pdf.

28. Did it begin with twentieth-century tastemaker and Chicagoan Frank Lloyd Wright, who chose a spread of Scottsdale desert for Taliesin West, his winter compound?

29. Underscoring the challenge of pioneering a successful grocery store in downtown Phoenix, the Phoenix Public Market closed a few months after I visited. A newspaper article cited financial problems and too much of a niche appeal. The city continued to try to figure out how to make a downtown grocery store work.

Dustin Gardiner, "Urbanites Hunger for Grocery," *Arizona Republic*, November 29, 2012.

30. "Businesses of Light Rail," Arizona PIRG Education Fund.

31. A study of downtown parking in cities throughout the world indicated that of forty-four cities studied, Phoenix had the second-highest ratio of parking spots per job (beat out only by Canberra, Australia). This was by far the highest of the thirteen American cities included in the study, crushing even auto-oriented cities such as Houston, Los Angeles, and Sacramento, California. Phoenix's parking spots per job ratio of .91 was nearly three times the forty-four world cities' average. Michael Manville and Donald Shoup, "Parking, People, and Cities," *Journal of Urban Planning and Development* 131 (December 2005): 243.

32. "Copper Square Parking Study: Phoenix, Arizona," Downtown Phoenix Partnership, Inc., June 29, 2006, http://dtphx.org/downloads/downtown-phoenix-parking-study.pdf.

33. Eric Anderson (Maricopa Association of Governments), interview with author, March 7, 2012.

PART V

Adventure

LINCOLN HIGHWAY AND TIPPET'S RANCH, NV

1930

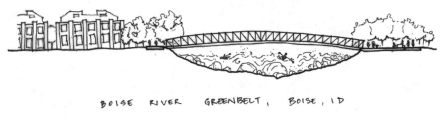

BOISE RIVER GREENBELT, BOISE, ID

2012

DOI: 10.7330/9780874219937.c005

Motoring

Traveling behind the wheel of a car felt strange. Usually the sensation of driving on the open road defined my sense of a road trip. Driving alone felt right. It was liberating. It was central to the adventure.

But driving out of Phoenix felt staid and ordinary. It did not feel liberating. It felt like I was using a necessary tool to accomplish a job.

Which I was. Boise was one thousand miles away. I could have taken the bus. But my only option was Greyhound, and not only would it take thirty-one hours but I would have to travel the interstates, probably through the night.

I wanted a different trip for this leg. I wanted to travel on the blue highways, the back roads. So I decided to rent a car. I could stop where I wanted, camp where I wanted, travel at my own pace, which was not possible with the extremely limited intercity mass transit in the West. On one hand, the Greyhound was an adventure. But on the other, its skeletal service and prison-like operations precluded choosing the kind adventure you wanted to have.

And so it didn't feel quite right to be back in a car, but safely out of the Phoenix metro area, I was bouncing along the rolling hills of the Sonoran outback. The corridor of travel between Phoenix and Boise wasn't popular, but the two cities were nearly at an identical longitude. Driving between them would take me through three of North America's four deserts—the Sonoran, the Mojave, and the Great Basin. While all driving adventures in the West etched in the country's collective memory seemed to be east-west, going north-south in the heart of the region was more interesting to me.

A few hours into the drive, I saw a sign pointing the way to "Old 93" and felt it my duty to take it. "Primitive Road," it said. I had been sleepy, but now I was awake, rolling down the dirt road and kicking up a tail of dust.

Trains allowed Americans to access and experience the West, but the automobile allowed us to explore it. When autos became available to consumers, they were less about mobility than adventure. In 1910, 95 percent of intercity travel in the United States was by train.[1] The first autos allowed travelers to extend the journey into country unknown to them.

When a train left the tracks it was a wreck, but autos were made to go off the grid. Motoring was a visceral thrill, the act of put-put-putting across the American dirt. For the first few decades, cars were open to the air, the driver and passengers exposed to the wind and the weather and the sounds and scents of the landscape. Without power steering and automatic transmissions, early cars were physically exerting to drive and control.[2]

Like riding the luxury trains of the Santa Fe, motoring was originally an upper-class pursuit because only the gentry had the leisure time to undertake such trips. At the turn of the century, when the first automobiles were coming off assembly lines, most Americans did not have vacations. In the early twentieth century, though, America's Puritanical roots had faded enough and new spiritual movements urged Americans to recuperate on longer breaks from work. The middle classes suddenly had time to travel, and increasingly affordable autos gave them the means, as auto camps opened across the country and especially in the West.[3]

For Americans of all kinds in the early 1900s, driving the West was a different kind of exploration than that of the previous century. America knew the layout of the West; even the most remote mountain ranges and rivers had been mapped. The geographic frontier of settlement was closed. This original American exploration had been driven by economic opportunity and national purpose.

But President Theodore Roosevelt, an outdoorsman himself, encouraged Americans to rediscover the benefits of the "strenuous life," to break open new frontiers. As one contemporary author wrote, "There is exhilaration in the onward rush of the biting wind. There is health and healing in the pure clean cold. There is tonic in the sweep of the crystal clean air, keen as a whetted scimitar and whipped home by the added impetus of flight of a fast moving motor car." Personal drama now drove the exploration of the western United States. Traveling Americans could see the same landscape a thousand different ways.[4]

From Old 93, I found my way to Route 66, cutting a line across the northern Arizona desert. This classic section of the Mother Road paralleled Interstate 40 but was far enough away from the freeway to have some distinct character and utility.

I turned west, and past Kingman the interstate swerved south to avoid the steep 2,000-foot rise of the Black Mountains. But 66 had not been deterred. As the road approached the mountains, it was unusually straight, as if it was working up the gumption for the climb. The view from here was so spectacular that I stopped the car and stepped out for a look. The two-lane road had no shoulder. The smaller scale of the old highway didn't dominate the landscape, like the freeway did. This road gave cars just enough space to move through, no more and no less. It was small, straight, and brave, and it struck me how different these old highways were from the ones we hurried on today. Like the Oregon Trail, they had ushered America across the West without much of a trace.

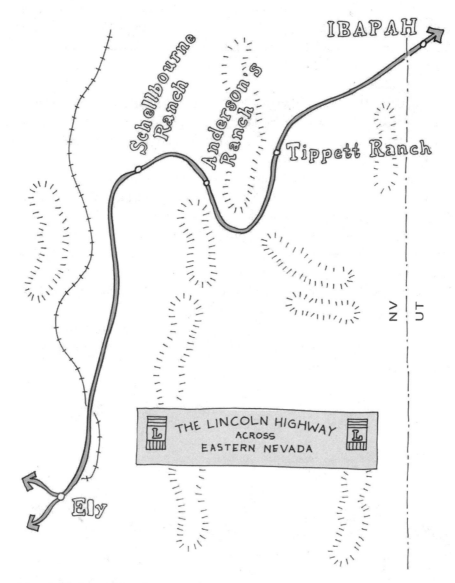

IBAPAH

Schellbourne Ranch

Anderson's Ranch

Tippett Ranch

NV | UT

THE LINCOLN HIGHWAY
ACROSS
EASTERN NEVADA

Ely

Lincoln Highway, Nevada.

By the Lincoln Highway

"What a tour it has been!" wrote a woman named Effie Gladding in 1914, about the 8,600 miles she had just driven across the United States. She and her husband, Thomas, were early adopters of a new road called the Lincoln Highway, which took them coast-to-coast from San Francisco to their home in New York City. The trip was so long that they needed two cars. They had driven a Studebaker from San Francisco as far as Denver and found a Franklin to take them the rest of the way. The next year Effie published *Across the Continent by the Lincoln Highway*, an account of her journey.[5]

If Route 66 was the most famous early highway in America, the Lincoln Highway was the most impressive. It was completed in autumn 1913 and took a more rugged route over the western mountains, crossing the Rockies, the Wasatch, and the Sierra at their thickest and highest. Today it is hard to consider these early roads—what amounted to a dirt track in many places—"highways." But compared to the condition of most American roads at the time, the Lincoln Highway was a magical ribbon of unprecedented connection. Effie thought it was "already what it is intended to be, a golden road of pleasure and usefulness, fitly dedicated, and destined to inspire a great patriotism and to honour a great patriot."[6]

As an adventurer, Effie Gladding was no joke. Her cross-country trip came after a year of touring in Europe, nearly a year of travel in Asia, six months in Australia and New Zealand, and three months in Honolulu. The journey on the Lincoln Highway was, in effect, a victory lap.

Effie knew that motoring in the United States was for the brave. "The Lincoln Highway," she wrote, "is not as yet a road for those motorists who wish only luxurious hotels, frequent stops, and all the cushioned comfort of the much-traveled main roads of the favorite tourist parts of Europe." As they pushed east from California, the Gladdings learned to love the red, white, and blue signs with a large letter L, which told them that they were on the right road. They carried chains, a shovel, an ax, jacks, tire casings and inner tubes, tools, and a pair of Lincoln Highway pennants.[7]

Their travel habits were modern in many ways. They usually ate at restaurants, even for their "luncheons," and they found great interest in some of the characters running the restaurants. When they couldn't find a restaurant, they approached a ranch for a meal. There they might dine on offerings of fried bacon and eggs, potatoes, lettuce, radishes, preserved cherries, stewed prunes, milk, tea, and pie. The adventure was always the people as well as the land.

She explained her and Thomas's rules of the road. First, they did not wear their good clothes. Open-air driving spewed dust and dirt on them. Effie's standard outfit consisted of a lightweight tweed suit and plenty of washable blouses with rolling collars, covered by an ample "motor coat." By the end of the trip, the dust of the West was ground into the outfits she wore.

They did not travel by night. Effie loved driving in late afternoon because of the light on the land, but they ended their days as evening approached. In this way, she explained, "one does not miss the scenery of the country, and one is not over fatigued."[8] They usually ate dinner where they lodged for the night, but if they planned to arrive late, they tried to eat whatever they had at the proper supper hour.

They did not travel on Sunday. This was partly because they wanted to attend church in whatever town they were passing through and partly because the day of rest refreshed them for more sightseeing.

Finally, the Gladdings resolved to a zen-like fatalism of the road. They took "the days and the roads as they came." They did not look for luxury and kept themselves well satisfied with simplicity. "It is surprising," Effie wrote, "how one is fortified for the vicissitudes of the road by such a deliberate attitude of mind."[9]

—————————————————

The heart of Effie Gladding's adventure was the interior West, where, on one hand, "the whole day [was] so full of wide and happy promise," but on the other, the landscape produced "a very trying drive." It was at once hated and compelling: "dreary and desolate and yet had its own charm."[10]

After driving through Sacramento, up the American River, over the crest of the Sierra Nevada at Donner Pass, and down to Lake Tahoe (where "the road was very sandy, and as we drove among the pine trees it was in some places so narrow that the hubs of our machine just cleared the tree trunks"), the Gladdings faced the notorious road block of the Great Basin, which had challenged travelers for centuries, going back to the Dominguez-Escalante Expedition.[11] Even by the time the Gladdings drove the Lincoln Highway, America still hadn't figured out how to cross the Great Basin comfortably.

"The whole character of the country changed," Effie wrote. "The road was a narrow shelf along a barren, rocky mountain side. There were but few trees. The color of the rock and of patches of brilliant yellow flowers, growing along the roadside, gave variety to the landscape. Otherwise it was somewhat dreary and forbidding."[12]

Heavy rains had made the road through the first stretch of Great Basin muddy and uneven. They encountered a scene of wagons drawn by as many as sixteen horses and mules struggling hopelessly through the sticky mud. The drivers were "cracking their whips, yelling and swearing, and the poor animals' flanks and bellies were thick with mud and covered with the dried blood which had streamed down from the wounds made by a pitchfork in the hands of a desperate and angry teamster determined to get his team started out of a mud hole."[13]

But the broad tires and power of their Studebaker took them past the wagon quagmire and around the salt water holes and muddy playas. Effie began to understand the shape of the country, a feeling that comes over anyone who drives the width of Nevada—even now. "We were passing from one great valley into another, hour after hour," she wrote. "We were descending into a valley, crossing its immense width, coming up on to a more or less lofty pass, usually bare, and descending into another valley. It was very fascinating, this rising and falling with always the new vista of a new valley just opening before us."[14]

"I can completely understand how the desert casts its spell over cattlemen and sheepmen so that they love it and its freedom and are continually drawn back to it," Effie continued. "The mystery and glory of the desert plains have their devotees just as really as the mystery and glory of the great city have their worshippers who never wish to be far from its lights."[15]

Along the road they found a traveling companion, a young "commercial man" from San Francisco driving a Ford to Utah, who Effie called "Mr. N." They were glad to meet Mr. N, and the feeling was mutual. But once they had arrived at their place of lodging for the night, a place called Alpine Ranch, Mr. N told them he planned to keep driving into the night, which, of course, was against one of the Gladdings' (and many other travelers') strict rules of motoring. The Gladdings warned him that he might get into trouble, but he assured them that he often traveled at night and "enjoyed the stillness and the freedom to speed along." They watched him disappear down the valley, his car "finally hidden in acres of grey-green sage brush."[16]

On the road at about 10:00 the following morning, her husband called out, "I believe that's N's car!" N was stuck in a rut and had spent the night in the desert; he told them it had been utterly still and dark, that "not even a jack rabbit passed." With wood from a nearby ranch and the help of more pass-ersby, the Gladdings extracted Mr. N's car. It was past 1:00 when they climbed up the "bare road" to the old mining town of Austin and had their luncheon at a place called the International Hotel.[17]

"What with lack of sleep and his long fast Mr. N was quite worn out," Effie wrote. But "a good luncheon prepared by a Japanese cook and served by a natty and very debonair Japanese waiter put us all in better trim."[18]

━━━ ━ ━ ━ ━ ━ ━ ━ ━ ━ ━

The Gladdings' path met up with mine near Ely, one of the Great Basin's only real towns, almost smack in its center. I had camped the previous night about fifty miles north of Las Vegas, continuing in the morning up US 93 toward Idaho.

A few miles north of Ely, I turned east on a dirt road headed for the ghost town of Schellbourne, which had been founded as a short-lived Pony Express stop and became a mining boomtown with five saloons, a Wells Fargo office, two blacksmith shops, three stores, two restaurants, two lodging houses, and two law firms. It topped out at four hundred people but no more than twenty-five had lived in it for a century.

This section of the Lincoln Highway was divorced from the modern paving of the highway. Past the old ghost town, the road wound up to Schellbourne Pass, where I left the Steptoe Valley, and descended into Spring Valley, the road rising and falling with always the new vista of a new valley, like Effie noticed one hundred years earlier. Driving over the pass, I realized the effect of auto speeds—even at 30 or 40 miles per hour—on moving through the Great Basin: the massive scale, always changing. As a new technology, it must have been a stunning way to experience the West.

Effie left Ely on the morning of June 24, 1914. "We drove through Steptoe Valley for some forty miles," she wrote. "Where we turned off from the valley it still stretched on for another forty miles. It looked as if it might go on to the world's end." Out of Ely they passed through McGill and, being good tourists, visited the "immense" smelting works.[19]

They took a right toward Schellbourne, freshly abandoned, and drove up to the pass. They drove down into Spring Valley "under the shadow of the Schellbourne range."[20] They passed some young motorists from Detroit and men with burros taking supplies to the sheep ranchers in the mountains.

They had their luncheon at a place called Anderson's ranch, which was no longer there in 2012. The Andersons treated Effie and her husband hospitably. She judged that this was a Mormon household, as Mormon marriage certificates hung upon the wall and "as the Deseret Weekly was evidently its newspaper connection with the outside world."[21] They were still with Mr. N, who picked up a man from the ranch who wanted to get to Salt Lake City.

It struck me that even in a time ostensibly more connected and civilized, my drive through this country felt less animated than what Effie described, and more haunted. I passed no one in a car or on foot or horse. I found no places to eat luncheons. If I had passed someone, I likely would not have stopped to ask them where they were from, as the Gladdings had done. In the Gladdings' time, there existed a community of travelers even in this most far-flung American outback.

At the bottom of Spring Valley I passed a long-abandoned stone house. Perhaps this had been Anderson's ranch. Over another notch in the next mountain range called Tippets Pass, I found the famous Tippets Ranch, which had also begun as a Pony Express stop in the 1860s. By Effie Gladding's time, Tippets was a major stopping point. Having had lunch at Anderson's, the Gladdings merely pit stopped at Tippets, finding out that "its owner travels thirty-six miles for his mail and supplies."[22] Tippets had a general store, a post office, and a campground in the days of the Lincoln Highway.

Unlike Bent's Old Fort back in Colorado, Tippets Ranch was not a recreation. It was a pure ghost of itself. The former highway wrapped around a quarter of the circle of fields and ranch buildings, and I stopped my car. A fence of weathered trunks and branches and rusty barbed wire surrounded the property. Some of the buildings were made of stone, others of logs. Most no longer had roofs. I saw a few dead trees, a few living but leafless trees, and outside the fence, a small reservoir. Despite the appearance of no one being home, the ranch fields were bright green and being irrigated in the middle of the day.

Around the ranch, dirt tracks that were not quite roads whirled in all directions into the valley. Grazing cattle speckled the dry plains. In the distance I could see a lot of storm activity over the snowy mountain ranges. Above the ranch, old Model T–era auto bodies lay abandoned on the slope below the Tippets Range.

Wind whipped through the valley, rattling my parked car as I sat inside eating a bagel. I was surprised at how vulnerable I felt, even in my trusty Chevy rental with ten thousand miles on it that was ten thousand times as reliable as the Gladdings' or Mr. N's machines. I think I felt the expanse of time on the landscape. It was still scary to be that far out in a car. We let cars take us into the middle of nowhere. Of anywhere I had been thus far, Tippets Valley scared me the most; I was nervous and spooked.

Effie also saw the ghosts of the past. At a point where the new highway crossed the Overland Trail, she thought of the "forty-niner" gold seekers seeing the trail signs of their day. "In coming along the Lincoln Highway," she wrote, "we are simply traversing the old overland road along which the prairie schooners of the pioneers passed. How much heart-ache, heart-break, and hope deferred this old trail has seen! I think of it as we bowl along so comfortably over the somewhat rough but yet very passable road."[23]

"I can appreciate now," she continued, "the touching story in a San Francisco paper of an old lady who came to the rear platform of a fine overland train after passing a certain village station, and threw out some flowers upon the plain. Near here, she told her friends, her little baby had been buried in the desert forty years before, as she and her husband toiled with their little caravan along the trail. The years had passed and they were prosperous and old in California. And now as she went East on the swift and beautiful train she threw out her tribute to the little grave somewhere in the great desert."[24]

I kept driving through the valley. The sandy road sent rocks up into the undercarriage of my Chevy. I was incredibly relieved to arrive in the Goshute Indian town of Ibapah, just across the Utah border.

So was Effie Gladding. Toward evening, after a day through several basins and several ranges on lots of bad roads, the Gladdings crossed the Utah border and reached their "station for the night" in Ibapah.[25] They spent a comfortable night at a ranch house owned by a Mr. Sheridan, who also had a grocery store. Before leaving they purchased some Indian baskets.

They continued on across the Salt Flats to Salt Lake City, then carried on to Laramie, Denver, and points east, eventually taking a ferry across the Hudson River home to New York City.

Although Effie drove across the entire country, she dedicated two-thirds of her book to traveling across the West. "If I were crossing the Lincoln Highway again," she wrote, "I should take with me a spirit lamp, a little sauce pan, some boxes of biscuits, some excellent tea, some cocoa and other supplies. Not that this is a necessity. But it would be very pleasant to have a luncheon or a cup of afternoon tea al fresco, now and then."[26]

Back on the smooth asphalt of today's highway, I drove north. Rain was coming.

Packed Veronica

When I was growing up, my family went on frequent Effie Gladding-esque adventures. Several times a year—in the Isuzu Trooper, or otherwise—we drove five or six hours in all directions from Salt Lake. Spring and fall meant desert camping excursions to the Colorado Plateau. Summer took us north to the cool mountains of Idaho and Wyoming. Winter was an occasional ski trip to Grand Targhee or Steamboat Springs. There was nowhere better than somewhere we hadn't been.

In the years since the Lincoln Highway was built, the West had in many ways become synonymous with the adventure it promoted, the place to harvest drama out of the American countryside. Autos were the tools for these travels, and we had adapted our adventures to the scale of how far our cars could take us.

Only we had our luncheons at McDonald's or Wendy's, which did not typically employ debonair Japanese chefs. We knew the towns by their freeway gas station and fast food clusters, rarely taking the time to drive down their main streets. And when we did, we usually regretted it, passing scores of empty storefronts of little use to us. Even if we had investigated the local smelter, as Effie would have done, we would have found it closed down and chained up.

We didn't interact with anyone on the road but busted to "make good time," as my mom said. I didn't blame her. Five hours in the back seat really started to set off my brother and me. My parents preferred not to listen to music, enjoying the silence of being inside our car humming along the pavement as the antidote to a week of work. I remember once when our car broke down on I-15 near the small town of Santaquin, we tracked down some distant relatives who helped us get our vehicle to a service station, rolling it through the apple orchards along the old Mormon Trail. It was almost surreal to have any sort of human drama between the city and the destination.

As cars went faster and farther, the human landscape of the West had thinned and agglomerated into either large bruising metros or outdoor destinations us city slickers packed into our vacation time. The beginning of each weekend in the West's population centers featured a ritual of traffic congestion as people left the city for the real attractions outside of them.

We went to a lot of national parks. We explored Zion, Capitol Reef, Arches, Bryce Canyon, Mesa Verde, Yellowstone, and Grand Teton, and what stood out about these experiences to my young eyes was that they were so crowded. A hundred years after western leisure adventure was invented, America had caught on. This was what Ed Abbey called "industrial tourism." By the 1980s, when I was a kid, they were National Parking Lots.

"It's packed Veronica," my dad would always say when we arrived.

This was the conundrum that the western adventure had become. We needed our cars to get us into the backcountry because they gave us a much greater variety of experiences. But this tool to experience the West had become the experience itself, in its freeways, fast food, chain motels, and parking lots. We had brought urban congestion to wild places by making them auto accessible. Our cars and roads were built to be (boringly) predictable.

In my experience, the best motoring is the slowest, the hardest, in the backest of beyond. Once, some friends and I drove a caravan of trucks with days' worth of gas, food, and drink into the Maze District of Utah's Canyonlands, down into the canyon that contained the Colorado River and home to such mythic-sounding landmarks as the Chocolate Drops and the Doll House. It took us a full day to drive ninety miles into one of the state's most remote places. We switchbacked down a 1,000-foot-cliff on a 5-foot-wide dirt road.

Several in the party were so nervous they walked rather than ride in their truck as it banged along the dugway. At the end of the day none of us had walked a step, yet we all felt like we had gone on an expedition.

———————————

At some point, though, it occurred to me that perhaps the way to improve adventure in the West wasn't to keep driving farther out, but to stay home. Effie Gladding's travels had emphasized civility. She and her husband took days off, interacted with people, experienced the local culture. What that civility really meant was community in adventure, like they found with Mr. N and the ranch families they stayed with. We were hard pressed to find that in making good time or visiting National Parking Lots.

But what about in our cities? Western cities, by and large, had remained separate places from the spectacular landscapes of recreation that surrounded them. Roads and traffic bisected adventuring in the outdoors from daily life. By day and by week we were beings in a car, and by weekend and the occasional morning or evening we removed ourselves to the "real" West.

I wondered if we could reinvent adventure in the West's cities by getting out of our cars. Indeed, some national parks had banned autos from their most crowded districts. Zion National Park, for example, had experimented with banning cars in its namesake canyon, a cathedral of a valley in the heart of the park. It completely changed the character of the place to one of quiet serenity. Wildlife came closer to the empty parking lots. People got around fine.

In removing cars, places became more communal and urban. My wife and I had recently spent three days in Yosemite without using a car. Being saddled with an infant in a stroller, we were just like the thousands of other Americans there who usually drove, and we found that pushing our stroller along the walking paths made us want to stop along the Merced River and share the views of the falls with the people we bumped into. The Wasatch Mountains' recreational playground was occasionally called "Wasangeles" because of its heavy use by residents and tourists. But I wondered whether the problem was so much people as their automobiles. I liked bumping into people while hiking and touring the canyons, trading information and good tidings. I think Effie Gladding would have too.

The city is the real chance for the wild. I'd guess that we—and I include myself here—would continue to happily take our city lives beyond the wheels of cars and four-wheelers. But we could do the opposite too, to pull the "real" West back into the city. As with other aspects of the West, the city was the new frontier for adventure.

I searched for a place heading in this direction, and I found it in Boise. Idaho's capital was building a city based almost entirely on outdoor recreation, much of it right in the center of the city. In Boise the line between walking, running, biking, and getting around was blurring. Boise had been consistently rated as one of the nation's best mountain bike communities and whitewater boating towns. At the same time, Idaho had the third-highest bike mode share in the nation.[27] Its residents seemed happy to pay for open space and were restoring their waterways. Boise's rivers and parks were likely to be packed Veronica, but in the heart of the city that emphasized people and not cars, that was a good thing.

I arrived in Boise after dark and checked into the Shilo Inn Boise Riverside. I needed to drop off the car. One thousand miles later, it had served its purpose, a tool that needed to be put away. I was in the city now.

I put my stuff in my room, drove the car to the Boise Airport, and rode my bike back. As I reached the hotel, it started to hail.

I walked up to my room, which had a balcony that overlooked the Boise River. I could hear it before I even opened the sliding glass door. People were whizzing by on bikes. The water, black in the night, was overflowing.

Bank Full

The river was what river scientists called "bank full," a condition that usually happened once a year during the snowmelt in the mountains. In the case of the Boise, which, like the Jordan River in the Salt Lake Valley, had been dammed, channelized, and diverted beyond recognition, bank full occurred when the reservoirs had more water than they could hold and the water master needed to use the capacity of the riverbed. While the river ran at 250 cfs in the winter, today it was approaching 6,000 cfs.

Ralph Budwig, a mechanical engineering professor at the University of Idaho Boise explained this to me the next morning. We were commuting on bikes to Budwig's office downtown. We rode along the river on what was called the Greenbelt, a paved path that ran along the river for twenty-two miles. The rain had stopped, but the cold air that usually followed a storm had settled in. Water had flooded into wildlife areas between the braided river channels. We rode through the mist across bridges and wound through groves of cottonwood and willow. It did not feel like we were commuting to work in Idaho's largest city.

Budwig, like most of the people who live in Boise, was a self-described outdoorsman. "I'm not a sports club guy," he told me. "When I moved to

Boise.

Boise, I made a point of buying a house near mountain bike trails. When I get home, it's an hour of exercise."

He was also a committed bike commuter. Budwig lived just outside the city limits north of town, along the foothills. He rode despite a personal tragedy that happened fifteen years earlier. Budwig and his wife lived in Moscow, a small town that was home to the main campus of the University of Idaho, where Budwig worked. He and his wife would either walk or ride their bikes most places. One day, his wife was killed after a driver ran a red light.

Budwig didn't stop riding after his wife's death, but he was a lot more tentative. That was why he liked the Greenbelt. He took his route not for its shortness but for its safety. Other routes, like Hill Road, were shorter. But Hill Road had high volumes of fast-moving traffic and was a known location of traffic-related fatalities. He went extra miles to ride the Greenbelt.

His ten-mile commute took him about an hour, but he enjoyed it, at least once he was on the Greenbelt. Today he was dressed in a parka, fleece pants, and black gloves. We joined a parade of other commuters, most with stylish high-visibility yellow and green cycling outerwear.

As an engineer, Budwig specialized in fluid dynamics, the study of the flow of gases and liquids. Usually fluid dynamics is applied to water and air, but fluid dynamicists also study other fluids, like the way blood moves through the arteries; that had been Budwig's specialization before he moved to Boise. He studied blood flow and aneurysms and coronary arteries for most of his career at the U of I in Moscow.

But three years earlier, the Boise campus obtained a giant research flume as part of a new $2 million lab facility. They asked Budwig to come to Boise to help the new center study ecohydraulics, which is the way river water flows through its sediment bed and, consequently, how it hosts plants and animals. Rivers had not been part of Budwig's expertise, but the fluid dynamic principles were the same.

Since then, he had undertaken over a dozen projects with state and federal agencies like the Forest Service and the Bureau of Reclamation on all sorts of topics. He was currently working on a study measuring the effect of a river's flow on salmon eggs as it washed over rocks and nests. He and his colleagues were manipulating the water with a spatula to simulate a salmon tail and changing the gravel sizes and the topography of the riverbed to test the effects of different conditions.

Sometimes on his bike commute Budwig thought about the river, especially on a day like today. Supercritical flow, subcritical flow, fast and shallow, and slow and deep. When they mixed, it made a hydraulic jump: whitewater. Idaho's mountain streams were shallow and fast and had holes that caused hydraulic jumps. He watched kayakers and fishermen and thought about the amazing resource that was the Boise River; there just weren't that many urban places where people kayaked and fished on a river. His favorite part of the river was wide and braided. The trail wound through forests of black cottonwoods and geese swam in the side streams and eddies.

But more often, he thought about nothing. The Greenbelt allowed Budwig to go into what he called his "nothing box" for the better part of an hour. He just let his mind go. He didn't have to pay much attention. He moved through the forest and listened to the river. It was part of his spirituality. He was with people a lot—in meetings, with friends on the weekend—and he enjoyed being alone along the river. The Hill Road route did not let him go into his nothing box.

And so the Greenbelt had become a central thread of Ralph Budwig's life in a number of ways. He rode it. He studied it. He worked on it. His church ministered to the homeless in the Greenbelt parks, where they'd grill hamburgers for two hundred people.

Eventually, we emerged into a clearing on the river where a large plaza had been constructed on the riverbank. The plaza overlooked a small drop in the river that demonstrated the idea of the hydraulic jump and its production of whitewater. But what was happening underneath the roaring water was definitely not natural, and that was what I had wanted Budwig to show me.

This was one of his projects. He explained that a pile of industrial rubble had fallen into the river here. When the river was high, it formed a wave. At bank full, kayakers would come to surf the wave, an urban thrill that they'd usually find only after driving up Payette Canyon.

At lower flows, the wave was extremely dangerous. But instead of closing the attraction, the City of Boise had recognized the value of having a kayak park in the middle of town that could run year-round no matter the river's actual flow. The City joined with some boaters and decided to engineer a wave.

The city hired Denver's McLaughlin Whitewater Design Group to design and build the wave. McLaughlin had invented a contraption called a WaveShaper, which simulated the hydraulic jump between supercritical and subcritical flows by tricking the river into thinking the level of the riverbed was higher than it actually was. The adjustable nature of the WaveShaper meant someone could change the size of the wave it created by pushing a few buttons. The company wanted to push the envelope and make the wave even more adjustable, to make it either flat water or the Grand Canyon.

They needed Budwig to test the wave. He explained that in the winter the river ran at about 250 cfs. Bank full was 6,000 or 7,000 cfs, which usually occurred in May or June or, as it were, today, in April.

"That's a factor of thirty," Budwig said. We were leaning against the bar of the plaza, which was designed as a viewing platform. Spandexed cyclists whizzed by us. "To get a device to produce that change is not trivial."

McLaughlin produced the drop with a metal deck that they could raise and lower. Vanes on the turbine blade could alter both the magnitude and character of the wave—changing it, for example, from a low-hazard wave to one boaters feared, which they called a "keeper hole."

Budwig tested a miniature model of the WaveShaper. He and his students looked at how the vanes closed and opened. They invited kayakers to have a look at it. The final design had the vanes, but it was harder for someone or something to get caught under the deck. The City cleared out the industrial debris, installed two WaveShapers, and built the viewing platform to create another outdoor recreation amenity in Boise's center. Adventure had been scientifically engineered into the city just like roads and buildings. Boiseans increasingly came inward for their recreation, adventure, and nothing boxes. The River Recreation Park, as it was called, was another jewel on the Greenbelt.

The Greenbelt

Ralph Budwig and I kept riding toward downtown Boise, now a few miles up the river. As the morning warmed up, the Greenbelt filled up with bicyclists, joggers, walkers, and rollerbladers. I saw one kid riding a bike with a fishing rod attached to the back. They passed under the street overpasses, enjoying a smooth ribbon of a ride. It was bicycling's meditative version of a freeway, the constant hum of the river in the background instead of revving motors and honking and car stereos.

A lot of cities claimed to have a greenbelt, but this was often a matter of semantics, a way to mitigate suburban development and make the view a little better on the drive home from work. Boise's was the real thing, a green shot of high-country energy and life running down what felt like the very middle of the city of half a million people. It should have been called the Green-something else. It wasn't so much of a belt as a zipper.

The river was its centerpiece. Nothing epitomizes the West like a mountain river. Cold, clear water rushing over boulders, full of fish, slowly eroding the mountains above. A river could be enjoyed in so many ways, people and ecology side by side. The river brought a taste of the power, unpredictability and sublimity of the western landscape into the city.

But like Budwig emphasized, today's river wasn't a product of simply preserving what was there when white people arrived in the Treasure Valley. It was a human invention forged from a wrecked landscape, a tandem urban and ecological resurrection built from a vision for what the urban West should be.

"If you're starting with a pristine river," Budwig explained, "and you're starting to make improvements for boaters, it's not a good idea." Yet very few places in the West were pristine, least of all river corridors like the Boise that had been channelized and diverted. "But if you're starting with a river that's been channelized and diverted," he continued, "you can make things better for the kayakers and the habitat."

The Boise was a short, swift stream that began as three separate forks high in the Sawtooth Mountains of central Idaho. It ran through the Treasure Valley parallel to the foothills and then emptied into the mighty Snake River at the Oregon border forty miles northwest of where we were—right about where fur trappers traveling east from Astoria used to reach the river. Like the Jordan, the Colorado, and many other western rivers, the Boise was a ghost of itself. Farmers who used its water for their crops first diverted it in the 1800s. Then, throughout the twentieth century, Idahoans and the federal government built a series of dams along it, beginning with the 1909 Boise River Diversion Dam. Several other diversion projects followed, reaching their apex with the 1955 Lucky Peak Dam that the US Army Corps of Engineers built ten miles southeast of Boise, which eventually provided power for the city of Seattle.

Because the Boise River now flowed through a growing metropolitan area, Lucky Peak's primary purpose was not irrigation but flood control. The dam also made for a more consistent flow. Before the dam, floods of 20,000 cfs were commonplace. Now the largest storm events produced half that flow. The Army Corps also narrowed the floodplain so the city could more efficiently grow around it. Like so many other western rivers, the Boise was now a piece of a plumbing system rather than an ecological system.

Meanwhile, as it grew outward into the former agriculture of the Treasure Valley, the city turned its back on the river. While industry capitalized on the plumbed river, it also used it as a dumping ground. Agriculture and stockyards lined the banks and cast their refuse into the water. By the time industry began to leave, the center of the city had developed elsewhere. Although close to the river, downtown disregarded it.

In the 1960s, Boiseans began to understand what had happened to the river and what potential it still held. The city was starting to sprawl throughout the valley into the same kind of suburban development found anywhere in the United States. But the river set Boise apart as the kind of unique natural resource that people were beginning to notice. Throughout the United States, communities started to take back their cities from midcentury guttings and their environment from the industrial age.

The Greenbelt emerged from both of these movements. The city's 1962 general plan recommended a linear park along the river, and in 1968 the city created the Greenbelt Plan and Guidelines. In 1971 it passed a Greenbelt ordinance for the river corridor, which established setbacks along the river to help the riparian area regenerate itself.

The vision was large, but developers minded the details. The city built the first of two large parks along the river, naming them after the wives of the largest donors, Julia Davis and Ann Morrison, creating a tradition in Boise. They connected parks easements from the State of Idaho. A Greenbelt and Pathways Committee reviewed development proposals. Little by little, the flavor of the river changed.

For the first few decades of the Greenbelt, transportation was not part of the equation. Boiseans built the Greenbelt as a response to a decaying environment in order to address other challenges such as water quality, dying ecology, and the potential for recreation. Yet mitigating auto dependency—the factor that had led to this predicament as much as anything else—was not one of them.

But in the 1980s, it became clear that Boiseans were using the Greenbelt to get around, especially cyclists. Enough linear mileage connected neighborhoods and suburbs to downtown Boise. It happened that many businesses, because of the peaceful environment, had located on the river corridor. Some of these were tech behemoths-in-the-making, like Hewlett-Packard. Bicyclists figured out that if they could get to the Greenbelt, they could get to the downtown core. Bike counts in 2012 documented over five hundred cyclists in the afternoon rush hour riding along the Greenbelt downtown, a number that would put it in the top handful of bike volumes in Seattle and comparable to many popular bike corridors in downtown San Francisco, a cycling mecca and the center of a metro area ten times as large.[28]

The Greenbelt became such a popular bicycle commute route that the city had to alter its maintenance practices because so many people traveled along it. It stopped irrigating before 9:00 a.m. and cleared snow for cyclists even in the winter. The city began widening the path from six or eight feet to twelve feet, with 2-foot shoulders and a stripe down the middle, like a bicycle highway.

Transportation reinforced environmental concerns, providing a way to reduce auto emissions in a sprawling city and an alternative way to work. The Greenbelt became the torch for a citizenry concerned about the environmental impacts of urbanization on the western landscape and the desire for an enjoyable place to live.

The city treated the Greenbelt like a complex urban artery. It was a major street—only this corridor was a river and a trail instead of a freeway and light rail. It was even more complex because nature had to be part of the balance. The city worried about the riparian zone being trampled and pollution in storm water runoff.

On the Greenbelt, transportation and recreation snowballed. Now almost twenty parks lined the river, and many in the Boise metro area found they could walk to at least one of them. You could bike to freestyle BMX parks and ride home. With improved water quality, people began to use the river more to fish and kayak, some 10,000 strong floated down it on a hot summer weekend. The Greenbelt had become more than a destination at the end of a car trip; it was one continuous experience, immersed in a community of other people moving through it.

Perhaps best of all, like all great urban public spaces, the Greenbelt was an economic equalizer. Usually, the socioeconomically elite undertake outdoor sports like kayaking or skiing in the mountains outside of town. But the Greenbelt was in the center, a civic seam appealing to rich and poor. Everyone could find something in it, and almost everyone did.

What was Boise's secret? Boiseans gave me a simple answer: the people. Nearly everyone I talked to spoke about the culture of volunteering that ran through the city. A study on volunteering in America undertaken by the Corporation for National & Community Service found that Idaho had the second highest rate of volunteering in the United States, with almost 40 percent of its residents volunteering for a civic, religious, educational, sports, arts, or social service organization.[29]

The Greenbelt was a central thread of Boise's volunteer culture. On a daily basis, people pitched in to keep it vital, safe, and beautiful. Even in my short time along the Greenbelt, I saw volunteer police riding on bikes and volunteer Rotary Club members picking up trash. Boise was able to reinject wildness into its core through civility.

Volunteers had also largely built the Greenbelt. I rode downriver later in the morning and met a few of the hundreds of people who had put together this trail. The motley group of old bureaucrats, nonprofit activists, and Treasure Valley citizens was led by Judy Peavey-Derr, a former Ada County commissioner who was currently running for the Idaho Senate.

I met them at a newly built segment of the Greenbelt near Eagle, about seven miles from downtown Boise. Under the moniker Foundation for Ada/Canyon Trail Systems (F.A.C.T.S.), they had constructed a three-mile segment that wound through groves of cottonwood trees and willows. All of it was volunteer time. "Our mission is simple," the F.A.C.T.S. website said. It was "to close the gap on the Green Belt along the Boise River. Creating one path, from Lucky Peak Dam to where the Boise River meets the Snake River."[30]

Peavey-Derr had begun advocating for the Greenbelt over thirty years earlier when her kids were in grade school. She didn't actually own a bike, but her kids did. They'd go down to the river and make a day of it. All kids ought to be doing this, she thought.

But at the same time, as a politician, she was shrewd about the Greenbelt as an economic development tool. She'd once suggested to a cofounder of the Boise tech company Micron that the company should bring potential hires to the river path and parks.

"If we continue the path to the Snake River, people can make a vacation of the whole experience," Peavey-Derr said, as we walked along the trail. "You start out at Lucky Peak, camp at Eagle Island, go to the Snake, and then hop in a boat."

Indeed, the Greenbelt was a complicated, growing organism, as attested by this most recent branch of it. The simple enthusiasm of volunteers was belied by the inescapable complexity of building the trail. In 2009 F.A.C.T.S. members decided to pursue the section of trail from Garden City to Eagle. They drew on one another's different skills and connections and found all kinds of people to help them with the expensive and time-consuming task of building a seemingly simple path along the river. Nancy had the money through her connection at Idaho Parks and Recreation. Don obtained the easements from private property owners he'd been working with for the last thirty years. Judy, as Don said, "knew where the sleeping dogs lay." They wrangled $118,000 from the Federal Highway Administration, which gave them enough to get started.

They enlisted the master negotiation skills of a shopping center developer one of them knew. The Ada County surveyor agreed to resurvey the path to determine the location of the easement amid all the brush. The all-volunteer Eagle Fire Department cleared the path. The list went on.

We walked through the black cottonwoods, gravel crunching under our feet. Most of the group hadn't been back for several months, since the work had been done. While pleased, they were focused on the next stage—getting the trail paved—which would cost another $140,000 and untold volunteer hours. And they kept pushing the Greenbelt along the river. This time next year, they told me, they expected to build the path another few miles.

These folks were like a bizarro Robert Moses, New York City's powerful midcentury road builder, aggressively harnessing the will of Boise's empowered citizenry to build this little superhighway for people.

The Boise Bicycle Project

With the Greenbelt established in the center of their city, Boiseans were finding ways to reconnect outdoor recreation and urban life without the annoyance of the car. Many of the city's recreational cyclists found that Boise could be a city within cities for bicycling.

Around midday I visited a place called the Boise Bicycle Project. It was crowded with kids and adults hunching over bikes, hard at work. A dad watched as a ten-year-old boy tried to fix his brakes. An entire Indian family showed up. The dad said he worked at Micron and came to the shop after he got a flat tire and didn't know how to fix it. He rode in India but rode much more here because the whole family could do it. They came in here every week and today he was looking for a mountain bike. Next to them, a twenty-something girl worked on a baby blue road bike. She explained that she had crashed her old bike after drinking at the bars. Because she bent the frame, she needed a new bike. She had been visiting her home in Idaho Falls, and while her grandpa was showing off his new Firebird she noticed a bunch of bike frames. She asked him what he was going to do with those, and he said he planned to throw them away. So she took one with her to fix up at Boise Bicycle Project, where she was a member.

Jimmy Hallyburton presided over all of this, in brown corduroy pants, a T-shirt, and a cap. Along with his friend Brian Anderson, Hallyburton had started the Boise Bicycle Project as a meeting place for Boise's varied cycling community.

He led me out in back of the building to a 15-foot-high mountain of old bikes, like you might see composed of trash at the dump. He explained that when the shop received bike donations, mechanics inspected them. Then they donated them to six- to twelve-year-old-kids if they agreed to go through a class. Otherwise they sold the bikes or gave them away in exchange for work-trade, where people would take bikes apart or patch tubes. For the bikes that couldn't be fixed, a man picked them up to sell as scrap metal.

"We want to offer something to everybody," Hallyburton said. "A lot of it is the social aspect. They get the sense of community here."

Much of Hallyburton's philosophy was driven by the same sense of value that drove Aaron Kimberlin in Phoenix. He explained that the Boise Bicycle Project had stopped letting its members get cheap-o Walmart bikes because, long term, they were "doing themselves a disservice."

"It's much better to turn a mountain bike from the 1990s into a commuter bike because you're getting a good steel frame," he said. "We use the term 'serviceable.' It's more about the long-term value of things than the short-term bells and whistles like disc brakes or shocks."

Hallyburton agreed to take me on a ride through central Boise. He didn't bother to suit up in Lycra, bike shoes, or even a helmet. He just pulled his bike off one of the walls, tucked in his pant leg, and we rode down the street.

Hallyburton had always loved riding bikes. He had grown up on a dairy farm outside Eagle. It was the 1980s, before suburban development had reached as far as Eagle. The farm was a few miles away from the foothills, where a web of Jeep tracks and Forest Service roads provided an endless realm of exploration and thrill.

In Eagle, the primary access point for mountain biking in the foothills was State Street, a wide, nasty asphalt road with no bike lanes and speeding cars and trucks. Hallyburton and his friends were hesitant to ride on State Street. The Greenbelt hadn't reached Eagle yet; it was still six miles away. So he and his friends usually loaded their bikes in someone's truck and drove to the trailhead.

When he began to attend college at Boise State University, though, he realized that the bikes he had loved all his life were also a very cheap and dependable form of transportation. Eventually, because he lived downtown, he noticed that he didn't need a car.

Hallyburton had always taken for granted that a rural lifestyle was preferable to an urban one. Living in the country allowed you to have the freedom to go mountain biking in the mountains. He didn't think anything of all the miles he drove. Gas cost a dollar a gallon, and he and everyone he knew drove everywhere.

But after he moved out of his parents' house, he realized that, especially in Boise, the city was better for biking, even for the outdoor recreation that was his lifeblood. The mountain bike trails he had grown up riding were even more accessible from central Boise, where they shot up into the foothills from downtown. The streets he rode to access them were urban residential streets, not scary rural highways. The Greenbelt took him up or down the river to more trails or to other parts of town. Pretty soon, living a rural lifestyle didn't make sense.

In the summer of 2007, Hallyburton and Anderson acted on their idea to create a bike shop accessible to a wider segment of the population than hardcore mountain or road bikers. Instead of cycling being a testosterone-fueled appendage of the city, they wanted to make it its soul—and the Boise Bicycle Project was born. They started fixing kids' bikes. They taught bicycle safety and mechanics courses. They sold memberships; $50 a year allowed you to use the shop's tools and knowledge to work on your bike. Boise had become home to a large population of refugees from war-torn countries such as Ghana, Bosnia, Iraq, and Bhutan; when they arrived, the majority of them did not have cars. Hallyburton reached out to them. By 2011 the Boise Bicycle Project was closing in on one thousand members. In Boise, the adventures of outdoor recreation could be concentrated and community-oriented as well as dispersed and solitary.

We rode into nearby Ann Morrison Park, then entered the Greenbelt and rode it for a little while alongside Boise State University. Hallyburton rode what he described as his "dream bike"—a Bridgestone lug frame he built up to be a touring bike. It was comfortable riding, and Jimmy rode with the ease of someone walking from his bedroom to his kitchen. He rode slowly and said "hi" to the people he encountered, whether Spandexed racers or dog walkers.

We crossed the river and emerged from the Greenbelt into downtown.[31] When Hallyburton was growing up, his family never went into downtown

Boise, going there only when they had to. Bicycles had given him a new belief in the power of downtown. Pockets of it were full of businesses that openly catered to cyclists, with rows of bike parking out in front; sometimes they even placed bike racks below the curbs, where cars used to park.[32] As Hallyburton had come to learn, the bicycle could do a lot of things, but perhaps their most powerful trick was that they were re-creating the city itself.

Then again, Jimmy Hallyburton still rode his mountain bike. The trail network accessible from central Boise neighborhoods was staggering. In 2001 Boise voters approved a two-year tax levy that generated $10 million for open space conservation that, combined with federal funds and private donations, protected over 10,000 acres of foothills for public use, immediately adjacent to the central city. These foothill lands were a vast repository of mountain bike, hiking, and horse trails just outside the city. Together with the relative density of Boise, they largely removed the auto from the outdoor recreation equation. The city conducted a study of how trail users accessed the trailheads and found that almost two-thirds did not use a car, with 27 percent walking and 34 percent biking to the trailhead.[33]

Hallyburton was one of these people. He recently bought a house in Boise's North End, one of the city's only pre-auto neighborhoods. As one of the city's more expensive neighborhoods, its steep prices reflected its easy access to both downtown and the foothills, and Hallyburton paid more for a 1,100-square-foot house than he would have for a much larger one in a location farther away. It was worth it. He could walk or bike to town and reach the foothills on foot in three minutes. When he biked to the grocery store, his trailer carried six grocery bags.

He also had begun to expand the revelation that had led him to the Boise Bicycle Project, illuminating the power of outdoor recreation to city kids who only knew the bike as a mode of transportation. Through an organization named the Southwest Idaho Mountain Biking Association, he was introducing kids from low-income families to mountain biking and other outdoor recreation. The other day, he took a kid on his first hike.

The City's Front Door

Boise's Greenbelt raised the same question as Phoenix's light rail: How was the city building around its beautiful alternative transportation route? Throughout my journey, I saw how changes in transportation were beginning to lead to a different way of building cities to leverage their transportation investments. Was the same thing happening along Boise's new spine of river recreation and bicycle transportation?

Surrounding the Greenbelt and its engineered adventure were the beginnings of new urban investment. A boating store had moved to within a few hundred yards of the River Recreation Park; in the summertime, the store rented thirty to sixty paddleboards, canoes, or kayaks for use on the adjacent pond.[34] Some artists had built cooperative studios and show spaces. A couple of wineries and breweries had opened in the last few years. City officials believed that the Greenbelt played a huge role in these changes because bicycling made up part of the lifestyle lived by the people starting these ventures. This spot was designed to be a place that blended the outdoors and urbanism. It could potentially be the corollary to Effie Gladding's community of travelers. She brought community to western adventure; Boise could bring western adventure into its community.

At the head of a new footbridge that spanned the river at the River Park were rows of townhouses that looked out of place, like they belonged in San Francisco. The project had a story worth telling as much for its failures as for its successes. In the mid-2000s, a land use attorney named Jim Neill was roaming through the area, in the rather industrial municipality of Garden City, and found 17 acres of open ground on what had been a meatpacking plant. The property had almost half a mile of frontage on the river. He saw the Greenbelt running alongside it. A beautiful spot. Neill stood there and realized that it was a natural place for infill development because it was two miles from downtown Boise.

Neill got the property under contract and began developing a design for the project, which he called the Waterfront District. He envisioned what he called "an old city situation," where the stoops of the townhouses would step right down to the Greenbelt. There might be some retail or restaurants along the way, with patios along the path. It would be dense and active and comfortable and beautiful.

Neill wanted to include a design aspect in his development—something that, I soon realized, would be the most important element guiding the transformation of the Boise River Greenbelt into a city of recreation: put the front door on the river. Lots of buildings throughout Boise were located on the river, but almost all of them "backed" onto it—in other words, the address of the building was on a street and the back of the building faced the Greenbelt.

But the concept of the Boise River and the Greenbelt being the "front door" of the Waterfront District went against nearly every aspect of the established real estate machine. The retail lacked the needed traffic count. The only places this type of development worked were in downtowns or touristy areas, which Garden City was decidedly not. There was no precedent in Boise for urban townhouses accessed mainly by a bike path. The whole vision depended on people using alternative transportation. With walkable downtowns and neighborhoods surging in popularity across the United States, people expected this kind of development to simply happen, but making it happen in most places flew in the face of a century's worth of standards and practices in the real estate, finance, and engineering fields. This would not be an overnight transformation but a slow, uphill grind.

Partway through the district's development process, the nationwide real estate market meltdown occurred. The project was not finding buyers.[35]

Neill's partners gave up in disgust. They had to pay $90,000 in taxes and they couldn't find buyers. And the public infrastructure to support their private risk—a street connection and a footbridge over the river—was not materializing.

"That's why we have sprawl," Neill told me when I had talked to him on the phone a few weeks earlier. "It makes sense for developers."

Neill sold his interest in the project. But in the ensuing years, the two cities did indeed build the footbridge (with American Recovery Act money), and the River Park was completed. The Waterfront District filled in with down-sized empty nesters. And the Greenbelt and its parks and bridges, and now the Waterfront District, were starting to shape the riverfront. More and more people were indeed moving to Garden City because of the river. The parents of elementary school students who used to be bused around the river were allowing their kids to walk to school over the new 36th Street footbridge. Recent area buyers appeared with kayaks over their shoulders.

The Waterfront District had pushed Garden City to rewrite its development code to mandate the vision that Neill and the planners had for the river. The city had quietly reduced its setbacks, increased its allowable building heights, and eliminated its parking requirements for Greenbelt sites.

Above all else, city planners wanted to make sure the space felt public. "We don't want it to be hard to access," one planner told me a few weeks before. "We don't want to have fences. I'm certain that someday the Greenbelt will be the city's front door."

A Low-Friction Lifestyle

But perhaps even more than shaping the form of its cityscape, Boise's trails were feeding the city's economy. Across the river from my Shilo Inn, an inconspicuous office building housed Inovus Solar, a small company that made solar streetlights and was founded by a gregarious Idahoan named Clay Young. When I contacted Young out of the blue, he responded by saying that what I was asking about—the nexus between outdoor recreation and economic development—was something to which he had given a lot of thought and energy. Young was an outdoor junkie. He rode mountain and road bikes; he skied and fly-fished. A freestyle kayaker, he was excited about the completion of the River Recreation Park. He was considering bringing his boat into the office and stashing it alongside his bikes and fishing equipment. Inovus's location right on the Greenbelt was no coincidence.

It was noon, and I planned to join Clay Young on the mountain bike ride he took with some of his staff members most days during lunchtime. I rode into the parking lot and took my bike up the elevator to the second floor. The office suite had the bare look of a start-up in new office space, with no time to decorate. Why would you decorate when there were trails to ride?

As I walked in, I saw bikes leaned haphazardly against walls and then Clay Young emerged from one of the offices, dressed in full Spandex and cleats. He called to one of his sales employees down the hall who also emerged in a bicycling outfit.

While looking for office space, they told potential landlords of their requirement to build a shower, for washing off after bike rides. "The Greenbelt is the reason our office is located where it is," Young said. "There are parks all around us, bird life, deer. There's an elk feeding station outside my window that I can see."

We rode down the Greenbelt and started to wind through downtown, much as I had done with Jimmy Hallyburton. Young's easy pedaling had the feel of an airplane taxiing on the runway before takeoff. He was sneakily fast. I struggled to keep up. Seeing Young in his outfit riding through downtown made me appreciate Hallyburton's vision of cyclists of all stripes, wearing everything from Lycra to cords, pedaling through Boise.

Young was from Idaho Falls, in eastern Idaho, and had attended Boise State University as an undergraduate. After college he had worked at Hewlett-Packard but knew he wanted to start a company. His business intelligence company was successful, and he sold it to Microsoft. Then he built another company and sold it. Inovus Solar came about because clean energy interested Young.

He had a theory about Boise's success as a tech and innovation hub. Although he spent his entire career living in Boise, Young had spent plenty of time in Silicon Valley and, during one period, had worked in Seattle nearly full time. Considering these cities' size and traffic, he noticed that everything he wanted to do required significant planning.

Young called the life he experienced in places like Silicon Valley and Seattle "high friction." High friction was hour-long commutes surrounded by cars, horns, and lines.

"I live in a pretty stressful world, in tech, and I'm really interested in being somewhere where I can live a low-stress lifestyle," he said. "I've gotten to the point where I love spending time with family and friends. Life in the big city is not as interesting."

The opposite of a high-friction lifestyle was, of course, a low-friction lifestyle. Boise was the essence of low friction. Low friction was a shorter bike commute on the Greenbelt, waders and a fly rod in the office. Young lived in

Eagle, like Ralph Budwig, about ten miles from his office. Unlike Budwig, he rode hard; he biked to work on the Greenbelt in about half an hour.

When hiring for Inovus Solar, Young found he attracted workers who felt the same way he did. He ended up with a young, well-educated workforce interested in both technology work and an outdoor lifestyle. The majority of his employees had come from towns or small cities looking for a more urban life culturally and economically but with the same benefits of the outdoors they grew up with. They were looking for a low-friction lifestyle. As a consequence, half of the staff rode their bikes to work—if not daily, then every other day—and most used the Greenbelt. Young imagined there must be thousands of people looking for that Boise lifestyle, a slightly larger place with the economic opportunities of a city (which, as we remember from my exploration of Wyoming and Denver, has always created opportunity in the West) but that fostered the same outdoor life. That was why he thought that adventure, and the lifestyle it fostered, was the fast-beating heart of the growing Boise economy.

Outdoor recreation is indeed an economic giant—to the size of $650 billion a year. According to an outdoor industry study, Americans spend $81 billion alone on bicycling gear and trips—more than they do on airplane tickets. Businesses tied to outdoor recreation account for 13 percent of Idaho's jobs.[36] The outdoor industry often measures outdoor recreation's impact through gear purchases and vehicle travel—a lens that sees adventure as an extension of the auto industry and a vision of outdoor recreation as separate from the day-to-day metropolitan life of most westerners.

But also powerful is the emerging force of active living. A synthesis of research by Active Living Research found that metropolitan development patterns that emphasized open space, recreation, and walking in metropolitan areas raised property values and often saved municipal governments money, and that urban residents in dense neighborhoods located near downtowns place substantially more value on proximity to open space. American homeowners are willing to pay a premium of $9,000 on houses that are within 1,000 feet of bike paths. These preferences play out in city economies. In Golden, Colorado, for example, a whitewater park brings together the Front Range's hunger for outdoor recreation with a desire for active urban living and contributes an estimated $2 million annually to the city's economy.[37] Ogden, Utah, has linked its spending on public space restoration to creating high numbers of jobs, lowering crime by 33 percent, and securing more than $1.2 billion in investment. In the spectacular landscapes of the West, adventure's ability to power urban economies and their transportation networks kicks in when outdoor recreation meets this emerging active lifestyle—and provides an alternative to the auto and highway-focused side of the outdoor industry. Boise is aware of this and is investing accordingly in assets like the Greenbelt, its foothills trails system, and open spaces like the River Recreation Park.

We suddenly left the city and were riding up a dirt road that wound up a canyon. An hour into the ride, Young kept charging forward uphill. We broke off the dirt road and climbed up a single-track trail that ran in the bottom of a dry creek drainage.

Apparently, a two-hour ride was normal. "We don't enforce 9 to 5," Young said. "It's more about meeting objectives. You meet your objectives and we're happy."

We switchbacked up a hillside and arrived at a place overlooking Boise, the city curled into the foothills like a yin-yang symbol. Dark clouds had gathered around the hills, and it began to sprinkle. It was time to turn around. I wondered if the weather had been better whether Young would have kept going. We could have ridden for days in these mountains.

After putting on their windbreakers, both men mounted their bikes and bunny-hopped down to the line of single track and were off. My cyclocross bike could not compete against their full suspension bikes. We rode down the ribbon along the green foothills, the grass just emerging from winter. I slowed down to take the periodic, small rocky drop-offs; my companions plowed over them at full speed through the sheets of rain. The trail dropped into the willowy creek drainage and then emptied out onto the dirt road we had ridden up. Then they went even faster.

It began to hail. Young did not slow down. Risking a disastrous wipeout, I caught up with him and shouted into the wind the question that remained, the one that had been forming during my time in Boise.

"What do people seeking outdoor lifestyles in the West really want?"

"Connection!" Young shouted back.

Then he sped off ahead, through the storm and down to the city.

Greyhound VI: Boise to Portland

By the time we returned to downtown Boise, which took about a tenth of the time as it did to climb up, it was sunny again. Young stopped at a sandwich shop he liked on a downtown corner, dismounted, and walked in. He didn't lock his bike, just leaned it against the building.

I thanked him for the ride and pedaled back through downtown toward my hotel. I had time to kill until my bus left that night for Portland. I checked out, loaded up my rig, and went to an alehouse on 8th Street, which the city occasionally closed to cars. I watched some NBA for a few hours.

The Greyhound terminal was a few blocks away. I found a bike box at a bike store on the way over and carried it with me. I approached the counter and unsurprisingly, but annoyingly, the man at the counter charged me $35 to check my bike. I explained what had happened at Flagstaff. He didn't budge.

Then I told him what I thought of Greyhound. I told him what I thought of it being the only option to get around the West without a car.

"Write your congressman," he said. "I used to live a block from Amtrak. It was always full. I had no idea why they shut it down."

I sat down on a bench and an old guy came over and sat down next to me. He wore a fishing vest and a blue denim shirt. He had a thick white mustache and a lazy eye.

"I couldn't help but overhear your conversation. I don't goddamn blame you for being mad," he said. "But why in the hell are you taking a bike on the Greyhound?"

I told him.

"You could ride that bike to Portland faster than taking the Greyhound," he said.

"I tell you, the only way to travel is by motorbike," he continued, now wistful. "When I was younger, I rode across the country. I had a tent, cook kit, sleeping bag, the whole thing. When it was raining I'd get a motel. Otherwise, I'd pitch a tent. I once ran into this guy riding a bike across the country. This son-of-a-bitch was eighty years old. From Holland."

He told me he was traveling to Las Vegas on the Greyhound from Lewiston, in northern Idaho, to pick up a car and drive it back, as a favor for a friend.

"Probably more than a favor," he said. "But this guy stayed with me through my operation."

I told him about my train trip that I liked.

"I once took the train across the country," he reminisced again. "All in a Pullman car. 1955."

"I'll bet that was nice," I said.

"It was stinky," he said. "Some scenery I never care to see again. But I found some other GIs and we drank some whiskey and chased girls. I could do that back then. We went through dry counties, and they'd have to shut down the club car. Kansas, Indiana. I was in the service for twenty years and I tell you, I don't like the direction this country's going in."

I recounted my journey. I told him that I thought good things were happening in the cities I had visited, that I thought many of them were headed in the right direction.

"Good luck," he said.

I warned him about the poor quality of the Vegas Greyhound terminal and said goodbye. It was dark when we pushed off toward Oregon.

Notes

1. Carlos Arnaldo Schwantes, *Going Places: Transportation Redefines the Twentieth-Century West* (Bloomington: Indiana University Press, 2003), 172–73.

2. John A. Jakle and Keith A. Sculle, *Motoring: The Highway Experience in America* (Athens: University of Georgia Press, 2008), 24.

3. Schwantes, *Going Places*, 182.

4. "The Invention of the American Vacation: The Automobile 1914–1932," American Studies at the University of Virginia, http://xroads.virginia.edu/~ug02/barnes/rough.html, accessed March 28, 2015; Jakle and Sculle, *Motoring*, 25; and Schwantes, *Going Places*, 183.

5. Effie Price Gladding, *Across the Continent by the Lincoln Highway* (New York: Brentano's, 1915). Gladding's book has been revived digitally by Project Gutenberg, http://www.gutenberg.org/files/33320/33320-h/33320-h.htm.

6. Ibid., ix.

7. Ibid., 261.

8. Ibid., 261.

9. Ibid., 261.

10. Ibid., 125.

11. Ibid., 114.

12. Ibid., 116.

13. Ibid., 124.

14. Ibid., 133.

15. Ibid., 138.

16. Ibid., 127.

17. Ibid., 131.

18. Ibid., 132.

19. Ibid., 147.

20. Ibid., 149.

21. Ibid., 149.

22. Ibid., 150.

23. Ibid., 146.

24. Ibid., 146.

25. Ibid., 150.

26. Ibid., 260.

27. One 2012 report ranked Idaho third in the proportion of commuters biking to work and ninth in cycling safety. Alliance for Biking & Walking, "Bicycling and Walking in the United States: 2012 Benchmarking Report.

28. Twice each year, the Treasure Valley Cycling Alliance organizes a volunteer countywide bike count. "May Counts Tabulated and Summarized," ADA County Bicycle Counts, last modified June 27, 2012, http://adabikecount.wordpress.com/2012/06/27/may-counts-tabulated-and-summarized-2/ and "SFMTA 2013 Bicycle Count," San Francisco Municipal Transportation Agency, accessed July 18, 2014, http://sfmta.com/sites/default/files/2013%20Bike%20Count%20Report.pdf. For Seattle data see Puget Sound Regional Council, Seattle, WA—2010 Regionally Coordinated Two Hour Bike Counts.

29. "Volunteer Rates," Corporation for National & Community Service, accessed July 18, 2014, http://www.volunteeringinamerica.gov/rankings.cfm. The highest-ranking state is Utah, which appears to be influenced by the large number of Latter-day Saints; religious volunteering made up roughly two-thirds of its volunteering. It's possible that Idaho's high ranking is influenced by its Mormon community as well, though just about any state with a high ranking had a large chunk of religious volunteering.

30. F.A.C.T.S. homepage, accessed, http://factsidaho.org, accessed March 28, 2015.

31. Idaho has a unique law that allows cyclists to treat stop signs as yield signs. The law has been in effect since the early 1980s, when the state's administrative director of the courts, who also happened to be a cyclist, noticed that violations citing bicyclists for not stopping at stop signs were cluttering up the courts. He and others thought it was natural for cyclists to slow down at stop signs without stopping because of their larger field of vision than cars and their need to conserve momentum. They managed to push a new bike code bill though the Idaho legislature with the yield provision. Rick Bernardi, "Origins of Idaho's 'Stop as Yield' Law," BicycleLaw.com, last modified March 7, 2009, http://www.bicyclelaw.com/blog/index.cfm/2009/3/7/Origins-of-Idahos-Stop-as-Yield-Law.

32. Even if the City of Boise wanted to turn down the volume of automobiles in its downtown, it had to confront a unique obstacle. Unlike most cities, Boise did not manage its own streets. They were controlled by the Ada County Highway District and the Idaho Transportation Department, neither of which was historically much interested in bikeable local streets. Downtown had its own improvement district, which was the way it got projects done.

33. "Study: Foothills Provide $11.9 Million in Benefits in 2011," Ridge to Rivers, last modified January 11, 2013, http://www.ridgetorivers.org/news/2013/01/study-foothills-provide-$119-million-in-benefits-in-2011/ and www.ridgetorivers.org, accessed March 18, 2010.

34. Adam Behrman, "Outdoor Recreation Drives Idaho Economy," KBOI2.com, last modified November 26, 2013, http://www.kboi2.com/news/local/Boise-Idaho-outdoor-recreation-economy-195700611.html.

35. And the transportation connections Neill believed were necessary for the project's success—a reconnection of the industrial street grid and a footbridge across the Boise River—were stalled. Few believed the River Park would actually be built.

36. "The Outdoor Recreation Economy: Take it Outside for American Jobs and a Strong Economy," Outdoor Industry Association, 2012, http://outdoorindustry.org/pdf/OIA_OutdoorRecEconomyReport2012.pdf and Behrman, "Outdoor Recreation Drives Idaho Economy."

37. "The Economic Benefits of Open Space, Recreation Facilities and Walkable Community Design," Active Living Research, May 2010, http://atfiles.org/files/pdf/Economic-Benefits-Active.pdf and "Economic Impact," City of Boise, Idaho, accessed July 18, 2014, http://parks.cityofboise.org/parks-locations/parks/boise-river-park/economic-impact/.

PART VI

The New Mobility

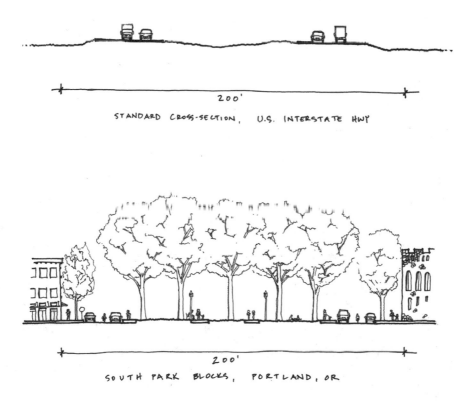

STANDARD CROSS-SECTION, U.S. INTERSTATE HWY

SOUTH PARK BLOCKS, PORTLAND, OR

DOI: 10.7330/9780874219937.c006

Moving in Place

The Columbia Gorge: the end of the old Oregon Trail. The Cascade Mountains tighten around the widening river and the brown hills begin to green with fir and spruce. White tops of volcanoes appear. The hardwoods, ▓▓▓ ▓▓ ▓▓▓ ▓▓ ▓▓▓▓ ▓▓▓▓▓▓▓ ▓▓▓▓ ▓▓ ▓▓▓ ▓▓▓ ▓▓▓▓ ▓▓▓▓ ▓▓▓ final stretch is some kind of endgame to a trip west. For emigrants traveling to the Oregon Country, it was the last two hundred miles, the last ten days of a six-month slog.

My bus rolled along I-84. It was a typical Greyhound experience. Every time we got out for a smoke—at Baker City, La Grande, Pendleton—one particular passenger screamed into a pay phone, then paced around. We got back on the interstate and everyone settled down and the lights went off until the next stop.

I had traveled about 3,700 miles, not counting the cities, in nine states, three of them twice. I count six modes: foot, bike, bus, train, boat, and car. I had nothing on Effie Gladding, but it was the longest road trip I had ever taken.

We've seen the stories of the creation of a western transportation network that started with the muddling of explorers through the American West's rugged landscape; the development of transportation corridors that grew from cart trails to stagecoach routes to transcontinental railroads; the expansion of the railroad into the farthest reaches of the West's cities and mountains only to be overtaken by roads for the automobile in the twentieth century. We've considered the networks and corridors of today, the role of the rail, the bicycle, the pedestrian, and economics and outdoor recreation in urban transportation and places.

We've explored how these aspects of the western transportation network can make the West great again and reinvent and revive the essential qualities of the region— the future, the land, opportunity, freedom, and adventure.

But the West would also have to reconsider its most dominant trait. In an essay titled "Living Dry," Wallace Stegner wrote that the American West is "a civilization in motion, driven by dreams." The whole intention of wagon trains, he reminded us, was to "get an early start, as soon as the grass greened up, and then get *through* the West as fast as possible."[1] Stegner argued that the most dominant trait of the American West was simply mobility. Getting around. Movement in its purest form.

"Ever since Daniel Boone took his first excursion over Cumberland Gap, Americans have been wanderers," Stegner wrote. "When Charles Dickens, in the Mississippi Valley, met a full-sized dwelling house coming down the road at a round trot, he was looking at the American people head-on. With a continent to take over and a Manifest Destiny to goad us, we could not have avoided being footloose. The initial act of emigration from Europe, an act of extreme, deliberate disaffiliation, was the beginning of a national habit."[2] And the road had always led west. American folk heroes and archetypical literary figures—Leatherstocking, Huck Finn, the Lone Ranger—were orphans and wanderers. Kids running away almost always ran west.

And from those early days of the wagon trains rolling through South Pass, mobility had endured. "The habit of mobility," Stegner wrote, "has only been reinforced by time."[3]

We've borne witness to this. Certainly, the last 3,700 miles have led us on roads and trails built simply to "get *through* the West as fast as possible," but this ethos has even more powerfully manifested in the cities. How many times have we seen places—the traffic sewers of North Las Vegas, I-25 and the Denver Tech Center, the anti-city of Phoenix—that were built with the goal of "extreme, deliberate disaffiliation"? Mobility ran through the places of the American West stronger than any other sense of common purpose or goal.

It was clear to me, as I neared the end of my trip, that in addition to changing the way we look at the future, the land, opportunity, freedom, and adventure, reinventing the West would also have to mean reinventing mobility.

———————————————————

The culmination of America's drive for mobility across its expanses was the building of the largest infrastructure project the world had ever seen. Looking out the windows of the Greyhound as it moved through the night, I knew the lane we were traveling in was at least twelve feet wide. I knew at least two lanes ran in our direction. And I knew we had a 4 foot shoulder on the left and a 10 foot breakdown lane on the right. Here in the Columbia Gorge, despite the tortured path of the road, the curves we traveled were designed to handle 70-mile-per-hour speeds, and it was not likely they would exceed a 1 degree curvature. In the Blue Mountains we climbed over, it was not likely I-84 had exceeded a 6 percent slope. I knew this despite not being able to see any of it.

This was the genius of the National System of Interstate and Defense Highways. The uniformity of the interstates was the ultimate vehicle for twentieth-century America. The 42,795 miles of the system were a quest for pure engineered mobility. The interstates composed a smooth, seamless web of pavement connecting the nation's cities. The system embodied efficiency, standardization, and safety.[4] I could be pretty sure that this was the straightest, flattest, and fastest route from Boise to Portland that a road could produce.

As the interstate map neared completion in the 1970s, nowhere benefited more than the West. Like the trains and early highways before it, the interstate system made the region more accessible to the rest of the nation and fueled the spacious expansion that lured hundreds of thousands of new residents to western metros each year. It enabled the relocation of the defense industries that helped tip growth away from the Rust Belt and toward the Sunbelt. A place that had always been about mobility had found the ultimate vehicle for it.

The interstate project moved 42 billion cubic yards of soil, the most in the history of the world. It generated an entire industry of earth-moving equipment. Huge pieces of machinery were invented solely for the interstates, such as scrapers that could pick up one thousand steam shovel loads. These machines cleared swaths two hundred feet wide. When building Interstate 40 through California, highway engineers even considered using nuclear bombs to eliminate a section of the Bristol Mountains.[5]

The interstate system was obsessed with standardization and speed, and these goals rubbed off on the places that clustered around the interstates. The freeways bypassed towns and chopped up inner-city neighborhoods while providing interchanges and off-ramps that shaped development in far-flung metro edges. The system was anti-city, but in the West, the cities were already anti-cities. They were so new that there was no retrofitting—just fitting.[6] They thrived with the pure mobility of the new freeways.

The interstate freeways cemented the West we know today. The West's wide-open spaces—now much more accessible and easy to travel—became less wild. For all of the adventure that had occurred in the Columbia Gorge, it was now a freeway, same as any other, especially in the dark. When I looked into the night outside the bus, I saw not the silent river and the increasingly forested hillsides but other vehicles on the road and the blinking lights of the dams and defense facilities that lined the freeway. The gorge was not a wild place; it was defined by fear and control and speed.

In "Living Dry," Stegner made the critical caveat about mobility in the West. "Being footloose has always exhilarated us," he wrote, but "the rootlessness that expresses energy and a thirst for the new and an aspiration toward freedom and personal fulfillment has just as often been a curse." He continued, "Our migratoriness has hindered us from becoming a people of communities and traditions . . . American individualism, much celebrated and cherished, has developed without its essential corrective, which is belonging."[7]

"The towns that are most western," Stegner wrote, "have had to strike a balance between mobility and stability."[8] It was clear that cities must bear this balance. They, to use Wendell Berry's turn of phrase, must be places, not displaces.

There is no doubt that mobility will always be an essential part of the West, but mobility should be a means to something else instead of an end in itself, as has become the case. Mobility as an end in itself has brought a wayward trajectory of degrading suburban sprawl across western land.

And the aspects of mobility that emerged out of the last century have been detrimental not only to the West's places but to mobility itself. Gridlock and unwalkable eight-lane arterial roads are now the centerpieces of western cities. Our transportation network has compromised the two most noteworthy aspects of our region: we are not rooted in our spectacular places, but we can't move about either. A region that has compromised everything for mobility is no longer mobile.

The bus arrived in Portland's old Union Pacific train station around 5:00 a.m. It was still pitch dark. I silently bid goodbye to the Greyhound as the line of my fellow road warriors filed out into the incongruously beautiful train station. I put my panniers and tent in a storage locker and headed out into the dark morning.

I rode up Lovejoy Street to an empty Starbucks that was open at this early hour. I collapsed at a table by the large windows and listened to music, soothing medicine after the Greyhound ride. A quiet, empty café, insulated from the outside by the darkness—this was my happy place right now.

I lived here for two years in the early 2000s, long enough to learn that Portland is different from both western cities and other cities in the United States. It's really a coastal city, belonging more to the blue-state swath of Cascadia than the red-state Mountain West, which make comparisons to Phoenix or Salt Lake unfair. But in many ways it is comparable to interior western cities—at least more so than New York City or San Francisco—because it isn't very big or particularly old or dense and it doesn't have any sort of pre-auto transit infrastructure. As a newer, smaller city, it is not as reliant on its pre-auto density and transit as on good planning and public policy. It serves as an example of how newer western cities like Salt Lake and Boise can cure their addictions to cars.

Portland was the end of the road for me. Today I'd fly back to California. Oregon had been a beginning for John Jacob Astor and an end for Abigail Scott. But for me, it was a coda on my trip, a brief, final passage to suggest ideas of a different future.

After an hour of decompressing at Starbucks, I returned to the bus station to get my stuff. Three different police incidents were occurring in front of the station, all of them involving passengers from my bus. The screaming/pacing woman was prone on the sidewalk, handcuffed, her stuff strewn over a 20-foot radius.

It was light now, so I loaded up my bike and rode from the station south toward downtown. I watched as the alphabetically named streets of Northwest Portland clicked by: Glisan, Flanders, Everett, Davis. If Portlanders had inherited one thing that gave them an advantage for a walkable city—and that differed from other western cities—it was their compact 200-foot long blocks. Most other city blocks are at least 300 feet on a side, many are 400 feet. Urbanists salivate over Portland's blocks because they are so easy to walk. And its streets are small. Portland's blocks and streets are the opposite of Salt Lake's. The small Portland grid is mighty, stretching all over the city. I always thought that biking in Portland works because rather than relying on a few major arterials to carry the traffic load and blocking off the neighborhoods, the Portland grid distributes traffic over hundreds of small streets. So, as a cyclist or pedestrian, you never have to cross a very big street or compete for space with heavy traffic.

Portland had plenty of freeways, but not as many as it was supposed to. In 1955 the Oregon Department of Transportation proposed a system of fourteen freeways for the Portland metro area. One of them, the Mount Hood Freeway, was planned to cut eastward from the Willamette River through the old neighborhoods of Southeast Portland. Practically every metro in the United States envisioned the rapidly growing suburbs having quick, uninterrupted access to the central business district. The destruction of the pre-auto neighborhoods in between was a cost of doing business in the modern world.

Portlanders disagreed. In the 1970s, when planners began taking steps to build the Mount Hood Freeway, people in the southeast Portland neighborhoods that would be torn up for the road spoke up. The freeway project was cancelled in 1974. Some of its funds were put toward the first MAX light rail line. The entire Portland freeway network had strange stubs of exits that never connected to new freeways. I first found out about the Mount Hood Freeway by talking to some old business owners on Division Street, where the freeway would have run. Division Street was now one of the city's many thriving neighborhood business districts full of car-free and local business zealots. Someone had even tried to firebomb a Starbucks that opened there.

The rejection of the Mount Hood Freeway became a galvanizing force against the tyranny of the automobile. The Portland alternative weekly

Willamette Week asserted in 2005 that nothing shaped Portland as much as the death of the Mount Hood Freeway.[9] The freeway revolt caused Portland to think about mobility differently than the rest of the nation. It was one of the first cities to reject pure mobility in preference for people and places.

In many ways, Portland was a classic western city. It had always marched to its own beat, free from the tradition of the East Coast or Midwest. Isolated like Boise, having a taste for new, unattached ways of thinking like Phoenix, geographically unconstrained like Denver. If the West could define freeway-driven mobility, why couldn't it redefine mobility? Portland had begun to do this.

And so Portland was where some of the most exciting work in street design and transportation was taking place. Portlanders had dedicated more space in their streets to other ways of getting around that just about any other American city. As I rode through the Pearl District into downtown, I saw that even more of Portland's streets had been carefully divvied up. A streetcar traveled up and down 11th and 12th Avenues. A protected cycle track went up Broadway, with special green "bike boxes" at every intersection for cyclists use to wait and turn. There was bike parking in the parking lane for cars. In the center of downtown, the city had turned 9th Avenue into a shared street along a new public plaza.

But Portland took its new definition of mobility even further. Using streets to get around without a car was great, but perhaps even better was using your streets to go nowhere at all. Portland had also given its streets to plazas and parks, to wetlands and commerce, adding even more connection and opportunity back into the mobility-driven street agenda. A "festival street" in Chinatown was designed to be blocked off for events. Tables occupied a street next to Voodoo Doughnuts.

Portland points the way toward the new definition of mobility. We need a mobility that balances the West's need for movement and opportunity and openness with the greater need for its communities and places. We need to rewrite the story of the West with belonging as the goal, with mobility as the means.

In the new mobility, cars are a burden. Not only are they an inefficient way of moving around, but they take up space in streets, which make up most of a city's public space. They separate you from the increasingly interesting world in the streets.

Telecommunications defines much more of our mobility today compared to physical movement. Our mobility is increasingly less about where we can travel quickly. One device gives you maps, delivery, parking, news, communication, and, in some cases, community. Modern technology enables a lighter, faster mobility and network, with information technology having rendered obsolete much of the physical mobility of concrete and rebar.

But the need for face-to-face contact is not obsolete. There is a reason Internet start-ups are beating down another gold rush in San Francisco, where young entrepreneurs are paying $500 a month to sleep in bathroom closets. They can be close to the action and each other using smartphones and bikes, proving again the timeless success of human density. As economist Edward Glaeser wrote in *Triumph of the City*, connections made among people and businesses in a dense urban environment are the "lifeblood of a 21st century city."[10]

Increasingly aware of this, cities are recalibrating their streets to reflect these new realities of mobility and connection to make places that connect people instead of simply trying to move them around, weaving back in the threads of the urban landscape—natural systems, economics, recreation, community—that had been cut out.

Many of the aims of the interstate system—efficiency, globalization, defense, standardization, and individualism—influence the world more than ever before. But now, freeways are an obsolete way of delivering these things. They can instead be carried through lighter, faster technologies that free up space for the things that humans have enjoyed for millennia. The things we need to accomplish individually largely happen through our modems and mobile devices. Now our streets can be for being together.

Most of all, the new mobility creates the opportunity for what I consider the most important quality of the West. It isn't mobility but its opposite. My favorite thing about the West has always been its places. The counterpoint to creating mobility in the West has always been valuing its places and making them better.

To me, places are synonymous with community. Places help community to happen and community creates places. In each of the places I visited, the people making the changes to how their cities get around had, as an often-unspoken directive, the betterment of community. It's a mulligan: westerners love freedom. We love opportunity, we love adventure, and we love mobility. But the people with whom I had spent the past three weeks were all trying to recast these things in a way that allowed people to enjoy them together. Reclaiming what people love about the places they live in the West is creating belonging in the West.

I had spent time with planners, engineers, developers, community activists, and entrepreneurs, and all of them were, to borrow from Stegner again, trying to find the angle of repose. America's frontier in the twenty-first century is simply belonging.

Portland is a great city for exploring. It's easy to get around and go long distances on a bike or car or train. But it is also a great city for being in the same place. It was Sunday, and after nearly a month on the road, I was staying put for the day.

I arrived at the South Park Blocks at a little past 7:00 a.m. The South Park Blocks were basically a street at the southern edge of downtown Portland. The street, at two hundred feet, was wide enough to be a massive arterial in any other city. Here though, the right of way consisted of mostly people space—a linear park. Seven rows of trees arched over the street. They were taller than almost all of the eight- or nine-story buildings on either side. This was a downtown neighborhood that specialized in museums and churches. But plenty of other things were going on here too. Offices were across the street. The *Oregonian* newsroom was a block away. Up the Park Blocks to the south was Portland State University.

I watched the city wake up. At 7:30, the first streetcar glided by on Market Street. Men ran by, a woman walked a dog. Someone walked past dressed for work. A woman set up to do solo tai chi.

At 8:30, the corner market opened, its front lights coming on. Someone at the First Christian Church across from me propped open its doors and swept its stairs.

By 9:00, more and more people walked by, a few occupied benches, most held smartphones. At 9:30, the sun came out. The birds in the trees still provided most of the sound. An old man read the Sunday paper.

By midday, a group of families in the middle of one of the Park Blocks staged an anti-lung cancer rally. Crowds of people filed into the Portland Art Museum. The owner of the corner store sat outside talking with a friend. A woman ate Whole Foods takeout on a bench. An older lady smoked and read a library book on another bench. When the streetcar pulled up, it looked like a little building in the middle of the park, people walking in and out.

It was time for me to go. I used my phone to check into my flight. A few blocks away, I obtained a nice large box from a bike shop to pack up my bike for the plane. Since I had reassembled my bike in the Las Vegas REI, I had ridden 652 miles, most of it on my tours in Utah, Arizona, and Wyoming. But a surprising amount happened in the cities; the little distances between neighborhoods and downtowns and business parks, in the cities within cities along the Greenbelt and the Valley Metro light rail.

I took my time packing my tired bike, removing the wheels, the seat, the pedals, the quick-releases on the hubs. I fished foam tubes out of the shop's scrap boxes to put around the frame. I wrapped everything in bubble wrap. I carefully lifted the parts into the box and taped it shut. I thanked the bike mechanic and walked out onto the street as evening approached.

I hefted the bike box and duffel bag a block to Yamhill Street and waited. After five minutes, a light rail train ambled down the hill and opened its doors.

Notes

1. Wallace Stegner, "Living Dry," in *The American West as Living Space*, 2nd ed. (Ann Arbor: University of Michigan Press, 1988), 20 (emphasis in original).

2. Ibid., 21.

3. Ibid.

4. At least what highway engineers considered safety, which was separating speeding traffic from pedestrians.

5. Dan McNichol, *The Roads that Built America: The Incredible Story of the U.S. Interstate System* (New York: Sterling, 2006), 127–33.

6. This, of course, is not entirely true. Even young western cities had old, often working-class or minority neighborhoods that succumbed to the interstate wrecking ball.

7. Stegner, "Living Dry," 22–23.

8. Ibid., 25.

9. Bob Young, "Highway to Hell: Nothing Shaped Portland So Much As the Murder of the Mount Hood Freeway," *Willamette Week*, March 9, 2005, http://www.wweek.com/portland/article-4212-highway_to_hell.html.

10. Edward Glaeser, *Triumph of the City: How Our Greatest Invention Makes Us Richer, Smarter, Greener, Healthier, and Happier* (New York: Penguin, 2011).

About the Author

Tim Sullivan is a city planner, urban designer, and writer whose professional focus is the reshaping of cities and communities through alternative transportation planning. He is the author of *No Communication with the Sea: Searching for an Urban Future in the Great Basin*. He lives in Salt Lake City with his wife and two children.

Index